D1640635

Lange/Rogers, Musterbriefe für den Auslandsbau

Die Deutsche Bibliothek – CIP-Einheitsaufnahme

Lange, Klaus:
Musterbriefe in Englisch für den Auslandsbau unter besonderer Berücksichtigung der FIDIC-
Bauvertragsbedinungen =
Standard letters in English for constructions work abroad with special reference to the FIDIC-
conditions of contract / Klaus Lange; F. Graham Rogers. – Wiesbaden; Berlin: Bauverl., 1994
ISBN 3-7625-2607-9
NE: Rogers, F. Graham·

Alle Rechte an den FIDIC-Vertragsbedingungen liegen bei der Fédération Internationale des
Ingénieurs Conseils (FIDIC). Wir danken dieser Organisation für die Erteilung der
Nachdruckgenehmigung. Exemplare der Vertragsbedingungen sind zu bestellen bei: Fédération
Internationale des Ingénieurs Conseils, P.O. Box 86, CH-1000 Lausanne 12 – Chailly.

All rights with regard to the FIDIC-conditions lie with the Fédération Internationale des
Ingénieurs Conseils (FIDIC). We thank this organization for granting reprinting permission.
Copies of the conditions can be ordered from the following address: Fédération Internationale
des Ingénieurs Conseils, P.O. Box 86, CH-Lausanne 12 – Chailly.

© 1994 Bauverlag GmbH, Wiesbaden und Berlin
Gesamtherstellung: Wetzlardruck GmbH, Wetzlar
ISBN 3-7625-2607-9

Prof. Dipl.-Ing. Klaus Lange
F. Graham Rogers

Musterbriefe in Englisch

für den Auslandsbau
unter besonderer Berücksichtigung der
FIDIC-Bauvertragsbedingungen

Standard Letters in English

for Construction Work Abroad
with Special Reference
to the FIDIC-Conditions of Contract

BAUVERLAG GMBH · WIESBADEN UND BERLIN

Inhaltsverzeichnis

Table of Contents

1. Vorwort

Bauleiter und Sachbearbeiter im Auslandsbau sind vielbeschäftigte Leute. Es ist deshalb nicht immer einfach, die bei internationalen Bauverträgen üblichen Formvorschriften und Fristen einzuhalten. Aus Fehlern können dem Auftragnehmer Nachteile z. B. infolge von nicht oder zu spät gestellten Nachforderungen entstehen. Auch der Beratende Ingenieur hat im Interesse des Auftraggebers auf die Einhaltung der Vertragsbestimmungen zu achten.

Das vorliegende Buch soll deshalb dem im Auslandsbau tätigen Sachbearbeiter, Bauleiter, Baukaufmann, Beratenden Ingenieur, Auftraggeber usw. eine zeit- und energiesparende Hilfe sein und auch den mit englischsprachiger Korrespondenz weniger Vertrauten die Abfassung entsprechender Schriftstücke ermöglichen, wobei naturgemäß gute Grundkenntnisse im Englischen vorausgesetzt werden müssen.

Die Verfasser danken der »Fédération Internationale des Ingénieurs Conseils« (FIDIC) für die Erlaubnis, die »Conditions of Contract for Works of Civil Engineering Construction« wiedergeben zu dürfen, sowie für die Beratung durch den Managing Director Dr. Marshall Gysi.

Tunbridge Wells/Wiesbaden im Frühjahr 1994

6

1. Preface

Site Engineers and managers in international construction are always busy. International Construction Contracts demand among other things the observation of certain formalities and limited periods. Mistakes may be detrimental to the Contractor in the event of missed or late claims. Adherence to all Conditions of Contract is equally important for the Consulting Engineer in order to safeguard the interests of his client.

Thus the present book shall offer help to the manager, site engineer, quantity surveyor and consulting engineer, employer, etc. engaged in international construction. The book shall save time and energy especially for those who are not familiar with correspondence in English and assist in the preparation of the documentation required. It goes without saying that a good knowledge of English will be required to make full use of the book.

The authors are indebted to the »Fédération Internationale des Ingénieurs Conseils« (FIDIC) for the permisson to reproduce the »Conditions of Contract for Works of Civil Engineering Construction« (Fourth Edition, 1987), their special thank goes to FIDIC's Managing Director, Dr. Marshall Gysi, for his help and advice.

Tunbridge Wells/Wiesbaden spring 1994

2. Hinweise zur Benutzung der Musterbriefe

Die Musterbriefe sind in der Reihenfolge der Klauseln des »Red Book« (Conditions of Contract for Works of Civil Engineering Construction) geordnet. Es wurde die vierte Auflage von 1987 (reprinted 1992 with further amendments) zugrunde gelegt. Sollten die Briefe im Zusammenhang mit einer anderen Auflage oder einem anderen Bauvertragstext geschrieben werden müssen, so sind sie sinngemäß zu modifizieren. Eine Gegenüberstellung der Änderungen in der vierten gegenüber der dritten Auflage findet sich in [20].
Die Musterbriefe gliedern sich in zwei Teile:

Abschnitt 9: Musterbriefe und Mitteilungen in englischer Sprache für den Auftragnehmer (mit Kommentar)

Abschnitt 10: Musterbriefe und Mitteilungen in englischer Sprache für den Beratenden Ingenieur (mit Kommentar)

Den FIDIC-Vertragsbedingungen sind in Abschnitt 3 kurzgefaßte Hinweise zu den Bedingungen vorangestellt. Zu den Vertragsbedingungen gibt es eine Vokabelliste typischer Adverbien, Adjektive und Konjunktionen der FIDIC-Bedingungen (Abschnitt 5), eine Übersetzung der Randbemerkungen der FIDIC-Bedingungen (Abschnitt 6) sowie ein Vokabelverzeichnis Englisch/Deutsch in der Reihenfolge des Auftretens (Abschnitt 7). Ein alphabetisches Vokabelverzeichnis (Englisch/Deutsch) der gesamten FIDIC-Bedingungen findet sich in Abschnitt 8. Für eine weitergehende Beschäftigung mit den FIDIC-Bedingungen ist ein Literaturverzeichnis beigefügt (Abschnitt 11). Veröffentlichungen und Wörterbücher, die bei der Abfassung der englischsprachigen Korrespondenz hilfreich sein können, sind in einem weiteren Verzeichnis aufgeführt (Abschnitt 12).

Ein lückenloses Bauberichtswesen – unterstützt durch Fotos – und eine übersichtliche Registratur ist für die Geltendmachung von Nachforderungen unerläßlich. Um Übersetzungsarbeiten zu vermeiden, sind die Unterlagen zweckmäßigerweise gleich in englischer oder der entsprechenden Vertragssprache abzufassen.

2.   Remarks on the Use of the Standard Letters

The standard letters are listed in the order of the clauses of the »Red Book« (Conditions of Contract for Works of Civil Engineering Construction). They are based on the fourth edition 1987 (reprinted 1992 with further amendments). Users who want to write letters in connection with another edition or another type of construction contract will have to modify the letters accordingly. For a »Marked up Copy« showing changes from the third edition to the fourth edition of the Conditions of Contract see literature [20].

The model letters are divided into two parts:

Chapter 9:   Standard Letters and Notices in English for use by the
               Contractor (with comments)

Chapter 10:   Standard Letters and Notices in English for use by the
               Engineer (with comments)

Chapter 3 contains short general remarks concerning the FIDIC Conditions. To facilitate the understanding the conditions are preceded by a list of typical adverbs and conjunctions frequently appearing in the conditions (Chapter 5), a translation of the marginal notes into German (Chapter 6), and a wordlist (English/German) in order of appearance in the FIDIC Clauses (Chapter 7). Chapter 8 comprises a word list (English/German) in alphabetical order.

Literature for a more detailed information on the FIDIC Conditions is listed in chapter 11.

Further publications and dictionaries which might be helpful in preparing correspondence and documents in English are contained in Chapter 12.

It is most important that a reliable und comprehensive system for recording correspondence and other information is established to assist in the contract administration. This will greatly assist in the substantiation of claims or other contract matters.

To avoid translation work the relevant documents should be drawn-up in the respective contract language.

3. Kurzgefaßte Hinweise zu den FIDIC-Bedingungen

FIDIC ist die Abkürzung für »Fédération Internationale des Ingénieurs Conseils«, das Sekretariat dieses internationalen Verbandes der Beratenden Ingenieure befindet sich in Lausanne (P.O. Box 86, CH 1000 Lausanne 12 – Chailly, Switzerland, Telex 454698 FIDI CH, Telefon +4121 6535003, Fax +4121 6535432).

Auch die 4. Fassung (1987) der »Conditions of Contract for Works of Civil Engineering Construction« (The Red Book) geht letztendlich zurück auf die alten ICE-Bedingungen (Institution of Civil Engineers, London).

Obwohl die Bedingungen ursprünglich mehr für den Ingenieurbau gedacht waren, werden sie in Ermangelung anderer passender Vertragsmuster auch für Hochbauprojekte verwendet. Bei entsprechender Ergänzung lassen sie sich auch für die maschinellen Einrichtungen im Rahmen eines Bauvertrages verwenden. Für größere Anlagenverträge werden im allgemeinen die ebenfalls von der FIDIC herausgegebenen »Conditions of Contract for Electrical and Mechanical Works (including erection on site)«, third edition 1987 (The Yellow Book) [21],[22] verwendet, auf die hier nicht näher eingegangen wird.

Die beiden Musterverträge sind zwar ähnlich, unterscheiden sich aber durch ihre unterschiedlichen Aufgaben; auch decken sich die Bezeichnungen in den beiden Verträgen nicht.

Um die FIDIC-Bedingungen für Bauarbeiten auch bei Verträgen zwischen einheimischen Partnern, vornehmlich in Entwicklungsländern, verwenden zu können, wurde die Bezeichnung »international« in der neuesten Fassung fortgelassen.

Zur Zeit wird an einem FIDIC-Mustervertrag gearbeitet, der die Vertragsgestaltung bei schlüsselfertigen Projekten oder bei Totalunternehmertätigkeit (Design and Build) regeln soll (The Orange Book). Weiterhin ist ein Mustervertrag für BOT-Projekte (Build, Operate, Transfer) vorgesehen.

Während es von der alten Fassung der FIDIC-Bedingungen Übersetzungen in die arabische, deutsche, französische und spanische Sprache gibt, liegt die neue Fassung in Englisch, Französich, Japanisch und Spanisch vor. Eine deutsche Fassung ist vorerst nicht geplant.

Nach dem Vorwort ~~der~~ *zu den* FIDIC-Bedingungen ist die englische Fassung die offizielle und authentische Fassung für Übersetzungen. In Teil II der Bedingungen (Conditions of Particular Application with Guidelines...) kann festgelegt werden, in welcher Sprache oder welchen Sprachen der Vertrag ausgefertigt werden soll, wobei die »Ruling Language« festzulegen ist, falls in mehreren Sprachen ausgefertigt wird. Hier sollte auch festgelegt werden, nach welchem Recht der Vertrag auszulegen ist.

Da die in der englischen Fassung verwendeten Begriffe aus dem englischen Rechtssystem stammen, können sich bei der Vereinbarung eines anderen Rechtssystems, das von dem englischen verschieden ist, große Probleme ergeben, da bestimmte Begriffe in den entsprechenden Rechtssystemen unbekannt sind oder eine andere Bedeutung haben.

Die Bedingungen gliedern sich in Teil I und Teil II. Teil I »General Conditions with Forms of Tender and Agreement« enthält die allgemeinen Bedingungen, die etwa Teil B der VOB [1] entsprechen. In Teil II finden sich Ergänzungen und Musterformulierungen für spezielle Umstände, wie z. B. Klauseln in bezug auf Währung, Sicherheiten, örtliche Umstände usw.

Zusätzlich sind in jedem Falle Vereinbarungen zu treffen, wie die Arbeiten aufgemessen und abgerechnet werden; Aufmaßregeln, wie sie in Teil C der VOB [1] enthalten sind, fehlen in den FIDIC-Bedingungen. Als englischsprachige Aufmaßregeln kann die »Standard Method of Measurement – SMM7« [2] und der SMM7- A Code of Procedure for Measurement of Building Works« [3] verwendet werden (für Hochbauprojekte).
Für den Ingenieurbau kann der Civil Engineering Standard of Measurement Third Edition CESMM 3 [18] vereinbart werden.

Weiterhin fehlen in den FIDIC-Bedingungen Normenangaben, diese sind ebenfalls zusätzlich in den Vertragsunterlagen zu vereinbaren, z. B. DIN, BS, AFNOR, ASTM.

Bestimmte Auftraggeber oder Finanzierungsinstitute modifizieren die Original-FIDIC-Bedingungen. So unterscheidet die Weltbank in ihren »Sample Bidding Documents« [4] zwischen Modifizierungen, die unbedingt verlangt werden, die empfohlen werden und die freigestellt sind (Mandatory, Recommended, Optional).

Eine Besonderheit der FIDIC-Bedingungen ist die Stellung und Rolle des »Engineer«, d. h. des Beratenden Ingenieurs. Nach der anglo-amerikanischen Tradition hat er neben den auch in anderen Ländern üblichen Aufgaben der Planung, Ausschreibung und Bauüberwachung noch den Status eines sachkundigen, unparteiischen und fairen Schiedsrichters in erster Instanz bei Meinungsverschiedenheiten zwischen Unternehmer und Bauherr.
Abgesehen von der allgemeinen Problematik, daß der »Engineer« letztlich in einem wirtschaftlichen Abhängigkeitsverhältnis zum Bauherrn steht, bedeutet die Veränderung der Original-FIDIC-Vertragsbedingungen bezüglich der Rechte und

Aufgaben des »Engineer« nahezu immer eine Benachteiligung des Unternehmers und ein erhöhtes Konfliktpotential.

Umfangreiche Kommentare wie etwa zur VOB [5],[6],[7] gibt es zu den FIDIC-Bedingungen nicht, überdies werden nahezu alle Schiedsgerichtsurteile nicht veröffentlicht, da sie vertraulich sind.

Eine außerordentlich detaillierte Behandlung der FIDIC-Bedingungen mit zahlreichen Diagrammen und der Darstellung des rechtlichen Umfeldes vieler Länder findet sich in dem Werk von N. Bunni, The FIDIC Form of Contract [8].

Einzelartikel zu den Problemen des FIDIC-Vertrages werden in folgenden Zeitschriften veröffentlicht:
International Construction Law Review [9],
Arbitration – The Journal of the Chartered Institute of Arbitrators, London [10],
World Arbitration & Mediation Report [11].
Arbitration & Dispute Resolution Law Journal [12].
Weitere Literaturangaben finden sich in den Abschnitten 11 und 12.

3. ~~Short~~ *Brief* General Remarks concerning the FIDIC-Conditions

"FIDIC" is the acronym of the "Fédération Internationale des Ingénieurs-Conseils", the secretariat of this international federation of Consulting Engineers is based in Lausanne (P.O. Box 86, CH 1000 Lausanne 12 – Chailly, Switzerland, Telex 454698 FIDI CH, Telephone +4121 6535003, Fax +4121 6535432).

The present 4th edition (1987) of the "Conditions of Contract for Works of Civil Engineering Construction" originated from the old ICE-Conditions (Institution of Civil Engineers, London).

Though the conditions are more suitable for civil engineering construction projects they are also used for building projects because appropriate international contract conditions are not available. With respective amendments they can also be applied to projects with certain mechanical installations.

For larger contracts of industrial plants FIDIC offers the "Conditions of Contract for Electrical and Mechanical Works (including erection on site)", third edition, 1987 (The Yellow Book). This contract is not dealt with in this book.

The two contracts mentioned above are similar but there are differences which are not only a consequence of the different contractual subjects.

Among other things the definitions of some words differ in the two conditions of contract.

In order to facilitate the use of the "Red Book" also for contracts with parties of the same nationality, preferably in developing countries, the adjective »international« has been deleted in the newest edition.

FIDIC has under preparation conditions of contract for "Design and Build" or turnkey projects to be called the "Orange Book" and is also considering a contract for BOT (Build, Operate, Transfer) projects.

Whereas the previous edition of the FIDIC-Conditions has been translated into Arabic, French, German and Spanish the latest edition is only available in English, French, Japanese and Spanish. A German version is not envisaged at present.

According to the foreword of of the FIDIC-Conditions the version in English is considered by FIDIC as the official and authentic text for the purpose of translation.

In part II (Conditions of particular application with guidelines...) it can be stated in which language or languages the contract shall be written and which the "Ruling Language" shall be, in case more than one language is stated. Furthermore in Part II the law that is in force in a certain country has to be stated in order to clarify according to which law the contract is to be interpreted and construed.

The terms used in the English version of the FIDIC-Conditions originate from the English judicial system, in cases where the law of a country other than England is stated in the contract great problems may arise as certain terms are unknown in the respective other judicial systems or they may have another meaning.

The FIDIC-Conditions consist of Part I and Part II. Part I "General Conditions with Forms of Tender and Agreement" comprises the general conditions which are comparable with the German VOB-Contract Teil B [1]. Part II contains additions and model clauses for certain circumstances e.g. clauses concerning currency, securities, bonds, local circumstances etc.

Furthermore agreements have to be made how the works shall be measured and paid for. The FIDIC-Conditions do not contain such rules as are to be found in VOB, Teil C [1].

As rules in English for the measurement of construction and building works the "Standard Method of Measurement of Building Works" can be used (SMM7) [2], together with the Code of Procedure for Measurement of Building Works [3]. The Civil Engineering Standard of Measurement Third Edition (CESMM 3) [18] is suitable for civil engineering works.

Standards and Specifications are also not included in the FIDIC-Conditions therefore special agreements regarding standards, e.g. ASTM, AFNOR, BS, DIN, are required.

Certain employers or financing institutions modify the original FIDIC-Conditions. E.g. the World Bank distinguishes between modifications which are mandatory, recommended and optional (Sample Bidding Documents) [4].

A special feature of all FIDIC-Conditions is the position and role of the "Engineer", i.e. of the Consulting Engineer. According to the Anglo-American tradition he has the status of a competent and impartial authority to decide in the first instance disputes between Employer and Contractor, this task is additional to the normal duties of planning, design, working out of tender documents and site supervision which are common tasks of consulting engineers in other countries.

Apart from the problem that the "Engineer" is in a state of economic dependency to the Employer, any change in the original FIDIC-conditions regarding the Engineer's powers and authority nearly always means a disadvantage to the Contractor and an increased potential for conflict.

There are no comprehensive commentaries on the FIDIC-Conditions comparable with those for the German VOB-Contract, this is mainly due to the fact that arbitration awards are normally confidential and therefore not published.

A very detailed and comprehensive survey of the FIDIC-Contract with numerous flow-charts and description of the legal environment of several countries is to be found in the work of N. Bunni "The FIDIC Form of Contract" [8].
Individual articles on the problems in connection with the FIDIC-Conditions are published in the following magazines:
International Construction Law Review [9],
Arbitration – The Journal of the Chartered Institute of Arbitrators, London [10],
World Arbitration and & Mediation Report [11],
Arbitration & Dispute Resolution Law Journal [12].
For further literature see chapter 11 and 12.

4. FIDIC-Bedingungen Teil 1 und Teil 2 (Red Book, 4. Auflage)
4. FIDIC-Conditions Part I und Part II (Red Book, 4th edition)

FEDERATION INTERNATIONALE DES INGENIEURS-CONSEILS

CONDITIONS OF CONTRACT
FOR WORKS OF CIVIL
ENGINEERING CONSTRUCTION

PART I GENERAL CONDITIONS
WITH FORMS OF TENDER AND AGREEMENT

FOURTH EDITION 1987

REPRINTED 1988 WITH EDITORIAL AMENDMENTS
REPRINTED 1992 WITH FURTHER AMENDMENTS

FOREWORD

The terms of the Fourth Edition of the Conditions of Contract for Works of Civil Engineering Construction have been prepared by the Fédération Internationale des Ingénieurs Conseils (FIDIC) and are recommended for general use for the purpose of construction of such works where tenders are invited on an international basis. The Conditions, subject to minor modifications, are also suitable for use on domestic contracts.

The version in English of the Conditions is considered by FIDIC as the official and authentic text for the purpose of translation.

In the preparation of the Conditions it was recognised that while there are numerous Clauses which will be generally applicable there are some Clauses which must necessarily vary to take account of the circumstances and locality of the Works. The Clauses of general application have been grouped together in this document and are referred to as Part I – General Conditions. They have been printed in a form which will facilitate their inclusion as printed in the contract documents normally prepared.

The General Conditions are linked with the Conditions of Particular Application, referred to as Part II, by the corresponding numbering of the Clauses, so that Parts I and II together comprise the Conditions governing the rights and obligations of the parties.

Part II must be specially drafted to suit each individual Contract.

When dredging and certain types of reclamation work are involved special consideration must be given to Part II.

To assist in the preparation of Part II explanatory material and example clauses are published with the Conditions in a separately bound document entitled "Conditions of Contract for Works of Civil Engineering Construction, Part II – Conditions of Particular Application, with Guidelines for preparation of Part II Clauses, Fourth Edition".

FIDIC has published a "Guide to the Use of FIDIC Conditions of Contract for Works of Civil Engineering Construction" which includes comments on the provisions of the Fourth Edition of the Conditions. Users of the Fourth Edition may find it helpful to refer to this Guide.

It may also be helpful for users to refer to other FIDIC publications, such as:

Tendering Procedure (First Edition 1982)
Construction, Insurance and Law (1986)

FIDIC gratefully acknowledges the suggestions and comments it has received during the preparation of this edition from European International Contractors (EIC) as mandatory of Confederation of International Contractors Associations (CICA) with participation of Associated General Contractors of America (AGC).

CONTENTS

PART I: GENERAL CONDITIONS

Definitions and Interpretation

Engineer and Engineer's Representative

Assignment and Subcontracting

Contract Documents

General Obligations

© FIDIC 1987

Release from Performance

Settlement of Disputes

Notices

Default of Employer

Changes in Cost and Legislation

Currency and Rates of Exchange

REFERENCE TO PART II
INDEX
TENDER
AGREEMENT
EDITORIAL AMENDMENTS IN 1988
FURTHER AMENDMENTS IN 1992

PART I - GENERAL CONDITIONS

Definitions and Interpretation

Definitions **1.1** In the Contract (as hereinafter defined) the following words and expressions shall have the meanings hereby assigned to them, except where the context otherwise requires:

(a) (i) "Employer" means the person named as such in Part II of these Conditions and the legal successors in title to such person, but not (except with the consent of the Contractor) any assignee of such person.

(ii) "Contractor" means the person whose tender has been accepted by the Employer and the legal successors in title to such person, but not (except with the consent of the Employer) any assignee of such person.

(iii) "Subcontractor" means any person named in the Contract as a Subcontractor for a part of the Works or any person to whom a part of the Works has been subcontracted with the consent of the Engineer and the legal successors in title to such person, but not any assignee of any such person.

(iv) "Engineer" means the person appointed by the Employer to act as Engineer for the purposes of the Contract and named as such in Part II of these Conditions.

(v) "Engineer's Representative" means a person appointed from time to time by the Engineer under Sub-Clause 2.2.

(b) (i) "Contract" means these Conditions (Parts I and II), the Specification, the Drawings, the Bill of Quantities, the Tender, the Letter of Acceptance, the Contract Agreement (if completed) and such further documents as may be expressly incorporated in the Letter of Acceptance or Contract Agreement (if completed).

(ii) "Specification" means the specification of the Works included in the Contract and any modification thereof or addition thereto made under Clause 51 or submitted by the Contractor and approved by the Engineer.

(iii) "Drawings" means all drawings, calculations and technical information of a like nature provided by the Engineer to the Contractor under the Contract and all drawings, calculations, samples, patterns, models, operation and maintenance manuals and other technical information of a like nature submitted by the Contractor and approved by the Engineer.

(iv) "Bill of Quantities" means the priced and completed bill of quantities forming part of the Tender.

(v) "Tender" means the Contractor's priced offer to the Employer for the execution and completion of the Works and the remedying of any defects therein in accordance with the provisions of the Contract, as accepted by the Letter of Acceptance.

(vi) "Letter of Acceptance" means the formal acceptance by the Employer of the Tender.

(vii) "Contract Agreement" means the contract agreement (if any) referred to in Sub-Clause 9.1.

(viii) "Appendix to Tender" means the appendix comprised in the form of Tender annexed to these Conditions.

(c) (i) "Commencement Date" means the date upon which the Contractor receives the notice to commence issued by the Engineer pursuant to Clause 41.

(ii) "Time for Completion" means the time for completing the execution of and passing the Tests on Completion of the Works or any Section or part thereof as stated in the Contract (or as extended under Clause 44) calculated from the Commencement Date.

(d) (i) "Tests on Completion" means the tests specified in the Contract or otherwise agreed by the Engineer and the Contractor which are to be made by the Contractor before the Works or any Section or part thereof are taken over by the Employer.

(ii) "Taking-Over Certificate" means a certificate issued pursuant to Clause 48.

(e) (i) "Contract Price" means the sum stated in the Letter of Acceptance as payable to the Contractor for the execution and completion of the Works and the remedying of any defects therein in accordance with the provisions of the Contract.

(ii) "Retention Money" means the aggregate of all monies retained by the Employer pursuant to Sub-Clause 60.2(a).

(iii) "Interim Payment Certificate" means any certificate of payment issued by the Engineer other than the Final Payment Certificate.

(iv) "Final Payment Certificate" means the certificate of payment issued by the Engineer pursuant to Sub-Clause 60.8.

(f) (i) "Works" means the Permanent Works and the Temporary Works or either of them as appropriate.

(ii) "Permanent Works" means the permanent works to be executed (including Plant) in accordance with the Contract.

(iii) "Temporary Works" means all temporary works of every kind (other than Contractor's Equipment) required in or about the execution and completion of the Works and the remedying of any defects therein.

(iv) "Plant" means machinery, apparatus and the like intended to form or forming part of the Permanent Works.

(v) "Contractor's Equipment" means all appliances and things of whatsoever nature (other than Temporary Works) required for the execution and completion of the Works and the remedying of any defects therein, but does not include Plant, materials or other things intended to form or forming part of the Permanent Works.

(vi) "Section" means a part of the Works specifically identified in the Contract as a Section.

(vii) "Site" means the places provided by the Employer where the Works are to be executed and any other places as may be specifically designated in the Contract as forming part of the Site.

(g) (i) "cost" means all expenditure properly incurred or to be incurred, whether on or off the Site, including overhead and other charges properly allocable thereto but does not include any allowance for profit.

(ii) "day" means calendar day.

(iii) "foreign currency" means a currency of a country other than that in which the Works are to be located.

(iv) "writing" means any hand-written, type-written, or printed communication, including telex, cable and facsimile transmission.

Headings and Marginal Notes	1.2	The headings and marginal notes in these Conditions shall not be deemed part thereof or be taken into consideration in the interpretation or construction thereof or of the Contract.
Interpretation	1.3	Words importing persons or parties shall include firms and corporations and any organisation having legal capacity.
Singular and Plural	1.4	Words importing the singular only also include the plural and vice versa where the context requires.

2

Notices,	1.5	Wherever in the Contract provision is made for the giving or issue of any notice,
Consents,		consent, approval, certificate or determination by any person, unless otherwise
Approvals,		specified such notice, consent, approval, certificate or determination shall be in
Certificates and		writing and the words "notify", "certify" or "determine" shall be construed
Determinations		accordingly. Any such consent, approval, certificate or determination shall not

Wherever in the Contract provision is made for the giving or issue of any notice, consent, approval, certificate or determination by any person, unless otherwise specified such notice, consent, approval, certificate or determination shall be in writing and the words "notify", "certify" or "determine" shall be construed accordingly. Any such consent, approval, certificate or determination shall not unreasonably be withheld or delayed.

Engineer and Engineer's Representative

Engineer's Duties and Authority

2.1 (a) The Engineer shall carry out the duties specified in the Contract.

(b) The Engineer may exercise the authority specified in or necessarily to be implied from the Contract, provided, however, that if the Engineer is required, under the terms of his appointment by the Employer, to obtain the specific approval of the Employer before exercising any such authority, particulars of such requirements shall be set out in Part II of these Conditions. Provided further that any requisite approval shall be deemed to have been given by the Employer for any such authority exercised by the Engineer.

(c) Except as expressly stated in the Contract, the Engineer shall have no authority to relieve the Contractor of any of his obligations under the Contract.

Engineer's Representative

2.2 The Engineer's Representative shall be appointed by and be responsible to the Engineer and shall carry out such duties and exercise such authority as may be delegated to him by the Engineer under Sub-Clause 2.3.

Engineer's Authority to Delegate

2.3 The Engineer may from time to time delegate to the Engineer's Representative any of the duties and authorities vested in the Engineer and he may at any time revoke such delegation. Any such delegation or revocation shall be in writing and shall not take effect until a copy thereof has been delivered to the Employer and the Contractor.

Any communication given by the Engineer's Representative to the Contractor in accordance with such delegation shall have the same effect as though it had been given by the Engineer. Provided that:

(a) any failure of the Engineer's Representative to disapprove any work, materials or Plant shall not prejudice the authority of the Engineer to disapprove such work, materials or Plant and to give instructions for the rectification thereof; and

(b) if the Contractor questions any communication of the Engineer's Representative he may refer the matter to the Engineer who shall confirm, reverse or vary the contents of such communication.

Appointment of Assistants

2.4 The Engineer or the Engineer's Representative may appoint any number of persons to assist the Engineer's Representative in the carrying out of his duties under Sub-Clause 2.2. He shall notify to the Contractor the names, duties and scope of authority of such persons. Such assistants shall have no authority to issue any instructions to the Contractor save in so far as such instructions may be necessary to enable them to carry out their duties and to secure their acceptance of materials, Plant or workmanship as being in accordance with the Contract, and any instructions given by any of them for those purposes shall be deemed to have been given by the Engineer's Representative.

Instructions in Writing

2.5 Instructions given by the Engineer shall be in writing, provided that if for any reason the Engineer considers it necessary to give any such instruction orally, the Contractor shall comply with such instruction. Confirmation in writing of such oral instruction given by the Engineer, whether before or after the carrying out of the instruction, shall be deemed to be an instruction within the meaning of this Sub-Clause. Provided further that if the Contractor, within 7 days, confirms in writing to the Engineer any oral instruction of the Engineer and such confirmation is not contradicted in writing within 7 days by the Engineer, it shall be deemed to be an instruction of the Engineer.

The provisions of this Sub-Clause shall equally apply to instructions given by the Engineer's Representative and any assistants of the Engineer or the Engineer's Representative appointed pursuant to Sub-Clause 2.4.

Engineer to Act Impartially **2.6** Wherever, under the Contract, the Engineer is required to exercise his discretion by:

(a) giving his decision, opinion or consent,

(b) expressing his satisfaction or approval,

(c) determining value, or

(d) otherwise taking action which may affect the rights and obligations of the Employer or the Contractor

he shall exercise such discretion impartially within the terms of the Contract and having regard to all the circumstances. Any such decision, opinion, consent, expression of satisfaction, or approval, determination of value or action may be opened up, reviewed or revised as provided in Clause 67.

Assignment and Subcontracting

Assignment of Contract **3. 1** The Contractor shall not, without the prior consent of the Employer (which consent, notwithstanding the provisions of Sub-Clause 1.5, shall be at the sole discretion of the Employer), assign the Contract or any part thereof, or any benefit or interest therein or thereunder, otherwise than by:

(a) a charge in favour of the Contractor's bankers of any monies due or to become due under the Contract, or

(b) assignment to the Contractor's insurers (in cases where the insurers have discharged the Contractor's loss or liability) of the Contractor's right to obtain relief against any other party liable.

Subcontracting **4. 1** The Contractor shall not subcontract the whole of the Works. Except where otherwise provided by the Contract, the Contractor shall not subcontract any part of the Works without the prior consent of the Engineer. Any such consent shall not relieve the Contractor from any liability or obligation under the Contract and he shall be responsible for the acts, defaults and neglects of any Subcontractor, his agents, servants or workmen as fully as if they were the acts, defaults or neglects of the Contractor, his agents, servants or workmen.

Provided that the Contractor shall not be required to obtain such consent for:

(a) the provision of labour, or

(b) the purchase of materials which are in accordance with the standards specified in the Contract, or

(c) the subcontracting of any part of the Works for which the Subcontractor is named in the Contract.

Assignment of Subcontractors' Obligations **4.2** In the event of a Subcontractor having undertaken towards the Contractor in respect of the work executed, or the goods, materials, Plant or services supplied by such Subcontractor, any continuing obligation extending for a period exceeding that of the Defects Liability Period under the Contract, the Contractor shall at any time, after the expiration of such Period, assign to the Employer, at the Employer's request and cost, the benefit of such obligation for the unexpired duration thereof.

Contract Documents

Language/s and Law **5. 1** There is stated in Part II of these Conditions:

(a) the language or languages in which the Contract documents shall be drawn up, and

(b) the country or state the law of which shall apply to the Contract and according to which the Contract shall be construed.

4

If the said documents are written in more than one language, the language according to which the Contract shall be construed and interpreted is also stated in Part II of these Conditions, being therein designated the "Ruling Language".

Priority of Contract Documents

5.2 The several documents forming the Contract are to be taken as mutually explanatory of one another, but in case of ambiguities or discrepancies the same shall be explained and adjusted by the Engineer who shall thereupon issue to the Contractor instructions thereon and in such event, unless otherwise provided in the Contract, the priority of the documents forming the Contract shall be as follows:

(1) The Contract Agreement (if completed);

(2) The Letter of Acceptance;

(3) The Tender;

(4) Part II of these Conditions;

(5) Part I of these Conditions; and

(6) Any other document forming part of the Contract.

Custody and Supply of Drawings and Documents

6.1 The Drawings shall remain in the sole custody of the Engineer, but two copies thereof shall be provided to the Contractor free of charge. The Contractor shall make at his own cost any further copies required by him. Unless it is strictly necessary for the purposes of the Contract, the Drawings, Specification and other documents provided by the Employer or the Engineer shall not, without the consent of the Engineer, be used or communicated to a third party by the Contractor. Upon issue of the Defects Liability Certificate, the Contractor shall return to the Engineer all Drawings, Specification and other documents provided under the Contract.

The Contractor shall supply to the Engineer four copies of all Drawings, Specification and other documents submitted by the Contractor and approved by the Engineer in accordance with Clause 7, together with a reproducible copy of any material which cannot be reproduced to an equal standard by photocopying. In addition the Contractor shall supply such further copies of such Drawings, Specification and other documents as the Engineer may request in writing for the use of the Employer, who shall pay the cost thereof.

One Copy of Drawings to be Kept on Site

6.2 One copy of the Drawings, provided to or supplied by the Contractor as aforesaid, shall be kept by the Contractor on the Site and the same shall at all reasonable times be available for inspection and use by the Engineer and by any other person authorised by the Engineer in writing.

Disruption of Progress

6.3 The Contractor shall give notice to the Engineer, with a copy to the Employer, whenever planning or execution of the Works is likely to be delayed or disrupted unless any further drawing or instruction is issued by the Engineer within a reasonable time. The notice shall include details of the drawing or instruction required and of why and by when it is required and of any delay or disruption likely to be suffered if it is late.

Delays and Cost of Delay of Drawings

6.4 If, by reason of any failure or inability of the Engineer to issue, within a time reasonable in all the circumstances, any drawing or instruction for which notice has been given by the Contractor in accordance with Sub-Clause 63, the Contractor suffers delay and/or incurs costs then the Engineer shall, after due consultation with the Employer and the Contractor, determine:

(a) any extension of time to which the Contractor is entitled under Clause 44, and

(b) the amount of such costs, which shall be added to the Contract Price,

and shall notify the Contractor accordingly, with a copy to the Employer.

Failure by Contractor to Submit Drawings

6.5 If the failure or inability of the Engineer to issue any drawings or instructions is caused in whole or in part by the failure of the Contractor to submit Drawings, Specification or other documents which he is required to submit under the Contract, the Engineer shall take such failure by the Contractor into account when making his determination pursuant to Sub-Clause 6.4.

Supplementary Drawings and Instructions	7.1	The Engineer shall have authority to issue to the Contractor, from time to time, such supplementary Drawings and instructions as shall be necessary for the purpose of the proper and adequate execution and completion of the Works and the remedying of any defects therein. The Contractor shall carry out and be bound by the same.
Permanent Works Designed by Contractor	7.2	Where the Contract expressly provides that part of the Permanent Works shall be designed by the Contractor, he shall submit to the Engineer, for approval:

(a) such drawings, specifications, calculations and other information as shall be necessary to satisfy the Engineer as to the suitability and adequacy of that design, and

(b) operation and maintenance manuals together with drawings of the Permanent Works as completed, in sufficient detail to enable the Employer to operate, maintain, dismantle, reassemble and adjust the Permanent Works incorporating that design. The Works shall not be considered to be completed for the purposes of taking over in accordance with Clause 48 until such operation and maintenance manuals, together with drawings on completion, have been submitted to and approved by the Engineer.

Responsibility Unaffected by Approval	7.3	Approval by the Engineer, in accordance with Sub-Clause 7.2, shall not relieve the Contractor of any of his responsibilities under the Contract.

General Obligations

Contractor's General Responsibilities	8.1	The Contractor shall, with due care and diligence, design (to the extent provided for by the Contract), execute and complete the Works and remedy any defects therein in accordance with the provisions of the Contract. The Contractor shall provide all superintendence, labour, materials, Plant, Contractor's Equipment and all other things, whether of a temporary or permanent nature, required in and for such design, execution, completion and remedying of any defects, so far as the necessity for providing the same is specified in or is reasonably to be inferred from the Contract.

The Contractor shall give prompt notice to the Engineer, with a copy to the Employer, of any error, omission, fault or other defect in the design of or Specification for the Works which he discovers when reviewing the Contract or executing the Works.

Site Operations and Methods of Construction	8.2	The Contractor shall take full responsibility for the adequacy, stability and safety of all Site operations and methods of construction. Provided that the Contractor shall not be responsible (except as stated hereunder or as may be otherwise agreed) for the design or specification of Permanent Works, or for the design or specification of any Temporary Works not prepared by the Contractor. Where the Contract expressly provides that part of the Permanent Works shall be designed by the Contractor, he shall be fully responsible for that part of such Works, notwithstanding any approval by the Engineer.
Contract Agreement	9.1	The Contractor shall, if called upon so to do, enter into and execute the Contract Agreement, to be prepared and completed at the cost of the Employer, in the form annexed to these Conditions with such modification as may be necessary.
Performance Security	10.1	If the Contract requires the Contractor to obtain security for his proper performance of the Contract, he shall obtain and provide to the Employer such security within 28 days after the receipt of the Letter of Acceptance, in the sum stated in the Appendix to Tender. When providing such security to the Employer, the Contractor shall notify the Engineer of so doing. Such security shall be in the form annexed to these Conditions or in such other form as may be agreed between the Employer and the Contractor. The institution providing such security shall be subject to the approval of the Employer. The cost of complying with the requirements of this Clause shall be borne by the Contractor, unless the Contract otherwise provides.

Period of Validity of Performance Security   **10.2**   The performance security shall be valid until the Contractor has executed and completed the Works and remedied any defects therein in accordance with the Contract. No claim shall be made against such security after the issue of the Defects Liability Certificate in accordance with Sub-Clause 62.1 and such security shall be returned to the Contractor within 14 days of the issue of the said Defects Liability Certificate.

Claims under Performance Security   **10.3**   Prior to making a claim under the performance security the Employer shall, in every case, notify the Contractor stating the nature of the default in respect of which the claim is to be made.

Inspection of Site   **11.1**   The Employer shall have made available to the Contractor, before the submission by the Contractor of the Tender, such data on hydrological and sub-surface conditions as have been obtained by or on behalf of the Employer from investigations undertaken relevant to the Works but the Contractor shall be responsible for his own interpretation thereof.

The Contractor shall be deemed to have inspected and examined the Site and its surroundings and information available in connection therewith and to have satisfied himself (so far as is practicable, having regard to considerations of cost and time) before submitting his Tender, as to:

(a) the form and nature thereof, including the sub-surface conditions,

(b) the hydrological and climatic conditions,

(c) the extent and nature of work and materials necessary for the execution and completion of the Works and the remedying of any defects therein, and

(d) the means of access to the Site and the accommodation he may require,

and, in general, shall be deemed to have obtained all necessary information, subject as above mentioned, as to risks, contingencies and all other circumstances which may influence or affect his Tender.

The Contractor shall be deemed to have based his Tender on the data made available by the Employer and on his own inspection and examination, all as aforementioned.

Sufficiency of Tender   **12.1**   The Contractor shall be deemed to have satisfied himself as to the correctness and sufficiency of the Tender and of the rates and prices stated in the Bill of Quantities, all of which shall, except insofar as it is otherwise provided in the Contract, cover all his obligations under the Contract (including those in respect of the supply of goods, materials, Plant or services or of contingencies for which there is a Provisional Sum) and all matters and things necessary for the proper execution and completion of the Works and the remedying of any defects therein.

Not Foreseeable Physical Obstructions or Conditions   **12.2**   If, however, during the execution of the Works the Contractor encounters physical obstructions or physical conditions, other than climatic conditions on the Site, which obstructions or conditions were, in his opinion, not foreseeable by an experienced contractor, the Contractor shall forthwith give notice thereof to the Engineer, with a copy to the Employer. On receipt of such notice, the Engineer shall, if in his opinion such obstructions or conditions could not have been reasonably foreseen by an experienced contractor, after due consultation with the Employer and the Contractor, determine:

(a) any extension of time to which the Contractor is entitled under Clause 44, and

(b) the amount of any costs which may have been incurred by the Contractor by reason of such obstructions or conditions having been encountered, which shall be added to the Contract Price,

and shall notify the Contractor accordingly, with a copy to the Employer. Such determination shall take account of any instruction which the Engineer may issue to the Contractor in connection therewith, and any proper and reasonable measures acceptable to the Engineer which the Contractor may take in the absence of specific instructions from the Engineer.

Work to be in Accordance with Contract	**13.1**	Unless it is legally or physically impossible, the Contractor shall execute and complete the Works and remedy any defects therein in strict accordance with the Contract to the satisfaction of the Engineer. The Contractor shall comply with and adhere strictly to the Engineer's instructions on any matter, whether mentioned in the Contract or not, touching or concerning the Works. The Contractor shall take instructions only from the Engineer (or his delegate).
Programme to be Submitted	**14.1**	The Contractor shall, within the time stated in Part II of these Conditions after the date of the Letter of Acceptance, submit to the Engineer for his consent a programme, in such form and detail as the Engineer shall reasonably prescribe, for the execution of the Works. The Contractor shall, whenever required by the Engineer, also provide in writing for his information a general description of the arrangements and methods which the Contractor proposes to adopt for the execution of the Works.
Revised Programme	**14.2**	If at any time it should appear to the Engineer that the actual progress of the Works does not conform to the programme to which consent has been given under Sub-Clause 14.1, the Contractor shall produce, at the request of the Engineer, a revised programme showing the modifications to such programme necessary to ensure completion of the Works within the Time for Completion.
Cash Flow Estimate to be Submitted	**14.3**	The Contractor shall, within the time stated in Part II of these Conditions after the date of the Letter of Acceptance, provide to the Engineer for his information a detailed cash flow estimate, in quarterly periods, of all payments to which the Contractor will be entitled under the Contract and the Contractor shall subsequently supply revised cash flow estimates at quarterly intervals, if required to do so by the Engineer.
Contractor not Relieved of Duties or Responsibilities	**14.4**	The submission to and consent by the Engineer of such programmes or the provision of such general descriptions or cash flow estimates shall not relieve the Contractor of any of his duties or responsibilities under the Contract.
Contractor's Superintendence	**15. 1**	The Contractor shall provide all necessary superintendence during the execution of the Works and as long thereafter as the Engineer may consider necessary for the proper fulfilling of the Contractor's obligations under the Contract. The Contractor, or a competent and authorised representative approved of by the Engineer, which approval may at any time be withdrawn, shall give his whole time to the superintendence of the Works. Such authorised representative shall receive, on behalf of the Contractor, instructions from the Engineer.
		If approval of the representative is withdrawn by the Engineer, the Contractor shall, as soon as is practicable, having regard to the requirement of replacing him as hereinafter mentioned, after receiving notice of such withdrawal, remove the representative from the Works and shall not thereafter employ him again on the Works in any capacity and shall replace him by another representative approved by the Engineer.
Contractor's Employees	**16. 1**	The Contractor shall provide on the Site in connection with the execution and completion of the Works and the remedying of any defects therein :
		(a) only such technical assistants as are skilled and experienced in their respective callings and such foremen and leading hands as are competent to give proper superintendence of the Works, and
		(b) such skilled, semi-skilled and unskilled labour as is necessary for the proper and timely fulfilling of the Contractor's obligations under the Contract.
Engineer at Liberty to Object	**16.2**	The Engineer shall be at liberty to object to and require the Contractor to remove forthwith from the Works any person provided by the Contractor who, in the opinion of the Engineer, misconducts himself, or is incompetent or negligent in the proper performance of his duties, or whose presence on Site is otherwise considered by the Engineer to be undesirable, and such person shall not be again allowed upon the Works without the consent of the Engineer. Any person so removed from the Works shall be replaced as soon as possible.

8   © FIDIC 1987

Setting-out **17. 1** The Contractor shall be responsible for:

(a) the accurate setting-out of the Works in relation to original points, lines and levels of reference given by the Engineer in writing,

(b) the correctness, subject as above mentioned, of the position, levels, dimensions and alignment of all parts of the Works, and

(c) the provision of all necessary instruments, appliances and labour in connection with the foregoing responsibilities.

If, at any time during the execution of the Works, any error appears in the position, levels, dimensions or alignment of any part of the Works, the Contractor, on being required so to do by the Engineer, shall, at his own cost, rectify such error to the satisfaction of the Engineer, unless such error is based on incorrect data supplied in writing by the Engineer, in which case the Engineer shall determine an addition to the Contract Price in accordance with Clause 52 and shall notify the Contractor accordingly, with a copy to the Employer.

The checking of any setting-out or of any line or level by the Engineer shall not in any way relieve the Contractor of his responsibility for the accuracy thereof and the Contractor shall carefully protect and preserve all bench-marks, sight-rails, pegs and other things used in setting-out the Works.

Boreholes and Exploratory Excavation **18.1** If, at any time during the execution of the Works, the Engineer requires the Contractor to make boreholes or to carry out exploratory excavation, such requirement shall be the subject of an instruction in accordance with Clause 51, unless an item or a Provisional Sum in respect of such work is included in the Bill of Quantities.

Safety, Security and Protection of the Environment **19.1** The Contractor shall, throughout the execution and completion of the Works and the remedying of any defects therein:

(a) have full regard for the safety of all persons entitled to be upon the Site and keep the Site (so far as the same is under his control) and the Works (so far as the same are not completed or occupied by the Employer) in an orderly state appropriate to the avoidance of danger to such persons,

(b) provide and maintain at his own cost all lights, guards, fencing, warning signs and watching, when and where necessary or required by the Engineer or by any duly constituted authority, for the protection of the Works or for the safety and convenience of the public or others, and

(c) take all reasonable steps to protect the environment on and off the Site and to avoid damage or nuisance to persons or to property of the public or others resulting from pollution, noise or other causes arising as a consequence of his methods of operation.

Employer's Responsibilities **19.2** If under Clause 31 the Employer shall carry out work on the Site with his own workmen he shall, in respect of such work:

(a) have full regard to the safety of all persons entitled to be upon the Site, and

(b) keep the Site in an orderly state appropriate to the avoidance of danger to such persons.

If under Clause 31 the Employer shall employ other contractors on the Site he shall require them to have the same regard for safety and avoidance of danger.

Care of Works **20.1** The Contractor shall take full responsibility for the care of the Works and materials and Plant for incorporation therein from the Commencement Date until the date of issue of the Taking-Over Certificate for the whole of the Works, when the responsibility for the said care shall pass to the Employer. Provided that:

(a) if the Engineer issues a Taking-Over Certificate for any Section or part of the Permanent Works the Contractor shall cease to be liable for the care of that Section or part from the date of issue of the Taking-Over Certificate, when the responsibility for the care of that Section or part shall pass to the Employer, and

(b) the Contractor shall take full responsibility for the care of any outstanding Works and materials and Plant for incorporation therein which he undertakes to finish during the Defects Liability Period until such outstanding Works have been completed pursuant to Clause 49.

Responsibility to Rectify Loss or Damage	**20.2**

If any loss or damage happens to the Works, or any part thereof, or materials or Plant for incorporation therein, during the period for which the Contractor is responsible for the care thereof, from any cause whatsoever, other than the risks defined in Sub-Clause 20.4, the Contractor shall, at his own cost, rectify such loss or damage so that the Permanent Works conform in every respect with the provisions of the Contract to the satisfaction of the Engineer. The Contractor shall also be liable for any loss or damage to the Works occasioned by him in the course of any operations carried out by him for the purpose of complying with his obligations under Clauses 49 and 50.

Loss or Damage Due to Employer's Risks	**20.3**

In the event of any such loss or damage happening from any of the risks defined in Sub-Clause 20.4, or in combination with other risks, the Contractor shall, if and to the extent required by the Engineer, rectify the loss or damage and the Engineer shall determine an addition to the Contract Price in accordance with Clause 52 and shall notify the Contractor accordingly, with a copy to the Employer. In the case of a combination of risks causing loss or damage any such determination shall take into account the proportional responsibility of the Contractor and the Employer.

Employer's Risks	**20.4**

The Employer's risks are:

(a) war, hostilities (whether war be declared or not), invasion, act of foreign enemies,

(b) rebellion, revolution, insurrection, or military or usurped power, or civil war,

(c) ionising radiations, or contamination by radio-activity from any nuclear fuel, or from any nuclear waste from the combustion of nuclear fuel, radio-active toxic explosive or other hazardous properties of any explosive nuclear assembly or nuclear component thereof,

(d) pressure waves caused by aircraft or other aerial devices travelling at sonic or supersonic speeds,

(e) riot, commotion or disorder, unless solely restricted to employees of the Contractor or of his Subcontractors and arising from the conduct of the Works,

(f) loss or damage due to the use or occupation by the Employer of any Section or part of the Permanent Works, except as may be provided for in the Contract,

(g) loss or damage to the extent that it is due to the design of the Works, other than any part of the design provided by the Contractor or for which the Contractor is responsible, and

(h) any operation of the forces of nature against which an experienced contractor could not reasonably have been expected to take precautions.

Insurance of Works and Contractor's Equipment	**21.1**

The Contractor shall, without limiting his or the Employer's obligations and responsibilities under Clause 20, insure:

(a) the Works, together with materials and Plant for incorporation therein, to the full replacement cost (the term "cost" in this context shall include profit),

(b) an additional sum of 15 per cent of such replacement cost, or as may be specified in Part II of these Conditions, to cover any additional costs of and incidental to the rectification of loss or damage including professional fees and the cost of demolishing and removing any part of the Works and of removing debris of whatsoever nature, and

(c) the Contractor's Equipment and other things brought onto the Site by the Contractor, for a sum sufficient to provide for their replacement at the Site.

Scope of Cover   **21.2**   The insurance in paragraphs (a) and (b) of Sub-Clause 21.1 shall be in the joint names of the Contractor and the Employer and shall cover:

(a) the Employer and the Contractor against all loss or damage from whatsoever cause arising, other than as provided in Sub-Clause 21.4, from the start of work at the Site until the date of issue of the relevant Taking-Over Certificate in respect of the Works or any Section or part thereof as the case may be, and

(b) the Contractor for his liability:

     (i) during the Defects Liability Period for loss or damage arising from a cause occurring prior to the commencement of the Defects Liability Period, and

     (ii) for loss or damage occasioned by the Contractor in the course of any operations carried out by him for the purpose of complying with his obligations under Clauses 49 and 50.

Responsibility for   **21.3**   Any amounts not insured or not recovered from the insurers shall be borne by the
Amounts not   Employer or the Contractor in accordance with their responsibilities under
Recovered   Clause 20.

Exclusions   **21.4**   There shall be no obligation for the insurances in Sub-Clause 21.1 to include loss or damage caused by:

(a) war, hostilities (whether war be declared or not), invasion, act of foreign enemies,

(b) rebellion, revolution, insurrection, or military or usurped power, or civil war,

(c) ionising radiations, or contamination by radio-activity from any nuclear fuel, or from any nuclear waste from the combustion of nuclear fuel, radio-active toxic explosive or other hazardous properties of any explosive nuclear assembly or nuclear component thereof, or

(d) pressure waves caused by aircraft or other aerial devices travelling at sonic or supersonic speeds.

Damage to   **22.1**   The Contractor shall, except if and so far as the Contract provides otherwise,
Persons and   indemnify the Employer against all losses and claims in respect of:
Property

(a) death of or injury to any person, or

(b) loss of or damage to any property (other than the Works),

which may arise out of or in consequence of the execution and completion of the Works and the remedying of any defects therein, and against all claims, proceedings, damages, costs, charges and expenses whatsoever in respect thereof or in relation thereto, subject to the exceptions defined in Sub-Clause 22.2.

Exceptions   **22.2**   The "exceptions" referred to in Sub-Clause 22.1 are:

(a) the permanent use or occupation of land by the Works, or any part thereof,

(b) the right of the Employer to execute the Works, or any part thereof, on, over, under, in or through any land,

(c) damage to property which is the unavoidable result of the execution and completion of the Works, or the remedying of any defects therein, in accordance with the Contract, and

(d) death of or injury to persons or loss of or damage to property resulting from any act or neglect of the Employer, his agents, servants or other contractors, not being employed by the Contractor, or in respect of any claims, proceedings, damages, costs, charges and expenses in respect thereof or in relation thereto or, where the injury or damage was contributed to by the Contractor, his servants or agents, such part of the said injury or damage as may be just and equitable having regard to the extent of the responsibility of the Employer, his servants or agents or other contractors for the injury or damage.

Indemnity by Employer	22.3	The Employer shall indemnify the Contractor against all claims, proceedings, damages, costs, charges and expenses in respect of the matters referred to in the exceptions defined in Sub-Clause 22.2.
Third Party Insurance (including Employer's Property)	23.1	The Contractor shall, without limiting his or the Employer's obligations and responsibilities under Clause 22, insure, in the joint names of the Contractor and the Employer, against liabilities for death of or injury to any person (other than as provided in Clause 24) or loss of or damage to any property (other than the Works) arising out of the performance of the Contract, other than the exceptions defined in paragraphs (a), (b) and (c) of Sub-Clause 22.2.
Minimum Amount of Insurance	23.2	Such insurance shall be for at least the amount stated in the Appendix to Tender.
Cross Liabilities	23.3	The insurance policy shall include a cross liability clause such that the insurance shall apply to the Contractor and to the Employer as separate insureds.
Accident or Injury to Workmen	24.1	The Employer shall not be liable for or in respect of any damages or compensation payable to any workman or other person in the employment of the Contractor or any Subcontractor, other than death or injury resulting from any act or default of the Employer, his agents or servants. The Contractor shall indemnify and keep indemnified the Employer against all such damages and compensation, other than those for which the Employer is liable as aforesaid, and against all claims, proceedings, damages, costs, charges, and expenses whatsoever in respect thereof or in relation thereto.
Insurance Against Accident to Workmen	24.2	The Contractor shall insure against such liability and shall continue such insurance during the whole of the time that any persons are employed by him on the Works. Provided that, in respect of any persons employed by any Subcontractor, the Contractor's obligations to insure as aforesaid under this Sub-Clause shall be satisfied if the Subcontractor shall have insured against the liability in respect of such persons in such manner that the Employer is indemnified under the policy, but the Contractor shall require such Subcontractor to produce to the Employer, when required, such policy of insurance and the receipt for the payment of the current premium.
Evidence and Terms of Insurances	25.1	The Contractor shall provide evidence to the Employer prior to the start of work at the Site that the insurances required under the Contract have been effected and shall, within 84 days of the Commencement Date, provide the insurance policies to the Employer. When providing such evidence and such policies to the Employer, the Contractor shall notify the Engineer of so doing. Such insurance policies shall be consistent with the general terms agreed prior to the issue of the Letter of Acceptance. The Contractor shall effect all insurances for which he is responsible with insurers and in terms approved by the Employer.
Adequacy of Insurances	25.2	The Contractor shall notify the insurers of changes in the nature, extent or programme for the execution of the Works and ensure the adequacy of the insurances at all times in accordance with the terms of the Contract and shall, when required, produce to the Employer the insurance policies in force and the receipts for payment of the current premiums.
Remedy on Contractor's Failure to Insure	25.3	If the Contractor fails to effect and keep in force any of the insurances required under the Contract, or fails to provide the policies to the Employer within the period required by Sub-Clause 25.1, then and in any such case the Employer may effect and keep in force any such insurances and pay any premium as may be necessary for that purpose and from time to time deduct the amount so paid from any monies due or to become due to the Contractor, or recover the same as a debt due from the Contractor.
Compliance with Policy Conditions	25.4	In the event that the Contractor or the Employer fails to comply with conditions imposed by the insurance policies effected pursuant to the Contract, each shall indemnify the other against all losses and claims arising from such failure.

12

Compliance with Statutes, Regulations	26.1	The Contractor shall conform in all respects, including by the giving of all notices and the paying of all fees, with the provisions of:

(a) any National or State Statute, Ordinance, or other Law, or any regulation, or bye-law of any local or other duly constituted authority in relation to the execution and completion of the Works and the remedying of any defects therein, and

(b) the rules and regulations of all public bodies and companies whose property or rights are affected or may be affected in any way by the Works,

and the Contractor shall keep the Employer indemnified against all penalties and liability of every kind for breach of any such provisions. Provided always that the Employer shall be responsible for obtaining any planning, zoning or other similar permission required for the Works to proceed and shall indemnify the Contractor in accordance with Sub-Clause 22.3.

Fossils	27.1	All fossils, coins, articles of value or antiquity and structures and other remains or things of geological or archaeological interest discovered on the Site shall, as between the Employer and the Contractor, be deemed to be the absolute property of the Employer. The Contractor shall take reasonable precautions to prevent his workmen or any other persons from removing or damaging any such article or thing and shall, immediately upon discovery thereof and before removal, acquaint the Engineer of such discovery and carry out the Engineer's instructions for dealing with the same. If, by reason of such instructions, the Contractor suffers delay and/or incurs costs then the Engineer shall, after due consultation with the Employer and the Contractor, determine:

(a) any extension of time to which the Contractor is entitled under Clause 44, and

(b) the amount of such costs, which shall be added to the Contract Price,

and shall notify the Contractor accordingly, with a copy to the Employer.

Patent Rights	28.1	The Contractor shall save harmless and indemnify the Employer from and against all claims and proceedings for or on account of infringement of any patent rights, design trademark or name or other protected rights in respect of any Contractor's Equipment, materials or Plant used for or in connection with or for incorporation in the Works and from and against all damages, costs, charges and expenses whatsoever in respect thereof or in relation thereto, except where such infringement results from compliance with the design or Specification provided by the Engineer.
Royalties	28.2	Except where otherwise stated, the Contractor shall pay all tonnage and other royalties, rent and other payments or compensation, if any, for getting stone, sand, gravel, clay or other materials required for the Works.
Interference with Traffic and Adjoining Properties	29.1	All operations necessary for the execution and completion of the Works and the remedying of any defects therein shall, so far as compliance with the requirements of the Contract permits, be carried on so as not to interfere unnecessarily or improperly with:

(a) the convenience of the public, or

(b) the access to, use and occupation of public or private roads and footpaths to or of properties whether in the possession of the Employer or of any other person.

The Contractor shall save harmless and indemnify the Employer in respect of all claims, proceedings, damages, costs, charges and expenses whatsoever arising out of, or in relation to, any such matters insofar as the Contractor is responsible therefor.

Avoidance of Damage to Roads	**30.1** The Contractor shall use every reasonable means to prevent any of the roads or bridges communicating with or on the routes to the Site from being damaged or injured by any traffic of the Contractor or any of his Subcontractors and, in particular, shall select routes, choose and use vehicles and restrict and distribute loads so that any such extraordinary traffic as will inevitably arise from the moving of materials, Plant, Contractor's Equipment or Temporary Works from and to the Site shall be limited, as far as reasonably possible, and so that no unnecessary damage or injury may be occasioned to such roads and bridges.
Transport of Contractor's Equipment or Temporary Works	**30.2** Save insofar as the Contract otherwise provides, the Contractor shall be responsible for and shall pay the cost of strengthening any bridges or altering or improving any road communicating with or on the routes to the Site to facilitate the movement of Contractor's Equipment or Temporary Works and the Contractor shall indemnify and keep indemnified the Employer against all claims for damage to any such road or bridge caused by such movement, including such claims as may be made directly against the Employer, and shall negotiate and pay all claims arising solely out of such damage.
Transport of Materials or Plant	**30.3** If, notwithstanding Sub-Clause 30.1, any damage occurs to any bridge or road communicating with or on the routes to the Site arising from the transport of materials or Plant, the Contractor shall notify the Engineer with a copy to the Employer, as soon as he becomes aware of such damage or as soon as he receives any claim from the authority entitled to make such claim. Where under any law or regulation the haulier of such materials or Plant is required to indemnify the road authority against damage the Employer shall not be liable for any costs, charges or expenses in respect thereof or in relation thereto. In other cases the Employer shall negotiate the settlement of and pay all sums due in respect of such claim and shall indemnify the Contractor in respect thereof and in respect of all claims, proceedings, damages, costs, charges and expenses in relation thereto. Provided that if and so far as any such claim or part thereof is, in the opinion of the Engineer, due to any failure on the part of the Contractor to observe and perform his obligations under Sub-Clause 30.1, then the amount, determined by the Engineer, after due consultation with the Employer and the Contractor, to be due to such failure shall be recoverable from the Contractor by the Employer and may be deducted by the Employer from any monies due or to become due to the Contractor and the Engineer shall notify the Contractor accordingly, with a copy to the Employer. Provided also that the Employer shall notify the Contractor whenever a settlement is to be negotiated and, where any amount may be due from the Contractor, the Employer shall consult with the Contractor before such settlement is agreed.
Waterborne Traffic	**30.4** Where the nature of the Works is such as to require the use by the Contractor of waterborne transport the foregoing provisions of this Clause shall be construed as though "road" included a lock, dock, sea wall or other structure related to a waterway and "vehicle" included craft, and shall have effect accordingly.
Opportunities for Other Contractors	**31.1** The Contractor shall, in accordance with the requirements of the Engineer, afford all reasonable opportunities for carrying out their work to:
	(a) any other contractors employed by the Employer and their workmen,
	(b) the workmen of the Employer, and
	(c) the workmen of any duly constituted authorities who may be employed in the execution on or near the Site of any work not included in the Contract or of any contract which the Employer may enter into in connection with or ancillary to the Works.
Facilities for Other Contractors	**31.2** If, however, pursuant to Sub-Clause 31.1 the Contractor shall, on the written request of the Engineer:
	(a) make available to any such other contractor, or to the Employer or any such authority, any roads or ways for the maintenance of which the Contractor is responsible,

14   © FIDIC 1987

(b) permit the use, by any such, of Temporary Works or Contractor's Equipment on the Site, or

(c) provide any other service of whatsoever nature for any such,

the Engineer shall determine an addition to the Contract Price in accordance with Clause 52 and shall notify the Contractor accordingly, with a copy to the Employer.

Contractor to Keep Site Clear   **32.1**   During the execution of the Works the Contractor shall keep the Site reasonably free from all unnecessary obstruction and shall store or dispose of any Contractor's Equipment and surplus materials and clear away and remove from the Site any wreckage, rubbish or Temporary Works no longer required.

Clearance of Site on Completion   **33.1**   Upon the issue of any Taking-Over Certificate, the Contractor shall clear away and remove from that part of the Site to which such Taking-Over Certificate relates all Contractor's Equipment, surplus material, rubbish and Temporary Works of every kind, and leave such part of the Site and Works clean and in a workmanlike condition to the satisfaction of the Engineer. Provided that the Contractor shall be entitled to retain on Site, until the end of the Defects Liability Period, such materials, Contractor's Equipment and Temporary Works as are required by him for the purpose of fulfilling his obligations during the Defects Liability Period.

Labour

Engagement of Staff and Labour   **34.1**   The Contractor shall, unless otherwise provided in the Contract, make his own arrangements for the engagement of all staff and labour, local or other, and for their payment, housing, feeding and transport.

Returns of Labour and Contractor's Equipment   **35.1**   The Contractor shall, if required by the Engineer, deliver to the Engineer a return in detail, in such form and at such intervals as the Engineer may prescribe, showing the staff and the numbers of the several classes of labour from time to time employed by the Contractor on the Site and such information respecting Contractor's Equipment as the Engineer may require.

Materials, Plant and Workmanship

Quality of Materials, Plant and Workmanship   **36.1**   All materials, Plant and workmanship shall be:

(a) of the respective kinds described in the Contract and in accordance with the Engineer's instructions, and

(b) subjected from time to time to such tests as the Engineer may require at the place of manufacture, fabrication or preparation, or on the Site or at such other place or places as may be specified in the Contract, or at all or any of such places.

The Contractor shall provide such assistance, labour, electricity, fuels, stores, apparatus and instruments as are normally required for examining, measuring and testing any materials or Plant and shall supply samples of materials, before incorporation in the Works, for testing as may be selected and required by the Engineer.

Cost of Samples   **36.2**   All samples shall be supplied by the Contractor at his own cost if the supply thereof is clearly intended by or provided for in the Contract.

Cost of Tests   **36.3**   The cost of making any test shall be borne by the Contractor if such test is:

(a) clearly intended by or provided for in the Contract, or

(b) particularised in the Contract (in cases only of a test under load or of a test to ascertain whether the design of any finished or partially finished work is appropriate for the purposes which it was intended to fulfil) in sufficient detail to enable the Contractor to price or allow for the same in his Tender.

Cost of Tests not Provided for	**36.4**	If any test required by the Engineer which is :

(a) not so intended by or provided for,

(b) (in the cases above mentioned) not so particularised, or

(c) (though so intended or provided for) required by the Engineer to be carried out at any place other than the Site or the place of manufacture, fabrication or preparation of the materials or Plant tested,

shows the materials, Plant or workmanship not to be in accordance with the provisions of the Contract to the satisfaction of the Engineer, then the cost of such test shall be borne by the Contractor, but in any other case Sub-Clause 36.5 shall apply.

Engineer's Determination where Tests not Provided for	**36.5**	Where, pursuant to Sub-Clause 36.4, this Sub-Clause applies the Engineer shall, after due consultation with the Employer and the Contractor, determine:

(a) any extension of time to which the Contractor is entitled under Clause 44, and

(b) the amount of such costs, which shall be added to the Contract Price,

and shall notify the Contractor accordingly, with a copy to the Employer.

Inspection of Operations	**37.1**	The Engineer, and any person authorised by him, shall at all reasonable times have access to the Site and to all workshops and places where materials or Plant are being manufactured, fabricated or prepared for the Works and the Contractor shall afford every facility for and every assistance in obtaining the right to such access.

Inspection and Testing	**37.2**	The Engineer shall be entitled, during manufacture, fabrication or preparation to inspect and test the materials and Plant to be supplied under the Contract. If materials or Plant are being manufactured, fabricated or prepared in workshops or places other than those of the Contractor, the Contractor shall obtain permission for the Engineer to carry out such inspection and testing in those workshops or places. Such inspection or testing shall not release the Contractor from any obligation under the Contract.

Dates for Inspection and Testing	**37.3**	The Contractor shall agree with the Engineer on the time and place for the inspection or testing of any materials or Plant as provided in the Contract. The Engineer shall give the Contractor not less than 24 hours notice of his intention to carry out the inspection or to attend the tests. If the Engineer, or his duly authorised representative, does not attend on the date agreed, the Contractor may, unless otherwise instructed by the Engineer, proceed with the tests, which shall be deemed to have been made in the presence of the Engineer. The Contractor shall forthwith forward to the Engineer duly certified copies of the test readings. If the Engineer has not attended the tests, he shall accept the said readings as accurate.

Rejection	**37.4**	If, at the time and place agreed in accordance with Sub-Clause 37.3, the materials or Plant are not ready for inspection or testing or if, as a result of the inspection or testing referred to in this Clause, the Engineer determines that the materials or Plant are defective or otherwise not in accordance with the Contract, he may reject the materials or Plant and shall notify the Contractor thereof immediately. The notice shall state the Engineer's objections with reasons. The Contractor shall then promptly make good the defect or ensure that rejected materials or Plant comply with the Contract. If the Engineer so requests, the tests of rejected materials or Plant shall be made or repeated under the same terms and conditions. All costs incurred by the Employer by the repetition of the tests shall, after due consultation with the Employer and the Contractor, be determined by the Engineer and shall be recoverable from the Contractor by the Employer and may be deducted from any monies due or to become due to the Contractor and the Engineer shall notify the Contractor accordingly, with a copy to the Employer.

Independent Inspection	37.5	The Engineer may delegate inspection and testing of materials or Plant to an independent inspector. Any such delegation shall be effected in accordance with Sub-Clause 2.4 and for this purpose such independent inspector shall be considered as an assistant of the Engineer. Notice of such appointment (not being less than 14 days) shall be given by the Engineer to the Contractor.
Examination of Work before Covering up	38.1	No part of the Works shall be covered up or put out of view without the approval of the Engineer and the Contractor shall afford full opportunity for the Engineer to examine and measure any such part of the Works which is about to be covered up or put out of view and to examine foundations before any part of the Works is placed thereon. The Contractor shall give notice to the Engineer whenever any such part of the Works or foundations is or are ready or about to be ready for examination and the Engineer shall, without unreasonable delay, unless he considers it unnecessary and advises the Contractor accordingly, attend for the purpose of examining and measuring such part of the Works or of examining such foundations.
Uncovering and Making Openings	38.2	The Contractor shall uncover any part of the Works or make openings in or through the same as the Engineer may from time to time instruct and shall reinstate and make good such part. If any such part has been covered up or put out of view after compliance with the requirement of Sub-Clause 38.1 and is found to be executed in accordance with the Contract, the Engineer shall, after due consultation with the Employer and the Contractor, determine the amount of the Contractor's costs in respect of such of uncovering, making openings in or through, reinstating and making good the same, which shall be added to the Contract Price, and shall notify the Contractor accordingly, with a copy to the Employer. In any other case all costs shall be borne by the Contractor.
Removal of Improper Work, Materials or Plant	39.1	The Engineer shall have authority to issue instructions from time to time, for:

(a) the removal from the Site, within such time or times as may be specified in the instruction, of any materials or Plant which, in the opinion of the Engineer, are not in accordance with the Contract,

(b) the substitution of proper and suitable materials or Plant, and

(c) the removal and proper re-execution, notwithstanding any previous test thereof or interim payment therefor, of any work which, in respect of

　(i) materials, Plant or workmanship, or

　(ii) design by the Contractor or for which he is responsible,

is not, in the opinion of the Engineer, in accordance with the Contract.

Default of Contractor in Compliance	39.2	In case of default on the part of the Contractor in carrying out such instruction within the time specified therein or, if none, within a reasonable time, the Employer shall be entitled to employ and pay other persons to carry out the same and all costs consequent thereon or incidental thereto shall, after due consultation with the Employer and the Contractor, be determined by the Engineer and shall be recoverable from the Contractor by the Employer, and may be deducted by the Employer from any monies due or to become due to the Contractor and the Engineer shall notify the Contractor accordingly, with a copy to the Employer.

Suspension

Suspension of Work	40. 1	The Contractor shall, on the instructions of the Engineer, suspend the progress of the Works or any part thereof for such time and in such manner as the Engineer may consider necessary and shall, during such suspension, properly protect and secure the Works or such part thereof so far as is necessary in the opinion of the Engineer. Unless such suspension is:

(a) otherwise provided for in the Contract,

(b) necessary by reason of some default of or breach of contract by the Contractor or for which he is responsible,

(c) necessary by reason of climatic conditions on the Site, or

(d) necessary for the proper execution of the Works or for the safety of the Works or any part thereof (save to the extent that such necessity arises from any act or default by the Engineer or the Employer or from any of the risks defined in Sub-Clause 20.4),

Sub-Clause 40.2 shall apply.

Engineer's Determination following Suspension	40.2	Where, pursuant to Sub-Clause 40.1, this Sub-Clause applies the Engineer shall, after due consultation with the Employer and the Contractor, determine:

(a) any extension of time to which the Contractor is entitled under Clause 44, and

(b) the amount, which shall be added to the Contract Price, in respect of the cost incurred by the Contractor by reason of such suspension,

and shall notify the Contractor accordingly, with a copy to the Employer.

Suspension lasting more than 84 Days	40.3	If the progress of the Works or any part thereof is suspended on the instructions of the Engineer and if permission to resume work is not given by the Engineer within a period of 84 days from the date of suspension then, unless such suspension is within paragraph (a), (b), (c) or (d) of Sub-Clause 40.1, the Contractor may give notice to the Engineer requiring permission, within 28 days from the receipt thereof, to proceed with the Works or that part thereof in regard to which progress is suspended. If, within the said time, such permission is not granted, the Contractor may, but is not bound to, elect to treat the suspension, where it affects part only of the Works, as an omission of such part under Clause 51 by giving a further notice to the Engineer to that effect, or, where it affects the whole of the Works, treat the suspension as an event of default by the Employer and terminate his employment under the Contract in accordance with the provisions of Sub-Clause 69.1, whereupon the provisions of Sub-Clauses 69.2 and 69.3 shall apply.

Commencement and Delays

Commencement of Works	41.1	The Contractor shall commence the Works as soon as is reasonably possible after the receipt by him of a notice to this effect from the Engineer, which notice shall be issued within the time stated in the Appendix to Tender after the date of the Letter of Acceptance. Thereafter, the Contractor shall proceed with the Works with due expedition and without delay.

Possession of Site and Access Thereto	42.1	Save insofar as the Contract may prescribe:

(a) the extent of portions of the Site of which the Contractor is to be given possession from time to time,

(b) the order in which such portions shall be made available to the Contractor,

and, subject to any requirement in the Contract as to the order in which the Works shall be executed, the Employer will, with the Engineer's notice to commence the Works, give to the Contractor possession of

(c) so much of the Site, and

(d) such access as, in accordance with the Contract, is to be provided by the Employer as may be required to enable the Contractor to commence and proceed with the execution of the Works in accordance with the programme referred to in Clause 14, if any, and otherwise in accordance with such reasonable proposals as the Contractor shall, by notice to the Engineer with a copy to the Employer, make. The Employer will, from time to time as the Works proceed, give to the Contractor possession of such further portions of the Site as may be required to enable the Contractor to proceed with the execution of the Works with due dispatch in accordance with such programme or proposals, as the case may be.

© FIDIC 1987

| **Failure to Give Possession** | **42.2** | If the Contractor suffers delay and/or incurs costs from failure on the part of the Employer to give possession in accordance with the terms of Sub-Clause 42. 1, the Engineer shall, after due consultation with the Employer and the Contractor, determine: |

(a) any extension of time to which the Contractor is entitled under Clause 44, and

(b) the amount of such costs, which shall be added to the Contract Price,

and shall notify the Contractor accordingly, with a copy to the Employer.

| **Rights of Way and Facilities** | **42.3** | The Contractor shall bear all costs and charges for special or temporary rights of way required by him in connection with access to the Site. The Contractor shall also provide at his own cost any additional facilities outside the Site required by him for the purposes of the Works. |

| **Time for Completion** | **43.1** | The whole of the Works and, if applicable, any Section required to be completed within a particular time as stated in the Appendix to Tender, shall be completed, in accordance with the provisions of Clause 48, within the time stated in the Appendix to Tender for the whole of the Works or the Section (as the case may be), calculated from the Commencement Date, or such extended time as may be allowed under Clause 44. |

| **Extension of Time for Completion** | **44.1** | In the event of : |

(a) the amount or nature of extra or additional work,

(b) any cause of delay referred to in these Conditions,

(c) exceptionally adverse climatic conditions,

(d) any delay, impediment or prevention by the Employer, or

(e) other special circumstances which may occur, other than through a default of or breach of contract by the Contractor or for which he is responsible,

being such as fairly to entitle the Contractor to an extension of the Time for Completion of the Works, or any Section or part thereof, the Engineer shall, after due consultation with the Employer and the Contractor, determine the amount of such extension and shall notify the Contractor accordingly, with a copy to the Employer.

| **Contractor to Provide Notification and Detailed Particulars** | **44.2** | Provided that the Engineer is not bound to make any determination unless the Contractor has |

(a) within 28 days after such event has first arisen notified the Engineer with a copy to the Employer, and

(b) within 28 days, or such other reasonable time as may be agreed by the Engineer, after such notification submitted to the Engineer detailed particulars of any extension of time to which he may consider himself entitled in order that such submission may be investigated at the time.

| **Interim Determination of Extension** | **44.3** | Provided also that where an event has a continuing effect such that it is not practicable for the Contractor to submit detailed particulars within the period of 28 days referred to in Sub-Clause 44.2(b), he shall nevertheless be entitled to an extension of time provided that he has submitted to the Engineer interim particulars at intervals of not more than 28 days and final particulars within 28 days of the end of the effects resulting from the event. On receipt of such interim particulars, the Engineer shall, without undue delay, make an interim determination of extension of time and, on receipt of the final particulars, the Engineer shall review all the circumstances and shall determine an overall extension of time in regard to the event. In both such cases the Engineer shall make his determination after due consultation with the Employer and the Contractor and shall notify the Contractor of the determination, with a copy to the Employer. No final review shall result in a decrease of any extension of time already determined by the Engineer. |

Restriction on Working Hours	**45.1**	Subject to any provision to the contrary contained in the Contract, none of the Works shall, save as hereinafter provided, be carried on during the night or on locally recognised days of rest without the consent of the Engineer, except when work is unavoidable or absolutely necessary for the saving of life or property or for the safety of the Works, in which case the Contractor shall immediately advise the Engineer. Provided that the provisions of this Clause shall not be applicable in the case of any work which it is customary to carry out by multiple shifts.
Rate of Progress	**46.1**	If for any reason, which does not entitle the Contractor to an extension of time, the rate of progress of the Works or any Section is at any time, in the opinion of the Engineer, too slow to comply with the Time for Completion, the Engineer shall so notify the Contractor who shall thereupon take such steps as are necessary, subject to the consent of the Engineer, to expedite progress so as to comply with the Time for Completion. The Contractor shall not be entitled to any additional payment for taking such steps. If, as a result of any notice given by the Engineer under this Clause, the Contractor considers that it is necessary to do any work at night or on locally recognised days of rest, he shall be entitled to seek the consent of the Engineer so to do. Provided that if any steps, taken by the Contractor in meeting his obligations under this Clause, involve the Employer in additional supervision costs, such costs shall, after due consultation with the Employer and the Contractor, be determined by the Engineer and shall be recoverable from the Contractor by the Employer, and may be deducted by the Employer from any monies due or to become due to the Contractor and the Engineer shall notify the Contractor accordingly, with a copy to the Employer.
Liquidated Damages for Delay	**47.1**	If the Contractor fails to comply with the Time for Completion in accordance with Clause 48, for the whole of the Works or, if applicable, any Section within the relevant time prescribed by Clause 43, then the Contractor shall pay to the Employer the relevant sum stated in the Appendix to Tender as liquidated damages for such default and not as a penalty (which sum shall be the only monies due from the Contractor for such default) for every day or part of a day which shall elapse between the relevant Time for Completion and the date stated in a Taking-Over Certificate of the whole of the Works or the relevant Section, subject to the applicable limit stated in the Appendix to Tender. The Employer may, without prejudice to any other method of recovery, deduct the amount of such damages from any monies due or to become due to the Contractor. The payment or deduction of such damages shall not relieve the Contractor from his obligation to complete the Works, or from any other of his obligations and liabilities under the Contract.
Reduction of Liquidated Damages	**47.2**	If, before the Time for Completion of the whole of the Works or, if applicable, any Section, a Taking-Over Certificate has been issued for any part of the Works or of a Section, the liquidated damages for delay in completion of the remainder of the Works or of that Section shall, for any period of delay after the date stated in such Taking-Over Certificate, and in the absence of alternative provisions in the Contract, be reduced in the proportion which the value of the part so certified bears to the value of the whole of the Works or Section, as applicable. The provisions of this Sub-Clause shall only apply to the rate of liquidated damages and shall not affect the limit thereof.

Taking-Over Certificate	**48.1**	When the whole of the Works have been substantially completed and have satisfactorily passed any Tests on Completion prescribed by the Contract, the Contractor may give a notice to that effect to the Engineer, with a copy to the Employer, accompanied by a written undertaking to finish with due expedition any outstanding work during the Defects Liability Period. Such notice and undertaking shall be deemed to be a request by the Contractor for the Engineer to issue a Taking-Over Certificate in respect of the Works. The Engineer shall, within 21 days of the date of delivery of such notice, either issue to the Contractor, with a copy to the Employer, a Taking-Over Certificate, stating the date on which, in his opinion, the Works were substantially completed in accordance with the Contract, or give instructions in writing to the Contractor specifying all the work which, in the Engineer's opinion, is required to be done by the Contractor before the issue of such Certificate. The Engineer shall also notify the Contractor of any defects in the Works affecting substantial completion that may appear after such instructions and before completion of the Works specified therein. The Contractor shall be entitled to receive such Taking-Over Certificate within 21 days of completion, to the satisfaction of the Engineer, of the Works so specified and remedying any defects so notified.

Taking Over of Sections or Parts **48.2** Similarly, in accordance with the procedure set out in Sub-Clause 48.1, the Contractor may request and the Engineer shall issue a Taking-Over Certificate in respect of:

(a) any Section in respect of which a separate Time for Completion is provided in the Appendix to Tender,

(b) any substantial part of the Permanent Works which has been both completed to the satisfaction of the Engineer and, otherwise than as provided for in the Contract, occupied or used by the Employer, or

(c) any part of the Permanent Works which the Employer has elected to occupy or use prior to completion (where such prior occupation or use is not provided for in the Contract or has not been agreed by the Contractor as a temporary measure).

Substantial Completion of Parts **48.3** If any part of the Permanent Works has been substantially completed and has satisfactorily passed any Tests on Completion prescribed by the Contract, the Engineer may issue a Taking-Over Certificate in respect of that part of the Permanent Works before completion of the whole of the Works and, upon the issue of such Certificate, the Contractor shall be deemed to have undertaken to complete with due expedition any outstanding work in that part of the Permanent Works during the Defects Liability Period.

Surfaces Requiring Reinstatement **48.4** Provided that a Taking-Over Certificate given in respect of any Section or part of the Permanent Works before completion of the whole of the Works shall not be deemed to certify completion of any ground or surfaces requiring reinstatement, unless such Taking-Over Certificate shall expressly so state.

Defects Liability

Defects Liability Period **49.1** In these Conditions the expression "Defects Liability Period" shall mean the defects liability period named in the Appendix to Tender, calculated from:

(a) the date of completion of the Works certified by the Engineer in accordance with Clause 48, or

(b) in the event of more than one certificate having been issued by the Engineer under Clause 48, the respective dates so certified,

and in relation to the Defects Liability Period the expression "the Works" shall be construed accordingly.

Completion of Outstanding Work and Remedying Defects	**49.2**	To the intent that the Works shall, at or as soon as practicable after the expiration of the Defects Liability Period, be delivered to the Employer in the condition required by the Contract, fair wear and tear excepted, to the satisfaction of the Engineer, the Contractor shall:

(a) complete the work, if any, outstanding on the date stated in the Taking-Over Certificate as soon as practicable after such date, and

(b) execute all such work of amendment, reconstruction, and remedying defects, shrinkages or other faults as the Engineer may, during the Defects Liability Period or within 14 days after its expiration, as a result of an inspection made by or on behalf of the Engineer prior to its expiration, instruct the Contractor to execute.

Cost of Remedying Defects	**49.3**	All work referred to in Sub-Clause 49.2 (b) shall be executed by the Contractor at his own cost if the necessity thereof is, in the opinion of the Engineer, due to:

(a) the use of materials, Plant or workmanship not in accordance with the Contract,

(b) where the Contractor is responsible for the design of part of the Permanent Works, any fault in such design, or

(c) the neglect or failure on the part of the Contractor to comply with any obligation, expressed or implied, on the Contractor's part under the Contract.

If, in the opinion of the Engineer, such necessity is due to any other cause, he shall determine an addition to the Contract Price in accordance with Clause 52 and shall notify the Contractor accordingly, with a copy to the Employer.

Contractor's Failure to Carry Out Instructions	**49.4**	In case of default on the part of the Contractor in carrying out such instruction within a reasonable time, the Employer shall be entitled to employ and pay other persons to carry out the same and if such work is work which, in the opinion of the Engineer, the Contractor was liable to do at his own cost under the Contract, then all costs consequent thereon or incidental thereto shall, after due consultation with the Employer and the Contractor, be determined by the Engineer and shall be recoverable from the Contractor by the Employer, and may be deducted by the Employer from any monies due or to become due to the Contractor and the Engineer shall notify the Contractor accordingly, with a copy to the Employer.

Contractor to Search	**50.1**	If any defect, shrinkage or other fault in the Works appears at any time prior to the end of the Defects Liability Period, the Engineer may instruct the Contractor, with copy to the Employer, to search under the directions of the Engineer for the cause thereof. Unless such defect, shrinkage or other fault is one for which the Contractor is liable under the Contract, the Engineer shall, after due consultation with the Employer and the Contractor, determine the amount in respect of the costs of such search incurred by the Contractor, which shall be added to the Contract Price and shall notify the Contractor accordingly, with a copy to the Employer. If such defect, shrinkage or other fault is one for which the Contractor is liable, the cost of the work carried out in searching as aforesaid shall be borne by the Contractor and he shall in such case remedy such defect, shrinkage or other fault at his own cost in accordance with the provisions of Clause 49.

Alterations, Additions and Omissions

Variations	**51.1**	The Engineer shall make any variation of the form, quality or quantity of the Works or any part thereof that may, in his opinion, be necessary and for that purpose, or if for any other reason it shall, in his opinion, be appropriate, he shall have the authority to instruct the Contractor to do and the Contractor shall do any of the following:

(a) increase or decrease the quantity of any work included in the Contract,

(b) omit any such work (but not if the omitted work is to be carried out by the Employer or by another contractor),

(c) change the character or quality or kind of any such work,

(d) change the levels, lines, position and dimensions of any part of the Works,

(e) execute additional work of any kind necessary for the completion of the Works, or

(f) change any specified sequence or timing of construction of any part of the Works.

No such variation shall in any way vitiate or invalidate the Contract, but the effect, if any, of all such variations shall be valued in accordance with Clause 52. Provided that where the issue of an instruction to vary the Works is necessitated by some default of or breach of contract by the Contractor or for which he is responsible, any additional cost attributable to such default shall be borne by the Contractor.

Instructions for Variations 51.2 The Contractor shall not make any such variation without an instruction of the Engineer. Provided that no instruction shall be required for increase or decrease in the quantity of any work where such increase or decrease is not the result of an instruction given under this Clause, but is the result of the quantities exceeding or being less than those stated in the Bill of Quantities.

Valuation of Variations 52.1 All variations referred to in Clause 51 and any additions to the Contract Price which are required to be determined in accordance with Clause 52 (for the purposes of this Clause referred to as "varied work"), shall be valued at the rates and prices set out in the Contract if, in the opinion of the Engineer, the same shall be applicable. If the Contract does not contain any rates or prices applicable to the varied work, the rates and prices in the Contract shall be used as the basis for valuation so far as may be reasonable, failing which, after due consultation by the Engineer with the Employer and the Contractor, suitable rates or prices shall be agreed upon between the Engineer and the Contractor. In the event of disagreement the Engineer shall fix such rates or prices as are, in his opinion, appropriate and shall notify the Contractor accordingly, with a copy to the Employer. Until such time as rates or prices are agreed or fixed, the Engineer shall determine provisional rates or prices to enable on-account payments to be included in certificates issued in accordance with Clause 60.

Power of Engineer to Fix Rates 52.2 Provided that if the nature or amount of any varied work relative to the nature or amount of the whole of the Works or to any part thereof, is such that, in the opinion of the Engineer, the rate or price contained in the Contract for any item of the Works is, by reason of such varied work, rendered inappropriate or inapplicable, then, after due consultation by the Engineer with the Employer and the Contractor, a suitable rate or price shall be agreed upon between the Engineer and the Contractor. In the event of disagreement the Engineer shall fix such other rate or price as is, in his opinion, appropriate and shall notify the Contractor accordingly, with a copy to the Employer. Until such time as rates or prices are agreed or fixed, the Engineer shall determine provisional rates or prices to enable on-account payments to be included in certificates issued in accordance with Clause 60.

Provided also that no varied work instructed to be done by the Engineer pursuant to Clause 51 shall be valued under Sub-Clause 52.1 or under this Sub-Clause unless, within 14 days of the date of such instruction and, other than in the case of omitted work, before the commencement of the varied work, notice shall have been given either:

(a) by the Contractor to the Engineer of his intention to claim extra payment or a varied rate or price, or

(b) by the Engineer to the Contractor of his intention to vary a rate or price.

Variations Exceeding 15 per cent 52.3 If, on the issue of the Taking-Over Certificate for the whole of the Works, it is found that as a result of:

(a) all varied work valued under Sub-Clauses 52.1 and 52.2, and

(b) all adjustments upon measurement of the estimated quantities set out in the Bill of Quantities, excluding Provisional Sums, dayworks and adjustments of price made under Clause 70,

but not from any other cause, there have been additions to or deductions from the Contract Price which taken together are in excess of 15 per cent of the "Effective Contract Price" (which for the purposes of this Sub-Clause shall mean the Contract Price, excluding Provisional Sums and allowance for dayworks, if any) then and in such event (subject to any action already taken under any other Sub-Clause of this Clause), after due consultation by the Engineer with the Employer and the Contractor, there shall be added to or deducted from the Contract Price such further sum as may be agreed between the Contractor and the Engineer or, failing agreement, determined by the Engineer having regard to the Contractor's Site and general overhead costs of the Contract. The Engineer shall notify the Contractor of any determination made under this Sub-Clause, with a copy to the Employer. Such sum shall be based only on the amount by which such additions or deductions shall be in excess of 15 per cent of the Effective Contract Price.

Daywork   **52.4**   The Engineer may, if in his opinion it is necessary or desirable, issue an instruction that any varied work shall be executed on a daywork basis. The Contractor shall then be paid for such varied work under the terms set out in the daywork schedule included in the Contract and at the rates and prices affixed thereto by him in the Tender.

The Contractor shall furnish to the Engineer such receipts or other vouchers as may be necessary to prove the amounts paid and, before ordering materials, shall submit to the Engineer quotations for the same for his approval.

In respect of such of the Works executed on a daywork basis, the Contractor shall, during the continuance of such work, deliver each day to the Engineer an exact list in duplicate of the names, occupation and time of all workmen employed on such work and a statement, also in duplicate, showing the description and quantity of all materials and Contractor's Equipment used thereon or therefor other than Contractor's Equipment which is included in the percentage addition in accordance with such daywork schedule. One copy of each list and statement will, if correct, or when agreed, be signed by the Engineer and returned to the Contractor.

At the end of each month the Contractor shall deliver to the Engineer a priced statement of the labour, materials and Contractor's Equipment, except as aforesaid, used and the Contractor shall not be entitled to any payment unless such lists and statements have been fully and punctually rendered. Provided always that if the Engineer considers that for any reason the sending of such lists or statements by the Contractor, in accordance with the foregoing provision, was impracticable he shall nevertheless be entitled to authorise payment for such work, either as daywork, on being satisfied as to the time employed and the labour, materials and Contractor's Equipment used on such work, or at such value therefor as shall, in his opinion, be fair and reasonable.

Procedure for Claims

Notice of Claims   **53.1**   Notwithstanding any other provision of the Contract, if the Contractor intends to claim any additional payment pursuant to any Clause of these Conditions or otherwise, he shall give notice of his intention to the Engineer, with a copy to the Employer, within 28 days after the event giving rise to the claim has first arisen.

Contemporary Records   **53.2**   Upon the happening of the event referred to in Sub-Clause 53.1, the Contractor shall keep such contemporary records as may reasonably be necessary to support any claim he may subsequently wish to make. Without necessarily admitting the Employer's liability, the Engineer shall, on receipt of a notice under Sub-Clause 53.1, inspect such contemporary records and may instruct the Contractor to keep any further contemporary records as are reasonable and may be material to the claim of which notice has been given. The Contractor shall permit the Engineer to inspect all records kept pursuant to this Sub-Clause and shall supply him with copies thereof as and when the Engineer so instructs.

Substantiation of Claims 53.3 Within 28 days, or such other reasonable time as may be agreed by the Engineer, of giving notice under Sub-Clause 53.1, the Contractor shall send to the Engineer an account giving detailed particulars of the amount claimed and the grounds upon which the claim is based. Where the event giving rise to the claim has a continuing effect, such account shall be considered to be an interim account and the Contractor shall, at such intervals as the Engineer may reasonably require, send further interim accounts giving the accumulated amount of the claim and any further grounds upon which it is based. In cases where interim accounts are sent to the Engineer, the Contractor shall send a final account within 28 days of the end of the effects resulting from the event. The Contractor shall, if required by the Engineer so to do, copy to the Employer all accounts sent to the Engineer pursuant to this Sub-Clause.

Failure to Comply 53.4 If the Contractor fails to comply with any of the provisions of this Clause in respect of any claim which he seeks to make, his entitlement to payment in respect thereof shall not exceed such amount as the Engineer or any arbitrator or arbitrators appointed pursuant to Sub-Clause 67.3 assessing the claim considers to be verified by contemporary records (whether or not such records were brought to the Engineer's notice as required under Sub-Clauses 53.2 and 53.3).

Payment of Claims 53.5 The Contractor shall be entitled to have included in any interim payment certified by the Engineer pursuant to Clause 60 such amount in respect of any claim as the Engineer, after due consultation with the Employer and the Contractor, may consider due to the Contractor provided that the Contractor has supplied sufficient particulars to enable the Engineer to determine the amount due. If such particulars are insufficient to substantiate the whole of the claim, the Contractor shall be entitled to payment in respect of such part of the claim as such particulars may substantiate to the satisfaction of the Engineer. The Engineer shall notify the Contractor of any determination made under this Sub-Clause, with a copy to the Employer.

Contractor's Equipment, Temporary Works and Materials

Contractor's Equipment, Temporary Works and Materials; Exclusive Use for the Works 54.1 All Contractor's Equipment, Temporary Works and materials provided by the Contractor shall, when brought on to the Site, be deemed to be exclusively intended for the execution of the Works and the Contractor shall not remove the same or any part thereof, except for the purpose of moving it from one part of the Site to another, without the consent of the Engineer. Provided that consent shall not be required for vehicles engaged in transporting any staff, labour, Contractor's Equipment, Temporary Works, Plant or materials to or from the Site.

Employer not Liable for Damage 54.2 The Employer shall not at any time be liable, save as mentioned in Clauses 20 and 65, for the loss of or damage to any of the said Contractor's Equipment, Temporary Works or materials.

Customs Clearance 54.3 The Employer will use his best endeavours in assisting the Contractor, where required, in obtaining clearance through the Customs of Contractor's Equipment, materials and other things required for the Works.

Re-export of Contractor's Equipment 54.4 In respect of any Contractor's Equipment which the Contractor has imported for the purposes of the Works, the Employer will use his best endeavours to assist the Contractor, where required, in procuring any necessary Government consent to the re-export of such Contractor's Equipment by the Contractor upon the removal thereof pursuant to the terms of the Contract.

Conditions of Hire of Contractor's Equipment	54.5	With a view to securing, in the event of termination under Clause 63, the continued availability, for the purpose of executing the Works, of any hired Contractor's Equipment, the Contractor shall not bring on to the Site any hired Contractor's Equipment unless there is an agreement for the hire thereof (which agreement shall be deemed not to include an agreement for hire purchase) which contains a provision that the owner thereof will, on request in writing made by the Employer within 7 days after the date on which any termination has become effective, and on the Employer undertaking to pay all hire charges in respect thereof from such date, hire such Contractor's Equipment to the Employer on the same terms in all respects as the same was hired to the Contractor save that the Employer shall be entitled to permit the use thereof by any other contractor employed by him for the purpose of executing and completing the Works and remedying any defects therein, under the terms of the said Clause 63.
Costs for the Purpose of Clause 63	54.6	In the event of the Employer entering into any agreement for the hire of Contractor's Equipment pursuant to Sub-Clause 54.5, all sums properly paid by the Employer under the provisions of any such agreement and all costs incurred by him (including stamp duties) in entering into such agreement shall be deemed, for the purpose of Clause 63, to be part of the cost of executing and completing the Works and the remedying of any defects therein.
Incorporation of Clause in Subcontracts	54.7	The Contractor shall, where entering into any subcontract for the execution of any part of the Works, incorporate in such subcontract (by reference or otherwise) the provisions of this Clause in relation to Contractor's Equipment, Temporary Works or materials brought on to the Site by the Subcontractor.
Approval of Materials not Implied	54.8	The operation of this Clause shall not be deemed to imply any approval by the Engineer of the materials or other matters referred to therein nor shall it prevent the rejection of any such materials at any time by the Engineer.

Measurement

Quantities	55.1	The quantities set out in the Bill of Quantities are the estimated quantities for the Works, and they are not to be taken as the actual and correct quantities of the Works to be executed by the Contractor in fulfilment of his obligations under the Contract.
Works to be Measured	56.1	The Engineer shall, except as otherwise stated, ascertain and determine by measurement the value of the Works in accordance with the Contract and the Contractor shall be paid that value in accordance with Clause 60. The Engineer shall, when he requires any part of the Works to be measured, give reasonable notice to the Contractor's authorised agent, who shall:

(a) forthwith attend or send a qualified representative to assist the Engineer in making such measurement, and

(b) supply all particulars required by the Engineer.

Should the Contractor not attend, or neglect or omit to send such representative, then the measurement made by the Engineer or approved by him shall be taken to be the correct measurement of such part of the Works. For the purpose of measuring such Permanent Works as are to be measured by records and drawings, the Engineer shall prepare records and drawings as the work proceeds and the Contractor, as and when called upon to do so in writing, shall, within 14 days, attend to examine and agree such records and drawings with the Engineer and shall sign the same when so agreed. If the Contractor does not attend to examine and agree such records and drawings, they shall be taken to be correct. If, after examination of such records and drawings, the Contractor does not agree the same or does not sign the same as agreed, they shall nevertheless be taken to be correct, unless the Contractor, within 14 days of such examination, lodges with the Engineer notice of the respects in which such records and drawings are claimed by him to be incorrect. On receipt of such notice, the Engineer shall review the records and drawings and either confirm or vary them.

| Method of Measurement | 57.1 | The Works shall be measured net, notwithstanding any general or local custom, except where otherwise provided for in the Contract. |

Method of Measurement   **57.1**   The Works shall be measured net, notwithstanding any general or local custom, except where otherwise provided for in the Contract.

Breakdown of Lump Sum Items   **57.2**   For the purposes of statements submitted in accordance with Sub-Clause 60.1, the Contractor shall submit to the Engineer, within 28 days after the receipt of the Letter of Acceptance, a breakdown for each of the lump sum items contained in the Tender. Such breakdowns shall be subject to the approval of the Engineer.

Provisional Sums

Definition of "Provisional Sum"   **58.1**   "Provisional Sum" means a sum included in the Contract and so designated in the Bill of Quantities for the execution of any part of the Works or for the supply of goods, materials, Plant or services, or for contingencies, which sum may be used, in whole or in part, or not at all, on the instructions of the Engineer. The Contractor shall be entitled to only such amounts in respect of the work, supply or contingencies to which such Provisional Sums relate as the Engineer shall determine in accordance with this Clause. The Engineer shall notify the Contractor of any determination made under this Sub-Clause, with a copy to the Employer.

Use of Provisional Sums   **58.2**   In respect of every Provisional Sum the Engineer shall have authority to issue instructions for the execution of work or for the supply of goods, materials, Plant or services by:

(a) the Contractor, in which case the Contractor shall be entitled to an amount equal to the value thereof determined in accordance with Clause 52, and

(b) a nominated Subcontractor, as hereinafter defined, in which case the sum to be paid to the Contractor therefor shall be determined and paid in accordance with Sub-Clause 59.4.

Production of Vouchers   **58.3**   The Contractor shall produce to the Engineer all quotations, invoices, vouchers and accounts or receipts in connection with expenditure in respect of Provisional Sums, except where work is valued in accordance with rates or prices set out in the Tender.

Nominated Subcontractors

Definition of "Nominated Subcontractors"   **59.1**   All specialists, merchants, tradesmen and others executing any work or supplying any goods, materials, Plant or services for which Provisional Sums are included in the Contract, who may have been or be nominated or selected or approved by the Employer or the Engineer, and all persons to whom by virtue of the provisions of the Contract the Contractor is required to subcontract shall, in the execution of such work or the supply of such goods, materials, Plant or services, be deemed to be subcontractors to the Contractor and are referred to in this Contract as "nominated Subcontractors".

Nominated Subcontractors; Objection to Nomination   **59.2**   The Contractor shall not be required by the Employer or the Engineer, or be deemed to be under any obligation, to employ any nominated Subcontractor against whom the Contractor may raise reasonable objection, or who declines to enter into a subcontract with the Contractor containing provisions:

(a) that in respect of the work, goods, materials, Plant or services the subject of the subcontract, the nominated Subcontractor will undertake towards the Contractor such obligations and liabilities as will enable the Contractor to discharge his own obligations and liabilities towards the Employer under the terms of the Contract and will save harmless and indemnify the Contractor from and against the same and from all claims, proceedings, damages, costs, charges and expenses whatsoever arising out of or in connection therewith, or arising out of or in connection with any failure to perform such obligations or to fulfil such liabilities, and

(b) that the nominated Subcontractor will save harmless and indemnify the Contractor from and against any negligence by the nominated Subcontractor, his agents, workmen and servants and from and against any misuse by him or them of any Temporary Works provided by the Contractor for the purposes of the Contract and from all claims as aforesaid.

Design Requirements to be Expressly Stated 59.3 If in connection with any Provisional Sum the services to be provided include any matter of design or specification of any part of the Permanent Works or of any Plant to be incorporated therein, such requirement shall be expressly stated in the Contract and shall be included in any nominated Subcontract. The nominated Subcontract shall specify that the nominated Subcontractor providing such services will save harmless and indemnify the Contractor from and against the same and from all claims, proceedings, damages, costs, charges and expenses whatsoever arising out of or in connection with any failure to perform such obligations or to fulfil such liabilities.

Payments to Nominated Subcontractors 59.4 For all work executed or goods, materials, Plant or services supplied by any nominated Subcontractor, the Contractor shall be entitled to:

(a) the actual price paid or due to be paid by the Contractor, on the instructions of the Engineer, and in accordance with the subcontract;

(b) in respect of labour supplied by the Contractor, the sum, if any, entered in the Bill of Quantities or, if instructed by the Engineer pursuant to paragraph (a) of Sub-Clause 58.2, as may be determined in accordance with Clause 52; and

(c) in respect of all other charges and profit, a sum being a percentage rate of the actual price paid or due to be paid calculated, where provision has been made in the Bill of Quantities for a rate to be set against the relevant Provisional Sum, at the rate inserted by the Contractor against that item or, where no such provision has been made, at the rate inserted by the Contractor in the Appendix to Tender and repeated where provision for such is made in a special item provided in the Bill of Quantities for such purpose.

Certification of Payments to Nominated Subcontractors 59.5 Before issuing, under Clause 60, any certificate, which includes any payment in respect of work done or goods, materials, Plant or services supplied by any nominated Subcontractor, the Engineer shall be entitled to demand from the Contractor reasonable proof that all payments, less retentions, included in previous certificates in respect of the work or goods, materials, Plant or services of such nominated Subcontractor have been paid or discharged by the Contractor. If the Contractor fails to supply such proof then, unless the Contractor:

(a) satisfies the Engineer in writing that he has reasonable cause for withholding or refusing to make such payments, and

(b) produces to the Engineer reasonable proof that he has so informed such nominated Subcontractor in writing,

the Employer shall be entitled to pay to such nominated Subcontractor direct, upon the certificate of the Engineer, all payments, less retentions, provided for in the nominated Subcontract, which the Contractor has failed to make to such nominated Subcontractor and to deduct by way of set-off the amount so paid by the Employer from any sums due or to become due from the Employer to the Contractor.

Provided that, where the Engineer has certified and the Employer has paid direct as aforesaid, the Engineer shall, in issuing any further certificate in favour of the Contractor, deduct from the amount thereof the amount so paid, direct as aforesaid, but shall not withhold or delay the issue of the certificate itself when due to be issued under the terms of the Contract.

Certificates and Payment

Monthly Statements   60.1   The Contractor shall submit to the Engineer after the end of each month six copies, each signed by the Contractor's representative approved by the Engineer in accordance with Sub-Clause 15.1, of a statement, in such form as the Engineer may from time to time prescribe, showing the amounts to which the Contractor considers himself to be entitled up to the end of the month in respect of:

(a) the value of the Permanent Works executed,

(b) any other items in the Bill of Quantities including those for Contractor's Equipment, Temporary Works, dayworks and the like,

(c) the percentage of the invoice value of listed materials, all as stated in the Appendix to Tender, and Plant delivered by the Contractor on the Site for incorporation in the Permanent Works but not incorporated in such Works,

(d) adjustments under Clause 70, and

(e) any other sum to which the Contractor may be entitled under the Contract or otherwise.

Monthly Payments   60.2   The Engineer shall, within 28 days of receiving such statement, deliver to the Employer an Interim Payment Certificate stating the amount of payment to the Contractor which the Engineer considers due and payable in respect of such statement, subject:

(a) firstly, to the retention of the amount calculated by applying the Percentage of Retention stated in the Appendix to Tender, to the amount to which the Contractor is entitled under paragraphs (a), (b), (c) and (e) of Sub-Clause 60.1 until the amount so retained reaches the Limit of Retention Money stated in the Appendix to Tender, and

(b) secondly, to the deduction, other than pursuant to Clause 47, of any sums which may have become due and payable by the Contractor to the Employer.

Provided that the Engineer shall not be bound to certify any payment under this Sub-Clause if the net amount thereof, after all retentions and deductions, would be less than the Minimum ·Amount of Interim Payment Certificates stated in the Appendix to Tender.

Notwithstanding the terms of this Clause or any other Clause of the Contract no amount will be certified by the Engineer for payment until the performance security, if required under the Contract, has been provided by the Contractor and approved by the Employer.

Payment of Retention Money   60.3   (a) Upon the issue of the Taking-Over Certificate with respect to the whole of the Works, one half of the Retention Money, or upon the issue of a Taking-Over Certificate with respect to a Section or part of the Permanent Works only such proportion thereof as the Engineer determines having regard to the relative value of such Section or part of the Permanent Works, shall be certified by the Engineer for payment to the Contractor.

(b) Upon the expiration of the Defects Liability Period for the Works the other half of the Retention Money shall be certified by the Engineer for payment to the Contractor. Provided that, in the event of different Defects Liability Periods having become applicable to different Sections or parts of the Permanent Works pursuant to Clause 48, the expression "expiration of the Defects Liability Period" shall, for the purposes of this Sub-Clause, be deemed to mean the expiration of the latest of such periods. Provided also that if at such time there shall remain to be executed by the Contractor any work instructed, pursuant to Clauses 49 and 50, in respect of the Works, the Engineer shall be entitled to withhold certification until completion of such work of so much of the balance of the Retention Money as shall, in the opinion of the Engineer, represent the cost of the work remaining to be executed.

Correction of Certificates   60.4   The Engineer may by any Interim Payment Certificate make any correction or modification in any previous Interim Payment Certificate which shall have been issued by him and shall have authority, if any work is not being carried out to his satisfaction, to omit or reduce the value of such work in any Interim Payment Certificate.

Statement at Completion	**60.5**	Not later than 84 days after the issue of the Taking-Over Certificate in respect of the whole of the Works, the Contractor shall submit to the Engineer six copies of a Statement at Completion with supporting documents showing in detail, in the form approved by the Engineer:

(a) the final value of all work done in accordance with the Contract up to the date stated in such Taking-Over Certificate,

(b) any further sums which the Contractor considers to be due, and

(c) an estimate of amounts which the Contractor considers will become due to him under the Contract.

The estimated amounts shall be shown separately in such Statement at Completion. The Engineer shall certify payment in accordance with Sub-Clause 60.2.

Final Statement	**60.6**	Not later than 56 days after the issue of the Defects Liability Certificate pursuant to Sub-Clause 62.1, the Contractor shall submit to the Engineer for consideration six copies of a draft final statement with supporting documents showing in detail, in the form approved by the Engineer:

(a) the value of all work done in accordance with the Contract, and

(b) any further sums which the Contractor considers to be due to him under the Contract or otherwise.

If the Engineer disagrees with or cannot verify any part of the draft final statement, the Contractor shall submit such further information as the Engineer may reasonably require and shall make such changes in the draft as may be agreed between them. The Contractor shall then prepare and submit to the Engineer the final statement as agreed (for the purposes of these Conditions referred to as the "Final Statement").

If, following discussions between the Engineer and the Contractor and any changes to the draft final statement which may be agreed between them, it becomes evident that a dispute exists, the Engineer shall deliver to the Employer an Interim Payment Certificate for those parts of the draft final statement, if any, which are not in dispute. The dispute may then be settled in accordance with Clause 67.

Discharge	**60.7**	Upon submission of the Final Statement, the Contractor shall give to the Employer, with a copy to the Engineer, a written discharge confirming that the total of the Final Statement represents full and final settlement of all monies due to the Contractor arising out of or in respect of the Contract. Provided that such discharge shall become effective only after payment due under the Final Payment Certificate issued pursuant to Sub-Clause 60.8 has been made and the performance security referred to in Sub-Clause 10.1, if any, has been returned to the Contractor.

Final Payment Certificate	**60.8**	Within 28 days after receipt of the Final Statement, and the written discharge, the Engineer shall issue to the Employer (with a copy to the Contractor) a Final Payment Certificate stating:

(a) the amount which, in the opinion of the Engineer, is finally due under the Contract or otherwise, and

(b) after giving credit to the Employer for all amounts previously paid by the Employer and for all sums to which the Employer is entitled other than under Clause 47, the balance, if any, due from the Employer to the Contractor or from the Contractor to the Employer as the case may be.

Cessation of Employer's Liability	**60.9**	The Employer shall not be liable to the Contractor for any matter or thing arising out of or in connection with the Contract or execution of the Works, unless the Contractor shall have included a claim in respect thereof in his Final Statement and (except in respect of matters or things arising after the issue of the Taking-Over Certificate in respect of the whole of the Works) in the Statement at Completion referred to in Sub-Clause 60.5.

Time for Payment	**60.10**	The amount due to the Contractor under any Interim Payment Certificate issued by the Engineer pursuant to this Clause, or to any other term of the Contract, shall, subject to Clause 47, be paid by the Employer to the Contractor within 28 days after such Interim Payment Certificate has been delivered to the Employer, or, in the case of the Final Payment Certificate referred to in Sub-Clause 60.8, within 56 days, after such Final Payment Certificate has been delivered to the Employer. In the event of the failure of the Employer to make payment within the times stated, the Employer shall pay to the Contractor interest at the rate stated in the Appendix to Tender upon all sums unpaid from the date by which the same should have been paid. The provisions of this Sub-Clause are without prejudice to the Contractor's entitlement under Clause 69 or otherwise.
Approval only by Defects Liability Certificate	**61.1**	Only the Defects Liability Certificate, referred to in Clause 62, shall be deemed to constitute approval of the Works.
Defects Liability Certificate	**62.1**	The Contract shall not be considered as completed until a Defects Liability Certificate shall have been signed by the Engineer and delivered to the Employer, with a copy to the Contractor, stating the date on which the Contractor shall have completed his obligations to execute and complete the Works and remedy any defects therein to the Engineer's satisfaction. The Defects Liability Certificate shall be given by the Engineer within 28 days after the expiration of the Defects Liability Period, or, if different defects liability periods shall become applicable to different Sections or parts of the Permanent Works, the expiration of the latest such period, or as soon thereafter as any works instructed, pursuant to Clauses 49 and 50, have been completed to the satisfaction of the Engineer. Provided that the issue of the Defects Liability Certificate shall not be a condition precedent to payment to the Contractor of the second portion of the Retention Money in accordance with the conditions set out in Sub-Clause 60.3.
Unfulfilled Obligations	**62.2**	Notwithstanding the issue of the Defects Liability Certificate the Contractor and the Employer shall remain liable for the fulfilment of any obligation incurred under the provisions of the Contract prior to the issue of the Defects Liability Certificate which remains unperformed at the time such Defects Liability Certificate is issued and, for the purposes of determining the nature and extent of any such obligation, the Contract shall be deemed to remain in force between the parties to the Contract.

Remedies

Default of Contractor	**63.1**	If the Contractor is deemed by law unable to pay his debts as they fall due, or enters into voluntary or involuntary bankruptcy, liquidation or dissolution (other than a voluntary liquidation for the purposes of amalgamation or reconstruction), or becomes insolvent, or makes an arrangement with, or assignment in favour of, his creditors, or agrees to carry out the Contract under a committee of inspection of his creditors, or if a receiver, administrator, trustee or liquidator is appointed over any substantial part of his assets, or if, under any law or regulation relating to reorganization, arrangement or readjustment of debts, proceedings are commenced against the Contractor or resolutions passed in connection with dissolution or liquidation or if any steps are taken to enforce any security interest over a substantial part of the assets of the Contractor, or if any act is done or event occurs with respect to the Contractor or his assets which, under any applicable law has a substantially similar effect to any of the foregoing acts or events, or if the Contractor has contravened Sub-Clause 3.1, or has an execution levied on his goods, or if the Engineer certifies to the Employer, with a copy to the Contractor, that, in his opinion, the Contractor:

(a) has repudiated the Contract,

(b) without reasonable excuse has failed

     (i) to commence the Works in accordance with Sub-Clause 41.1, or

     (ii) to proceed with the Works, or any Section thereof, within 28 days after receiving notice pursuant to Sub-Clause 46.1,

(c) has failed to comply with a notice issued pursuant to Sub-Clause 37.4 or an instruction issued pursuant to Sub-Clause 39.1 within 28 days after having received it,

(d) despite previous warning from the Engineer, in writing, is otherwise persistently or flagrantly neglecting to comply with any of his obligations under the Contract, or

(e) has contravened Sub-Clause 4.1,

then the Employer may, after giving 14 days' notice to the Contractor, enter upon the Site and the Works and terminate the employment of the Contractor without thereby releasing the Contractor from any of his obligations or liabilities under the Contract, or affecting the rights and authorities conferred on the Employer or the Engineer by the Contract, and may himself complete the Works or may employ any other contractor to complete the Works. The Employer or such other contractor may use for such completion so much of the Contractor's Equipment, Temporary Works and materials as he or they may think proper.

Valuation at Date of Termination **63.2** The Engineer shall, as soon as may be practicable after any such entry and termination by the Employer, fix and determine ex parte, or by or after reference to the parties or after such investigation or enquiries as he may think fit to make or institute, and shall certify:

a) what amount (if any) had, at the time of such entry and termination, been reasonably earned by or would reasonably accrue to the Contractor in respect of work then actually done by him under the Contract, and

(b) the value of any of the said unused or partially used materials, any Contractor's Equipment and any Temporary Works.

Payment after Termination **63.3** If the Employer terminates the Contractor's employment under this Clause, he shall not be liable to pay to the Contractor any further amount (including damages) in respect of the Contract until the expiration of the Defects Liability Period and there after until the costs of execution, completion and remedying of any defects, damages for delay in completion (if any) and all other expenses incurred by the Employer have been ascertained and the amount thereof certified by the Engineer. The Contractor shall then be entitled to receive only such sum (if any) as the Engineer may certify would have been payable to him upon due completion by him after deducting the said amount. If such amount exceeds the sum which would have been payable to the Contractor on due completion by him, then the Contractor shall, upon demand, pay to the Employer the amount of such excess and it shall be deemed a debt due by the Contractor to the Employer and shall be recoverable accordingly.

Assignment of Benefit of Agreement **63.4** Unless prohibited by law, the Contractor shall, if so instructed by the Engineer within 14 days of such entry and termination referred to in Sub-Clause 63.1, assign to the Employer the benefit of any agreement for the supply of any goods or materials or services and/or for the execution of any work for the purposes of the Contract, which the Contractor may have entered into.

Urgent Remedial Work **64.1** If, by reason of any accident, or failure, or other event occurring to, in, or in connection with the Works, or any part thereof, either during the execution of the Works, or during the Defects Liability Period, any remedial or other work is, in the opinion of the Engineer, urgently necessary for the safety of the Works and the Contractor is unable or unwilling at once to do such work, the Employer shall be entitled to employ and pay other persons to carry out such work as the Engineer may consider necessary. If the work or repair so done by the Employer is work which, in the opinion of the Engineer, the Contractor was liable to do at his own cost under the Contract, then all costs consequent thereon or incidental thereto shall, after due consultation with the Employer and the Contractor, be determined by the Engineer and shall be recoverable from the Contractor by the Employer, and may be deducted by the Employer from any monies due or to become due to the Contractor and the Engineer shall notify the Contractor accordingly, with a copy to the Employer. Provided that the Engineer shall, as soon after the occurrence of any such emergency as may be reasonably practicable, notify the Contractor thereof.

© FIDIC 1987

Special Risks

No Liability for Special Risks   **65.1**   The Contractor shall be under no liability whatsoever in consequence of any of the special risks referred to in Sub-Clause 65.2, whether by way of indemnity or otherwise, for or in respect of:

(a) destruction of or damage to the Works, save to work condemned under the provisions of Clause 39 prior to the occurrence of any of the said special risks,

(b) destruction of or damage to property, whether of the Employer or third parties, or

(c) injury or loss of life.

Special Risks   **65.2**   The special risks are:

(a) the risks defined under paragraphs (a), (c), (d) and (e) of Sub-Clause 20.4, and

(b) the risks defined under paragraph (b) of Sub-Clause 20.4 insofar as these relate to the country in which the Works are to be executed.

Damage to Works by Special Risks   **65.3**   If the Works or any materials or Plant on or near or in transit to the Site, or any of the Contractor's Equipment, sustain destruction or damage by reason of any of the said special risks, the Contractor shall be entitled to payment in accordance with the Contract for any Permanent Works duly executed and for any materials or Plant so destroyed or damaged and, so far as may be required by the Engineer or as may be necessary for the completion of the Works, to payment for:

(a) rectifying any such destruction or damage to the Works, and

(b) replacing or rectifying such materials or Contractor's Equipment,

and the Engineer shall determine an addition to the Contract Price in accordance with Clause 52 (which shall in the case of the cost of replacement of Contractor's Equipment include the fair market value thereof as determined by the Engineer) and shall notify the Contractor accordingly, with a copy to the Employer.

Projectile, Missile   **65.4**   Destruction, damage, injury or loss of life caused by the explosion or impact, whenever and wherever occurring, of any mine, bomb, shell, grenade, or other projectile, missile, munition, or explosive of war, shall be deemed to be a consequence of the said special risks.

Increased Costs arising from Special Risks   **65.5**   Save to the extent that the Contractor is entitled to payment under any other provision of the Contract, the Employer shall repay to the Contractor any costs of the execution of the Works (other than such as may be attributable to the cost of reconstructing work condemned under the provisions of Clause 39 prior to the occurrence of any special risk) which are howsoever attributable to or consequent on or the result of or in any way whatsoever connected with the said special risks, subject however to the provisions in this Clause hereinafter contained in regard to outbreak of war, but the Contractor shall, as soon as any such cost comes to his knowledge, forthwith notify the Engineer thereof. The Engineer shall, after due consultation with the Employer and the Contractor, determine the amount of the Contractor's costs in respect thereof which shall be added to the Contract Price and shall notify the Contractor accordingly, with a copy to the Employer.

Outbreak of War   **65.6**   If, during the currency of the Contract, there is an outbreak of war, whether war is declared or not, in any part of the world which, whether financially or otherwise, materially affects the execution of the Works, the Contractor shall, unless and until the Contract is terminated under the provisions of this Clause, continue to use his best endeavours to complete the execution of the Works. Provided that the Employer shall be entitled, at any time after such outbreak of war, to terminate the Contract by giving notice to the Contractor and, upon such notice being given, the Contract shall, except as to the rights of the parties under this Clause and Clause 67, terminate, but without prejudice to the rights of either party in respect of any antecedent breach thereof.

Removal of Contractor's Equipment on Termination 65.7 If the Contract is terminated under the provisions of Sub-Clause 65.6, the Contractor shall, with all reasonable dispatch, remove from the Site all Contractor's Equipment and shall give similar facilities to his Subcontractors to do so.

Payment if Contract Terminated 65.8 If the Contract is terminated as aforesaid, the Contractor shall be paid by the Employer, insofar as such amounts or items have not already been covered by payments on account made to the Contractor, for all work executed prior to the date of termination at the rates and prices provided in the Contract and in addition:

(a) the amounts payable in respect of any preliminary items referred to in the Bill of Quantities, so far as the work or service comprised therein has been carried out or performed, and a proper proportion of any such items which have been partially carried out or performed;

(b) the cost of materials, Plant or goods reasonably ordered for the Works which have been delivered to the Contractor or of which the Contractor is legally liable to accept delivery, such materials, Plant or goods becoming the property of the Employer upon such payments being made by him;

(c) a sum being the amount of any expenditure reasonably incurred by the Contractor in the expectation of completing the whole of the Works insofar as such expenditure has not been covered by any other payments referred to in this Sub-Clause;

(d) any additional sum payable under the provisions of Sub-Clauses 65.3 and 65.5;

(e) such proportion of the cost as may be reasonable, taking into account payments made or to be made for work executed, of removal of Contractor's Equipment under Sub-Clause 65.7 and, if required by the Contractor, return thereof to the Contractor's main plant yard in his country of registration or to other destination, at no greater cost; and

(f) the reasonable cost of repatriation of all the Contractor's staff and workmen employed on or in connection with the Works at the time of such termination.

Provided that against any payment due from the Employer under this Sub-Clause, the Employer shall be entitled to be credited with any outstanding balances due from the Contractor for advances in respect of Contractor's Equipment, materials and Plant and any other sums which, at the date of termination, were recoverable by the Employer from the Contractor under the terms of the Contract. Any sums payable under this Sub-Clause shall, after due consultation with the Employer and the Contractor, be determined by the Engineer who shall notify the Contractor accordingly, with a copy to the Employer.

Release from Performance

Payment in Event of Release from Performance 66.1 If any circumstance outside the control of both parties arises after the issue of the Letter of Acceptance which renders it impossible or unlawful for either or both parties to fulfil his or their contractual obligations, or under the law governing the Contract the parties are released from further performance, then the parties shall be discharged from the Contract, except as to their rights under this Clause and Clause 67 and without prejudice to the rights of either party in respect of any antecedent breach of the Contract, and the sum payable by the Employer to the Contractor in respect of the work executed shall be the same as that which would have been payable under Clause 65 if the Contract had been terminated under the provisions of Clause 65.

Settlement of Disputes

Engineer's Decision   **67.1**   If a dispute of any kind whatsoever arises between the Employer and the Contractor in connection with, or arising out of, the Contract or the execution of the Works, whether during the execution of the Works or after their completion and whether before or after repudiation or other termination of the Contract, including any dispute as to any opinion, instruction, determination, certificate or valuation of the Engineer, the matter in dispute shall, in the first place, be referred in writing to the Engineer, with a copy to the other party. Such reference shall state that it is made pursuant to this Clause. No later than the eighty-fourth day after the day on which he received such reference the Engineer shall give notice of his decision to the Employer and the Contractor. Such decision shall state that it is made pursuant to this Clause.

Unless the Contract has already been repudiated or terminated, the Contractor shall, in every case, continue to proceed with the Works with all due diligence and the Contractor and the Employer shall give effect forthwith to every such decision of the Engineer unless and until the same shall be revised, as hereinafter provided, in an amicable settlement or an arbitral award.

If either the Employer or the Contractor be dissatisfied with any decision of the Engineer, or if the Engineer fails to give notice of his decision on or before the eighty-fourth day after the day on which he received the reference, then either the Employer or the Contractor may, on or before the seventieth day after the day on which he received notice of such decision, or on or before the seventieth day after the day on which the said period of 84 days expired, as the case may be, give notice to the other party, with a copy for information to the Engineer, of his intention to commence arbitration, as hereinafter provided, as to the matter in dispute. Such notice shall establish the entitlement of the party giving the same to commence arbitration, as hereinafter provided, as to such dispute and, subject to Sub-Clause 67.4, no arbitration in respect thereof may be commenced unless such notice is given.

If the Engineer has given notice of his decision as to a matter in dispute to the Employer and the Contractor and no notice of intention to commence arbitration as to such dispute has been given by either the Employer or the Contractor on or before the seventieth day after the day on which the parties received notice as to such decision from the Engineer, the said decision shall become final and binding upon the Employer and the Contractor.

Amicable Settlement   **67.2**   Where notice of intention to commence arbitration as to a dispute has been given in accordance with Sub-Clause 67.1, the parties shall attempt to settle such dispute amicably before the commencement of arbitration. Provided that, unless the parties otherwise agree, arbitration may be commenced on or after the fifty-sixth day after the day on which notice of intention to commence arbitration of such dispute was given, even if no attempt at amicable settlement thereof has been made.

Arbitration   **67.3**   Any dispute in respect of which:

(a) the decision, if any, of the Engineer has not become final and binding pursuant to Sub-Clause 67.1, and

(b) amicable settlement has not been reached within the period stated in Sub-Clause 67.2,

shall be finally settled, unless otherwise specified in the Contract, under the Rules of Conciliation and Arbitration of the International Chamber of Commerce by one or more arbitrators appointed under such Rules. The said arbitrator/s shall have full power to open up, review and revise any decision, opinion, instruction, determination, certificate or valuation of the Engineer related to the dispute.

Neither party shall be limited in the proceedings before such arbitrator/s to the evidence or arguments put before the Engineer for the purpose of obtaining his said decision pursuant to Sub-Clause 67.1. No such decision shall disqualify the Engineer from being called as a witness and giving evidence before the arbitrator/s on any matter whatsoever relevant to the dispute.

Arbitration may be commenced prior to or after completion of the Works, provided that the obligations of the Employer, the Engineer and the Contractor shall not be altered by reason of the arbitration being conducted during the progress of the Works.

Failure to Comply with Engineer's Decision 67.4 Where neither the Employer nor the Contractor has given notice of intention to commence arbitration of a dispute within the period stated in Sub-Clause 67.1 and the related decision has become final and binding, either party may, if the other party fails to comply with such decision, and without prejudice to any other rights it may have, refer the failure to arbitration in accordance with Sub-Clause 67.3. The provisions of Sub-Clauses 67.1 and 67.2 shall not apply to any such reference.

Notices

Notice to Contractor 68.1 All certificates, notices or instructions to be given to the Contractor by the Employer or the Engineer under the terms of the Contract shall be sent by post, cable, telex or facsimile transmission to or left at the Contractor's principal place of business or such other address as the Contractor shall nominate for that purpose.

Notice to Employer and Engineer 68.2 Any notice to be given to the Employer or to the Engineer under the terms of the Contract shall be sent by post, cable, telex or facsimile transmission to or left at the respective addresses nominated for that purpose in Part II of these Conditions.

Change of Address 68.3 Either party may change a nominated address to another address in the country where the Works are being executed by prior notice to the other party, with a copy to the Engineer, and the Engineer may do so by prior notice to both parties.

Default of Employer

Default of Employer 69.1 In the event of the Employer:

(a) failing to pay to the Contractor the amount due under any certificate of the Engineer within 28 days after the expiry of the time stated in Sub-Clause 60.10 within which payment is to be made, subject to any deduction that the Employer is entitled to make under the Contract,

(b) interfering with or obstructing or refusing any required approval to the issue of any such certificate,

(c) becoming bankrupt or, being a company, going into liquidation, other than for the purpose of a scheme of reconstruction or amalgamation, or

(d) giving notice to the Contractor that for unforeseen economic reasons it is impossible for him to continue to meet his contractual obligations,

the Contractor shall be entitled to terminate his employment under the Contract by giving notice to the Employer, with a copy to the Engineer. Such termination shall take effect 14 days after the giving of the notice.

Removal of Contractor's Equipment 69.2 Upon the expiry of the 14 days' notice referred to in Sub-Clause 69.1, the Contractor shall, notwithstanding the provisions of Sub-Clause 54.1, with all reasonable despatch, remove from the Site all Contractor's Equipment brought by him thereon.

Payment on Termination 69.3 In the event of such termination the Employer shall be under the same obligations to the Contractor in regard to payment as if the Contract had been terminated under the provisions of Clause 65, but, in addition to the payments specified in Sub-Clause 65.8, the Employer shall pay to the Contractor the amount of any loss or damage to the Contractor arising out of or in connection with or by consequence of such termination.

Contractor's Entitlement to Suspend Work	69.4	Without prejudice to the Contractor's entitlement to interest under Sub-Clause 60.10 and to terminate under Sub-Clause 69.1, the Contractor may, if the Employer fails to pay the Contractor the amount due under any certificate of the Engineer within 28 days after the expiry of the time stated in Sub-Clause 60.10 within which payment is to be made, subject to any deduction that the Employer is entitled to make under the Contract, after giving 28 days' prior notice to the Employer, with a copy to the Engineer, suspend work or reduce the rate of work.

If the Contractor suspends work or reduces the rate of work in accordance with the provisions of this Sub-Clause and thereby suffers delay or incurs costs the Engineer shall, after due consultation with the Employer and the Contractor, determine:

(a) any extension of time to which the Contractor is entitled under Clause 44, and

(b) the amount of such costs, which shall be added to the Contract Price,

and shall notify the Contractor accordingly, with a copy to the Employer.

Resumption of Work	69.5	Where the Contractor suspends work or reduces the rate of work. having given notice in accordance with Sub-Clause 69.4, and the Employer subsequently pays the amount due, including interest pursuant to Sub-Clause 60.10, the Contractor's entitlement under Sub-Clause 69.1 shall, if notice of termination has not been given, lapse and the Contractor shall resume normal working as soon as is reasonably possible.

Changes in Cost and Legislation

Increase or Decrease of Cost	70.1	There shall be added to or deducted from the Contract Price such sums in respect of rise or fall in the cost of labour and/or materials or any other matters affecting the cost of the execution of the Works as may be determined in accordance with Part II of these Conditions.
Subsequent Legislation	70.2	If, after the date 28 days prior to the latest date for submission of tenders for the Contract there occur in the country in which the Works are being or are to be executed changes to any National or State Statute, Ordinance, Decree or other Law or any regulation or bye-law of any local or other duly constituted authority, or the introduction of any such State Statute, Ordinance, Decree, Law, regulation or bye-law which causes additional or reduced cost to the Contractor, other than under Sub-Clause 70.1, in the execution of the Contract, such additional or reduced cost shall, after due consultation with the Employer and the Contractor, be determined by the Engineer and shall be added to or deducted from the Contract Price- and the Engineer shall notify the Contractor accordingly, with a copy to the Employer.

Currency and Rates of Exchange

Currency Restrictions	71.1	If, after the date 28 days prior to the latest date for submission of tenders for the Contract, the Government or authorised agency of the Government of the country in which the Works are being or are to be executed imposes currency restrictions and/or transfer of currency restrictions in relation to the currency or currencies in which the Contract Price is to be paid, the Employer shall reimburse any loss or damage to the Contractor arising therefrom, without prejudice to the right of the Contractor to exercise any other rights or remedies to which he is entitled in such event.
Rates of Exchange	72.1	Where the Contract provides for payment in whole or in part to be made to the Contractor in foreign currency or currencies, such payment shall not be subject to variations in the rate or rates of exchange between such specified foreign currency or currencies and the currency of the country in which the Works are to be executed.

Currency Proportions   **72.2**   Where the Employer has required the Tender to be expressed in a single currency but with payment to be made in more than one currency and the Contractor has stated the proportions or amounts of other currency or currencies in which he requires payment to be made, the rate or rates of exchange applicable for calculating the payment of such proportions or amounts shall, unless otherwise stated in Part II of these Conditions, be those prevailing, as determined by the Central Bank of the country in which the Works are to be executed, on the date 28 days prior to the latest date for the submission of tenders for the Contract, as has been notified to the Contractor by the Employer prior to the submission of tenders or as provided for in the Tender.

Currencies of Payment for Provisional Sums   **72.3**   Where the Contract provides for payment in more than one currency, the proportions or amounts to be paid in foreign currencies in respect of Provisional Sums shall be determined in accordance with the principles set forth in Sub-Clauses 72.1 and 72.2 as and when these sums are utilised in whole or in part in accordance with the provisions of Clauses 58 and 59.

REFERENCE TO PART II

As stated in the Foreword at the beginning of this document, the FIDIC Conditions comprise both Part I and Part II. Certain Clauses, namely Sub-Clauses 1.1 paragraph (a) (i) and (iv), 5.1 (part), 14.1, 14.3, 68.2 and 70.1 must include additional wording in Part II for the Conditions to be complete. Other Clauses may require additional wording to supplement Part I or to cover particular circumstances or the type of work (dredging is an example).

Part II Conditions of Particular Application with guidelines for the preparation of Part II are printed in a separately bound document.

PART I – GENERAL CONDITIONS

Index

Clause

Index

Clause

Index

Index

Clause

Index

Clause

Index

Index

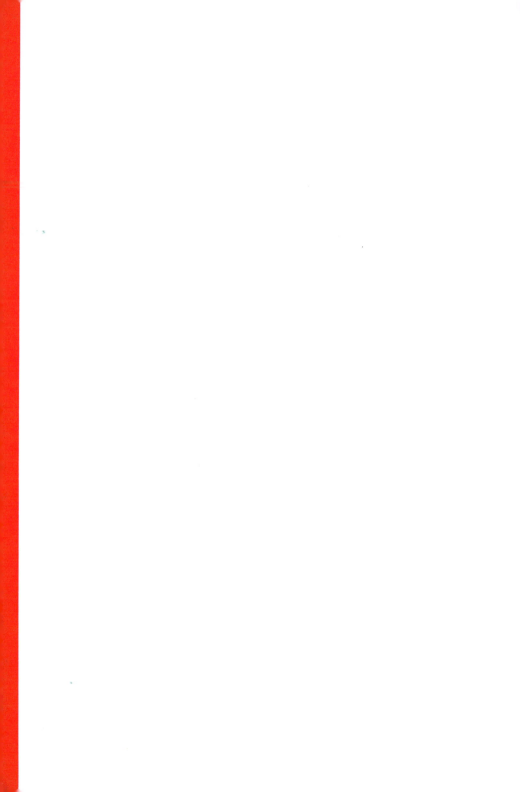

TENDER

NAME OF CONTRACT: * _____

_____

TO: * _____

_____

Gentlemen,

1. Having examined the Conditions of Contract, Specification, Drawings, and Bill of Quantities and Addenda Nos _____ for the execution of the above-named Works, we, the undersigned, offer to execute and complete such Works and remedy any defects therein in conformity with the Conditions of Contract, Specification, Drawings, Bill of Quantities and Addenda for the sum of

_____

_____

(_____)

   or such other sum as may be ascertained in accordance with the said Conditions.

2. We acknowledge that the Appendix forms part of our Tender.

3. We undertake, if our Tender is accepted, to commence the Works as soon as is reasonably possible after the receipt of the Engineer's notice to commence, and to complete the whole of the Works comprised in the Contract within the time stated in the Appendix to Tender.

4. We agree to abide by this Tender for the period of * _____ days from the date fixed for receiving the same and it shall remain binding upon us and may be accepted at any time before the expiration of that period.

5. Unless and until a formal Agreement is prepared and executed this Tender, together with your written acceptance thereof, shall constitute a binding contract between us.

6. We understand that you are not bound to accept the lowest or any tender you may receive.

   Dated this _____ day of _____ 19 ____

   Signature _____ in the capacity of _____

   duly authorised to sign tenders for and on behalf of _____

   _____

   (IN BLOCK CAPITALS)
   Address _____

   _____

   Witness _____

   Address _____

   _____

   Occupation _____

   (Note: All details marked * shall be inserted before issue of Tender documents.)

Appendix

Sub-Clause

	Sub-Clause	
Amount of security (if any) _____	10.1	_____ per cent of the Contract Price
Minimum amount of third party insurance	23.2	_____ per occurrence, with the number of occurrences unlimited
Time for issue of notice to commence	41.1	_____ days
Time for Completion _____	43.1	_____ days
Amount of liquidated damages _____	47.1	_____ per day
Limit of liquidated damages _____	47.1	_____
Defects Liability Period _____	49.1	_____ days
Percentage for adjustment of Provisional Sums	59.4(c)	_____ per cent
Percentage of invoice value of listed materials and Plant _____	60.1 (c)	_____ per cent
Percentage of Retention _____	60.2	_____ per cent
Limit of Retention Money _____	60.2	_____
Minimum Amount of Interim Payment Certificates _____	60.2	_____
Rate of interest upon unpaid sums _____	60.10	_____ per cent per annum

Initials of Signatory of Tender _____

(Notes: All details in the list above, other than percentage figure against Sub-Clause 59.4, shall be inserted before issue of Tender documents. Where a number of days is to be inserted, it is desirable, for consistency with the Conditions, that the number should be a multiple of seven.

Additional entries are necessary where provision is included in the Contract for:

(a) completion of Sections (Sub-Clauses 43.1 and 48.2(a))

(b) liquidated damages for Sections (Sub-Clause 47.1)

(c) a bonus (Sub-Clause 47.3 – Part II)

(d) payment for materials on Site (Sub-Clause 60.1(c))

(e) payment in foreign currencies (Clause 60 – Part II)

(f) an advance payment (Clause 60 – Part II)

(g) adjustments to the Contract Price on account of Specified Materials (Sub-Clause 70.1 – Part II)

(h) rates of exchange (Sub-Clause 72.2 – Part II))

Agreement

This Agreement made the _____ day of _____ 19 _____

Between _____

of _____

_____ (hereinafter called "the Employer") of the one part and

_____ of _____

(hereinafter called "the Contractor") of the other part

Whereas the Employer is desirous that certain Works should be executed by the

Contractor, viz _____

and has accepted a Tender by the Contractor for the execution and completion of such

Works and the remedying of any defects therein

Now this Agreement witnesseth as follows:

1. In this Agreement words and expressions shall have the same meanings as are respectively assigned to them in the Conditions of Contract hereinafter referred to.

2. The following documents shall be deemed to form and be read and construed as part of this Agreement, viz:

   (a) The Letter of Acceptance;

   (b) The said Tender;

   (c) The Conditions of Contract (Parts I and II);

   (d) The Specification;

   (e) The Drawings; and

   (f) The Bill of Quantities.

3. In consideration of the payments to be made by the Employer to the Contractor as hereinafter mentioned the Contractor hereby covenants with the Employer to execute and complete the Works and remedy any defects therein in conformity in all respects with the provisions of the Contract.

4. The Employer hereby covenants to pay the Contractor in consideration of the execution and completion of the works and the remedying of defects therein the Contract Price or such other sum as may become payable under the provisions of the Contract at the times and in the manner prescribed by the Contract.

   In Witness whereof the parties hereto have caused this Agreement to be executed the day and year first before written in accordance with their respective laws.

   The Common Seal of _____

   _____

   was hereunto affixed in the presence of:-

   or

   Signed Sealed and Delivered by the

   said _____
   in the presence of:

EDITORIAL AMENDMENTS IN 1988

Following publication of the Fourth Edition in 1987 of the Conditions of Contract for Works of Civil Engineering Construction, a number of editorial amendments were agreed by FIDIC. The amendments were incorporated during a 1988 reprinting and the list below clarifies the differences between the 1988 reprint and the original document.

Foreword   The last sentence of the first paragraph previously read "The Conditions are equally suitable for use on domestic contracts."

Page   **6**   Sub-Clause 10.1. A comma has been inserted after the word "Contract" in the second line.
The third sentence previously read "Such security shall be in such form as may be agreed between the Employer and the Contractor."

Page   **11**   Sub-Clause 22.1 (b) was previously one complete paragraph, ie there was no space between the words " . . . other than the Works), " and the remainder of the Sub-Clause.

Page   **15**   Sub-Clause 31.2 (c) was previously one complete paragraph, ie there was no space between the words "... nature for any such," and the remainder of the Sub-Clause.

Page   **20**   Sub-Clause 44.3. The penultimate sentence was previously, "In both such cases the Engineer shall notify the Contractor accordingly, with a copy to the Employer."

Page   **21**   Sub-Clause 49.1 (a). The word "substantial" has been deleted.

Page   **29**   Sub-Clause 60.3 (b) was previously two paragraphs, the second beginning with the words "Provided also that if at such time . . ."

Page   **30**   Sub-Clause 60.5. The word "The" has been inserted at the beginning of the final paragraph.

Page   **35**   Sub-Clause 67.1. In the eighth line of the third paragraph, a comma has been inserted after the word "provided". In the second line of the fourth paragraph, the word "notice" replaces the word "notification".

Page   **38**   Reference to Part II. In the third line, the words "and (iv)" have been inserted after paragraph (a) (i).

Tender

Item   **3.**   The word "Works" has been capitalised.

Agreement

Line   **4**   Inverted commas have been inserted following the words "the Employer."

Line   **6**   Inverted commas have been inserted before the word "the" instead of before the word "Contractor."

Line   **8**   The word "Contractor" has been capitalised.

Line   **9**   The words "Tender by the Contractor" were previously "Tender by Contractor."

Line   **11**   The word "Agreement" has been capitalised.

Last lines   The Agreement previously ended with the words "Binding Signature of Employer" and "Binding Signature of Contractor".

FURTHER AMENDMENTS IN 1992

The following amendments have been made to the 1988 Reprint of the Fourth Edition of the Conditions of Contract for Works of Civil Engineering Construction. The amendments of the 1988 Reprint are shown on the previous page. In addition, some minor changes in the use of punctuation marks (commas, semicolons, colons and stops), as well as the use of the words "or" and "and" have been introduced to attain uniformity in the style of all Clauses. These minor changes which improve the style, but which have no effect on the meaning of Clauses, have not been listed below.

FOREWORD The eighth paragraph previously referred to the anticipated publication of the "Guide to the Use of FIDIC Conditions of Contract for Works of Civil Engineering Construction".

Page 2 Sub-Clause 1.1, sub-para (e). Definitions (iii) "Interim Payment Certificate" and (iv) "Final Payment Certificate" have been added.

Page 6 Sub-Clause 8.1. Second paragraph has been added.

Page 7 Sub-Clause 12.2. Marginal note. The word "Adverse" has been changed to read "Not Foreseeable" (also amended in the Contents and the Index).

Page 8 Sub-Clause 13.1. Last sentence has been shortened by deleting the words "or, subject to the provisions of Clause 2, from the Engineer's Representative.", and adding the words "(or his delegate).".

Sub-Clause 15.1, para 1. Last sentence has been shortened by placing a full stop after the word "Engineer", deleting the words " or subject to the provisions of Clause 2, the Engineer's Representative."

Page 10 Sub-Clause 21.1, sub-para (a). The words "(the term "cost" in this context shall include profit)" have been added.

Page 11 Sub-Clause 21.4, sub-para (a). The word "where" has been corrected to read "whether".

Page 18 Sub-Clause 40.3. The word "written" has been deleted at the end of the first line.

Page 19 Sub-Clause 42.3. The word "wayleaves" has been changed to read "rights of way" in the text and marginal note (also amended in the Contents and the Index).

Page 29 Sub-Clause 60.1, sub-para (e). The words "or otherwise" have been added at the end

Sub-Clause 60.2. The words "certify to the Employer" have been changed to read "deliver to the Employer an Interim Payment Certificate stating", the word "thereof" has been changed to read "of such statement" and the word "he" has been changed to read "the Engineer". Sub-para (b). The words "Interim Certificates" have been changed to read "Interim Payment Certificates".

Sub-Clause 60.3, sub-para (b). In the eighth line, the word "ordered" has been changed to read "instructed".

Sub-Clause 60.4. The words "interim certificate" in the first and fourth lines, and the word "certificate" in the second line, have been changed to read "Interim Payment Certificate".

Page 30 Sub-Clause 60.5. In the second line, after the word "Engineer", the words "six copies of" have been added.

Sub-Clause 60.6. In the second line, after the word "consideration", the words "six copies of" have been added. Sub-para (b). The words "or otherwise" have been added at the end. At the end of the sub-clause, the final paragraph has been added.

Sub-Clause 60.7 and Sub-Clause 60.8 (text and marginal note). The words "Final Certificate" have been changed to read "Final Payment Certificate" (also amended in the Contents and the Index).

Sub-Clause 60.8 (a). The words "or otherwise" have been added. Sub-Clause 60.8 (b). The words "under the Contract other than Clause 47" have been changed to read "other than under Clause 47".
Sub-Clause 60.10. In the first and fourth lines, the words "interim certificate" have

Page	**31**	been changed to read "Interim Payment Certificate". In the fifth and sixth lines, the words "Final Certificate" have been changed to read "Final Payment Certificate". The words "or otherwise" have been added at the end.
Page	**33**	Sub-Clause 65.6. In the ninth line, the words "and to the operation of Clause 67" have been changed to read "and Clause 67".
Page	**34**	Sub-Clause 66.1. In the second line the word "party" has been changed to read "or both parties", in the third line between the words "his" and "contractual" the words "or their" have been added. In the fourth line after the word "then", the words "the parties shall be discharged from the Contract, except as to their rights under this Clause and Clause 67 and without prejudice to the rights of either party in respect of any antecedent breach of the Contract, and " have been added.
Page	**35**	Sub-Clause 67.2. The words "arbitration of such dispute shall not be commenced unless an attempt has first been made by the parties to settle such dispute amicably" have been changed to read " the parties shall attempt to settle such dispute amicably before the commencement of arbitration." The words "whether or not any attempt at amicable settlement thereof has been made" have been changed to read "even if no attempt at amicable settlement thereof has been made".
Page	**37**	Sub-Clause 69.1, Sub-para (d). The words "unforseen reasons, due to economic dislocation" have been changed to read "unforseen economic reasons".
		Sub-Clause 69.4. In the second line of the second paragraph, the word "cost" has been changed to read "costs".
Page	**38**	REFERENCE TO PART II. In the third line, the words "5.1 part" have been changed to read "5.1 (part)".
TENDER		Paragraph 1. In the last line, the word "sums" has been changed to read "sum".
Appendix		In the ninth line, the words "and Plant" have been added. In the twelth line, the word "Payment" has been added. In the thirteenth line, the words "per annum" have been added.
EDITORIAL AMENDMENTS		For page 35, after the words "Sub-Clause 67.1" the first sentence has been inserted.

FEDERATION INTERNATIONALE DES INGENIEURS-CONSEILS

CONDITIONS OF CONTRACT FOR WORKS OF CIVIL ENGINEERING CONSTRUCTION

PART II CONDITIONS OF PARTICULAR
APPLICATION WITH GUIDELINES FOR
PREPARATION OF PART II CLAUSES

FOURTH EDITION 1987
REPRINTED 1988 WITH EDITORIAL AMENDMENTS
REPRINTED 1992 WITH FURTHER AMENDMENTS

CONTENTS

PART II: CONDITIONS OF PARTICULAR APPLICATION

Page

INTRODUCTION

The terms of the Fourth Edition of the Conditions of Contract for Works of Civil Engineering Construction have been prepared by the Fédération Internationale des Ingénieurs Conseils (FIDIC) and are recommended for general use for the purpose of construction of such works where tenders are invited on an international basis. The Conditions, subject to minor modifications, are also suitable for use on domestic contracts.

The version in English of the Conditions is considered by FIDIC as the official and authentic text for the purpose of translation.

The Clauses of general application have been grouped together in a separately bound document and are referred to as Part I—General Conditions. They have been printed in a form which will facilitate their inclusion, as printed, in the contract documents normally prepared.

In the preparation of the Conditions it was recognised that while there are numerous Clauses which will be generally applicable there are some Clauses which must necessarily vary to take account of the circumstances and locality of the Works.

Part I – General Conditions and Part II – Conditions of Particular Application together comprise the Conditions governing the rights and obligations of the parties.

For this reason a Part II standard form has not been produced. It will be necessary to prepare a Part II document for each individual contract and the Guidelines are intended to aid in this task by giving options for various clauses where appropriate.

Part II clauses may arise for one or more reasons, of which the following are examples:

(i) Where the wording in Part I specifically requires that further information is to be included in Part II and the Conditions would not be complete without that information, namely in Sub-Clauses 1.1 paragraphs (a) (i) and (iv), 5.1 (part), 14.1, 14.3, 68.2 and 70.1

(ii) Where the wording in Part I indicates that supplementary information may be included in Part II, but the conditions would still be complete without any such information, namely in Sub-Clauses 2.1 paragraph (b), 5.1 (part), 21.1 paragraph (b) and 72.2.

(iii) Where the type, circumstances or locality of the Works necessitates additional Clauses or Sub-Clauses.

(iv) Where the law of the country or exceptional circumstances necessitate an alteration in Part I. Such alterations should be effected by stating in Part II that a particular Clause, or part of a Clause, in Part I is deleted and giving the substitute Clause, or part, as applicable.

As far as possible, in the Clauses that are mentioned hereunder, example wording is provided. In the case of some Clauses, however, only an aide-memoire for the preparation is given. Before incorporating any example wording it must be checked to ensure that it is wholly suitable for the particular circumstances and, if not, it must be varied. Where example wording is varied and in all cases where additional material is included in Part II, care must be taken that no ambiguity is created with Part I or between the Clauses in Part II.

Dredging and Reclamation Work

Special consideration must be given to Part II where dredging and certain types of reclamation work are involved. Dredgers are considerably more expensive than most items of Contractor's Equipment and the capital value of a dredger can often exceed the value of the Contract on which it is used.

For this reason, it is in the interests of both the Employer and the Contractor that a dredger is operated intensively in the most economic fashion, subject to the quality of work and any other over-riding factors. With this end in view, it is customary to allow the Contractor to execute dredging work continuously by day and by night seven days a week. Another difference from most civil engineering is that on dredging work the Contractor is not normally held responsible for the remedying of defects after the date of completion as certified under Clause 48. Part II contains explanations and example wording to cover the above points and others relating to dredging. Clauses 11, 12, 18, 19, 28, 40, 45, 49, 50 and 51 are those which most often require attention in Part II when dredging work is involved and reference is included under each of these Clauses. Other Clauses may also need additions in Part II in certain circumstances. Reclamation work varies greatly in character and each instance must be considered before deciding whether it is appropriate to introduce in Part II changes similar to those adopted for dredging, or to use the standard civil engineering form unaltered.

PART II CONDITIONS OF PARTICULAR APPLICATION

Clause 1

Sub-Clause 1.1 – Definitions

> *(a) (i) The Employer is (insert name)*

> *(a) (iv) The Engineer is (insert name)*

If further definitions are essential, additions should be made to the list.

Clause 2

Sub-Clause 2.1 – Engineer's Duties

> EXAMPLE
> *The Engineer shall obtain the specific approval of the Employer before carrying out his duties in accordance with the following Clauses of Part 1:*

> *(a) Clause (insert applicable number)*

> *(b) Clause (insert applicable number)*

> *(c) Clause (insert applicable number)*

This list should be extended or reduced as necessary.

In some cases the obligation to obtain the approval of the Employer may apply to only one Sub-Clause out of several in a Clause or approval may only be necessary beyond certain limits, monetary or otherwise. Where this is so, the example wording must be varied.

If the obligation to obtain the approval of the Employer could lead to the Engineer being unable to take action in an emergency, where matters of safety are involved, an additional paragraph may be necessary.

> EXAMPLE
> *Notwithstanding the obligation, as set out above, to obtain approval, if, in the opinion of the Engineer, an emergency occurs affecting the safety of life or of the Works or of adjoining property, he may, without relieving the Contractor of any of his duties and responsibilities under the Contract, instruct the Contractor to execute all such work or to do all such things as may, in the opinion of the Engineer, be necessary to abate or reduce the risk. The Contractor shall forthwith comply, despite the absence of approval of the Employer, with any such instruction of the Engineer. The Engineer shall determine an addition to the Contract Price, in respect of such instruction, in accordance with Clause 52 and shall notify the Contractor accordingly, with a copy to the Employer.*

Clause 5

Sub-Clause 5.1 – Language/s and Law

> *(a) The language is (insert as applicable)*

> *(b) The law is that in force in (insert name of country)*

If necessary (a) above should be varied to read:

> *The languages are (insert as applicable)*

and there should be added

> *The Ruling Language is (insert as applicable)*

Sub-Clause 5.2 – Priority of Contract Documents

Where it is decided that an order of precedence of all documents should be included, this Sub-Clause may be varied as follows:

> EXAMPLE
> *Delete the documents listed 1 - 6 and substitute:*
>
> *(1) the Contract Agreement (if completed);*
>
> *(2) the Letter of Acceptance;*
>
> *(3) the Tender;*
>
> *(4) the Conditions of Contract Part II;*
>
> *(5) the Conditions of Contract Part I;*
>
> *(6) the Specification;*
>
> *(7) the Drawings; and*
>
> *(8) the priced Bill of Quantities*

or

Where it is decided that no order of precedence of documents should be included, this Sub-Clause may be varied as follows:

> EXAMPLE
> *Delete the text of the Sub-Clause and substitute:*
>
> *The several documents forming the Contract are to be taken as mutually explanatory of one another, but in the case of ambiguities or discrepancies the priority shall be that accorded by law. If, in the opinion of the Engineer, such ambiguities or discrepancies make it necessary to issue any instruction to the Contractor in explanation or adjustment, the Engineer shall have authority to issue such instruction.*

Clause 9

Where it is decided that a Contract Agreement should be entered into and executed the form must be annexed to these Conditions as stated in Sub-Clause 9.1 of Part I of these Conditions.

A suitable form is annexed to Part I – General Conditions.

Clause 10

Sub-Clause 10.1 – Performance Security

Where it is decided that a performance security should be obtained by the Contractor, the form must be annexed to these Conditions as stated in Sub-Clause 10.1 of Part I of these Conditions.

Two example forms of performance security are given on pages 7, 8 and 9. The Clause and wording of the example forms may have to be varied to comply with the law of the Contract which may require the forms to be executed under seal.

Where there is provision in the Contract for payments to the Contractor to be made in foreign currency, Sub-Clause 10.1 of Part I of these Conditions may be varied.

> EXAMPLE
> *After the first sentence, insert the following sentence:*
>
> *The security shall be denominated in the types and proportions of currencies stated in the Appendix to Tender.*

Where the source of the performance security is to be restricted, an additional Sub-Clause may be added.

4

EXAMPLE SUB-CLAUSES

Source of 10.4 *The performance security, submitted by the Contractor in accordance with*
Performance *Sub-Clause 10.1, shall be furnished by an institution registered in (insert the*
Security *country where the Works are to be executed) or licensed to do business in such*
country.

or

Source of 10.4 *Where the performance security is in the form of a bank guarantee, it shall be*
Performance *issued by:*
Security
(a) a bank located in the country of the Employer, or

(b) a foreign bank through a correspondent bank located in the country of the
Employer.

Clause 11

Where the bulk or complexity of the data, or reasons of security enforced by the country where the Works are to be executed, makes it impracticable for the Employer to make all data available with the Tender Documents and inspection of some data by the Contractor at an office is therefore required, it would be advisable to make the circumstances clear.

EXAMPLE SUB-CLAUSE

Access 11.2 *Data made available by the Employer in accordance with Sub-Clause 11.1 shall*
to Data *be deemed to include data listed elsewhere in the Contract as open for inspection*
at (insert particulars of the office or offices where such data is stored)

Sub-Clause 11.1 – Inspection of Site

For a Contract comprising dredging and reclamation work the Clause may be varied as follows:

EXAMPLE
In the first paragraph, delete the words "hydrological and sub-surface" and substitute "hydrographic and sub-seabed".

In the second paragraph, under (a) delete the word "sub-surface" and substitute "sub-seabed" and under (b) delete the word "hydrological" and substitute "hydrographic".

Clause 12

Sub-Clause 12.2 – Not Foreseeable Obstructions or Conditions

For a Contract comprising dredging and some types of reclamation work the Sub-Clause may require to be varied.

EXAMPLE
Delete the words ", other than climatic conditions on the Site,

Clause 14

Sub-Clause 14.1 – Programme to be Submitted

The time within which the programme shall be submitted shall be (insert number) days.

Sub-Clause 14.3 – Cash Flow Estimate to be Submitted

The time within which the detailed cash flow estimate shall be submitted shall be (insert number) days.

In both examples given above it is desirable for consistency with the rest of the Conditions that the number of days inserted should be a multiple of seven.

EXAMPLE PERFORMANCE GUARANTEE

By this guarantee *We,* _____

whose registered office is at _____

(hereinafter called "the Contractor") and _____

whose registered office is at _____

(hereinafter called "the Guarantor") are held and firmly bound unto

_____ *(hereinafter called "the Employer")*

in the sum of _____ *for the payment of which sum*

the Contractor and the Guarantor bind themselves, their successors and assigns jointly and severally by these presents.

Whereas *the Contractor by an Agreement made between the Employer of the one part and the Contractor of the other part has entered into a Contract (hereinafter called "the said Contract") to execute and complete certain Works and remedy any defects therein as therein mentioned in conformity with the provisions of the said Contract.*

Now the Condition *of the above-written Guarantee is such that if the Contractor shall duly perform and observe all the terms provisions conditions and stipulations of the said Contract on the Contractor's part to be performed and observed according to the true purport intent and meaning thereof or if on default by the Contractor the Guarantor shall satisfy and discharge the damages sustained by the Employer thereby up to the amount of the above-written Guarantee then this obligation shall be null and void but otherwise shall be and remain in full force and effect but no alteration in terms of the said Contract or in the extent or nature of the Works to be executed, completed and defects therein remedied thereunder and no allowance of time by the Employer or the Engineer under the said Contract nor any forbearance or forgiveness in or in respect of any matter or thing concerning the said Contract on the part of the Employer or the said Engineer shall in any way release the Guarantor from any liability under the above-written Guarantee. Provided always that the above obligation of Guarantor to satisfy and discharge the damages sustained by the Employer shall arise only*

(a) on written notice from both the Employer and the Contractor that the Employer and the Contractor have mutually agreed that the amount of damages concerned is payable to the Employer or

(b) on receipt by the Guarantor of a legally certified copy of an award issued in arbitration proceeding carried out in conformity with the terms of the said Contract that the amount of the damages is payable to the Employer.

Signed on _____   *Signed on* _____

on behalf of _____   *on behalf of* _____

by _____   *by* _____

in the capacity of _____   *in the capacity of* _____

in the presence of _____   *in the presence of* _____

EXAMPLE SURETY BOND FOR PERFORMANCE

Know all Men by these Presents that (name and address of Contractor)

_____

as Principal (hereinafter called "the Contractor") and (name, legal title and address of Surety) _____

_____

as Surety (hereinafter called "the Surety"), are held and firmly bound unto (name and address of Employer) _____

_____ *as Obligee (hereinafter called "the Employer") in the amount of* _____ *for the payment of which sum, well and truly to be made, the Contractor and the Surety bind themselves, their successors and assigns, jointly and severally, firmly by these presents.*

Whereas the Contractor has entered into a written contract agreement with the Employer dated the _____ *day of* _____ *19__*

for(name of Works) _____
in accordance with the plans and specifications and amendments thereto, to the extent herein provided for, are by reference made part hereof and are hereinafter referred to as the Contract.

Now, therefore, the Condition of this Obligation is such that, if the Contractor shall promptly and faithfully perform the said Contract (including any amendments thereto) then this obligation shall be null and void; otherwise it shall remain in full force and effect.

Whenever Contractor shall be, and declared by Employer to be, in default under the Contract, the Employer having performed the Employer's obligations thereunder, the Surety may promptly remedy the default, or shall promptly:

(1) Complete the Contract in accordance with its terms and conditions; or

(2) Obtain a bid or bids for submission to the Employer for completing the Contract in accordance with its terms and conditions, and upon determination by Employer and Surety of the lowest responsible bidder, arrange for a contract between such bidder and Employer and make available as work progresses (even though there should be a default or a succession of defaults under the contract or contracts of completion arranged under this paragraph) sufficient funds to pay the cost of completion less the balance of the Contract Value; but not exceeding, including other costs and damages for which the Surety may be liable hereunder, the amount set forth in the first paragraph hereof. The term "balance of the Contract Value", as used in this paragraph, shall mean the total amount payable by Employer to Contractor under the Contract, less the amount properly paid by Employer to Contractor; or

(3) Pay the Employer the amount required by Employer to complete the Contract in accordance with its terms and conditions any amount up to a total not exceeding the amount of this Bond.

The Surety shall not be liable for a greater sum than the specified penalty of this Bond.

Any suit under this Bond must be instituted before the issue of the Defects Liability Certificate.

No right of action shall accrue on this Bond to or for the use of any person or corporation other than the Employer named herein or the heirs, executors, administrators or successors of the Employer.

Signed on _____ *Signed on* _____

on behalf of _____ *on behalf of* _____

by _____ *by* _____

in the capacity of _____ *in the capacity of* _____

in the presence of _____ *in the presence of* _____

Clause 15

Where the language in which the Contract documents have been drawn up is not the language of the country in which the Works are to be executed, or where for any other reason it is necessary to stipulate that the Contractor's authorised representative shall be fluent in a particular language, an additional Sub-Clause may be added.

EXAMPLE SUB-CLAUSES

Language Ability 15.2 *The Contractor's authorised representative shall be fluent in (insert name of*
of Contractor's *language).*
Representative

or

Interpreter to be 15.2 *If the Contractor's authorised representative is not, in the opinion of the*
Made Available *Engineer, fluent in (insert name of language), the Contractor shall have available on Site at all times a competent interpreter to ensure the proper transmission of instructions and information.*

Clause 16

Where the language in which the Contract documents have been drawn up is not the language of the country in which the Works are to be executed, or where for any other reason it is necessary to stipulate that members of the Contractor's superintending staff shall be fluent in a particular language, an additional Sub-Clause may be added.

EXAMPLE SUB-CLAUSE

Language Ability 16.3 *A reasonable proportion of the Contractor's superintending staff shall have a*
of Superintending *working knowledge of (insert name of language) or the Contractor shall have*
Staff *available on Site at all times a sufficient number of competent interpreters to ensure the proper transmission of instructions and information.*

Where there is a desire, but not a legal requirement, that the Contractor makes reasonable use of materials from or persons resident in the country in which the Works are to be executed, an additional Sub-Clause may be added.

EXAMPLE SUB-CLAUSE

Employment of 16.4 *The Contractor is encouraged, to the extent practicable and reasonable, to*
Local Personnel *employ staff and labour from sources within (insert name of country).*

Clause 18

Sub-Clause 18.1 – Boreholes and Exploratory Excavation

For a Contract comprising dredging and reclamation work the Sub-Clause may require to be varied.

EXAMPLE
Add second sentence as follows:

Such exploratory excavation shall be deemed to include dredging.

Clause 19

Sub-Clause 19.1 – Safety, Security and Protection of the Environment

Where a Contract includes dredging the possibility of pollution should be given particular attention and additional wording may be required. For example, where fishing and recreation areas might be influenced, the Contractor should be required to plan and execute the dredging so that the effect is kept to a minimum. Where there is a risk of chemical pollution from soluble sediments in the dredging area, for instance in a harbour, it is important that sufficient information is provided with the Tender documents. Responsibilities should be clearly defined.

Clause 21

Sub-Clause 21.1 – Insurance of Works and Contractor's Equipment

Where there is provision in the Contract for payments to the Contractor to be made in foreign currency, this Sub-Clause may be varied.

> EXAMPLE
> *Add final sentence as follows:*
>
> *The insurance in paragraphs (a) and (b) shall provide for compensation to be payable in the types and proportions of currencies required to rectify the loss or damage incurred.*

Where it is decided to state the deductible limits for the Employer's Risks, this Sub-Clause may be varied.

> EXAMPLE
> *Add to paragraph (a) as follows:*
>
> *and with deductible limits for the Employer's Risks not exceeding (insert amounts)*

Clauses 21, 23 and 25. Insurances Arranged by Employer

In certain circumstances, such as where a number of separate contractors are employed on a single project, or phased take-over is involved, it may be preferable for the Employer to arrange insurance of the Works, and Third Party insurance. In such case, it must be clear in the Contract that the Contractor is not precluded from taking out any additional insurance, should he desire to do so, over and above that to be arranged by the Employer.

Tenderers must be provided at the Tender stage with details of the insurance to be arranged by the Employer, in order to assess what provision to make in their rates and prices for any additional insurance, and for the amount of policy deductibles which they will be required to bear. Such details shall form part of the Contract between the Employer and the Contractor.

Example wording to allow for the arrangement of insurance by the Employer is as follows:

> EXAMPLE

Clause 21

Delete the text of the Clause and substitute the following re-numbered Sub-Clauses:

Insurance 21.1 of Works

Without limiting his or the Contractor's obligations and responsibilities under Clause 20, the Employer will insure:

(a) the Works, together with materials and Plant for incorporation therein, to the full replacement cost (the term "cost" in this context shall include profit), and

(b) an additional sum to cover any additional costs of and incidental to the rectification of loss or damage including professional fees and the cost of demolishing and removing any part of the Works and of removing debris of whatsoever nature.

Insurance of 21.2 Contractor's Equipment

The Contractor shall, without limiting his obligations and responsibilities under Clause 20, insure the Contractor's Equipment and other things brought onto the site by the Contractor, for a sum sufficient to provide for their replacement at the Site.

Scope of Cover 21.3

The insurance in Sub-Clause 21.1 shall be in the joint names of the Contractor and the Employer and shall cover:

10   © FIDIC 1987

(a) the Employer and the Contractor against loss or damage as provided in the details of insurance annexed to these Conditions, from the start of work at the Site until the date of issue of the relevant Taking-Over Certificate in respect of the Works or any Section or part thereof as the case may be, and

(b) the Contractor for his liability:
(i) during the Defects Liability Period for loss or damage arising from a cause occurring prior to the commencement of the Defects Liability Period, or

(ii) occasioned by the Contractor in the course of any operations carried out by him for the purpose of complying with his obligations under Clauses 49 and 50.

Responsibility for 21.4 Amounts not Recovered Any amounts not insured or not recovered from the insurers shall be borne by the Employer or the Contractor in accordance with their responsibilities under Clause 20.

Clause 23

Delete the text of the Clause and substitute:

Third Party 23.1 Insurance (including Employer's Property) Without limiting his or the Contractor's obligations and responsibilities under Clause 22, the Employer will insure in the joint names of the Contractor and the Employer, against liabilities for death of or injury to any person (other than as provided in Clause 24) or loss of or damage to any property other than the Works) arising out of the performance of the Contract, as provided in the details of insurance referred to in Sub-Clause 21.3.

Clause 25

Delete the text of the Clause and substitute:

Evidence 25.1 and Terms of Insurances The insurance policies to be arranged by the Employer pursuant to Clauses 21 and 23 shall be consistent with the general terms described in the Tender and copies of such policies shall when required be supplied by the Employer to the Contractor.

Adequacy of 25.2 Insurances The Employer shall notify the insurers of changes in the nature, extent or programme for execution of the Works and ensure the adequacy of the insurances at all times in accordance with the terms of the Contract and shall, when required, produce to the Contractor the insurance policies in force and the receipts for payment of the premiums. No variations shall be made to the insurances by the Employer without the prior approval of the Contractor.

Remedy on 25.3 Employer's Failure to Insure If and so far as the Employer fails to effect and keep in force any of the insurances referred to in Sub-Clause 25.1, then the Contractor may effect and keep in force any such insurance and pay any premium as may be necessary for that purpose and add the amount so paid to any monies due or to become due to the Contractor, or recover the same as a debt due from the Employer.

Compliance with 25.4 Policy Conditions In the event that the Contractor or the Employer fails to comply with conditions imposed by the insurance policies effected pursuant to the Contract, each shall indemnify the other against all losses and claims arising from such failure.

Clause 28

Sub-Clause 28.2 – Royalties

For a Contract comprising dredging and reclamation work and for any other Contract involving the dumping of materials the Sub-Clause may require to be varied.

EXAMPLE
Add second sentence as follows:

The Contractor shall also be liable for all payments or compensation, if any, levied in relation to the dumping of part or all of any such materials.

It is sometimes the case on dredging contracts for the Employer to bear the costs of tonnage and other royalties, rent and other payments or compensation. If such conditions are to apply, Sub-Clause 28.2 should be varied either by adding wording or by deleting the existing wording and substituting new wording.

Clause 31

Where the particular requirements of other contractors are known within reasonable limits at the time of preparation of the Contract documents, details must be stated. The Specification is usually the appropriate place to do so but, exceptionally, some reference may be desirable in the Conditions. In that case, an additional Sub-Clause or Sub-Clauses could be added to this Clause.

Clause 34

It will generally be necessary to add a number of Sub-Clauses, to take account of the circumstances and locality of the Works, covering such matters as: permits and registration of expatriate employees; repatriation to place of recruitment; provision of temporary housing for employees; requirements in respect of accommodation for staff of Employer and Engineer; standards of accommodation to be provided; provision of access roads, hospital, school, power, water, drainage, fire services, refuse collection, communal buildings, shops, telephones; hours and conditions of working; rates of pay; compliance with labour legislation; maintenance of records of safety and health.

EXAMPLE SUB-CLAUSES (to be numbered, as appropriate)

Rates of Wages and Conditions of Labour

34. *The Contractor shall pay rates of wages and observe conditions of labour not less favourable than those established for the trade or industry where the work is carried out. In the absence of any rates of wages or conditions of labour so established, the Contractor shall pay rates of wages and observe conditions of labour which are not less favourable than the general level of wages and conditions observed by other employers whose general circumstances in the trade or industry in which the Contractor is engaged are similar.*

Employment of Persons in the Service of Others

34. *The Contractor shall not recruit or attempt to recruit his staff and labour from amongst persons in the service of the Employer or the Engineer.*

Repatriation of Labour

34. *The Contractor shall be responsible for the return to the place where they were recruited or to their domicile of all such persons as he recruited and employed for the purposes of or in connection with the Contract and shall maintain such persons as are to be so returned in a suitable manner until they shall have left the Site or, in the case of persons who are not nationals of and have been recruited outside (insert name of country), shall have left (insert name of country).*

Housing for Labour

34. *Save insofar as the Contract otherwise provides, the Contractor shall provide and maintain such accommodation and amenities as he may consider necessary for all his staff and labour, employed for the purposes of or in connection with the Contract, including all fencing, water supply (both for drinking and other purposes), electricity supply, sanitation, cookhouses, fire prevention and fire-fighting equipment, air conditioning, cookers, refrigerators, furniture and other requirements in connection with such accommodation or amenities. On completion of the Contract, unless otherwise agreed with the Employer, the temporary camps/housing provided by the Contractor shall be removed and the site reinstated to its original condition, all to the approval of the Engineer.*

Accident Prevention Officer; Accidents

34. *The Contractor shall have on his staff at the Site an officer dealing only with questions regarding the safety and protection against accidents of all staff and labour. This officer shall be qualified for this work and shall have the authority to issue instructions and shall take protective measures to prevent accidents.*

© FIDIC 1987

Health and Safety	**34.**	Due precautions shall be taken by the Contractor, and at his own cost, to ensure the safety of his staff and labour and, in collaboration with and to the requirements of the local health authorities, to ensure that medical staff first aid equipment and stores, sick bay and suitable ambulance service are available at the camps, housing and on the Site at all times throughout the period of the Contract and that suitable arrangements are made for the prevention of epidemics and for all necessary welfare and hygiene requirements.
Measures against Insect and Pest Nuisance	**34.**	The Contractor shall at all times take the necessary precautions to protect all staff and labour employed on the site from insect nuisance, rats and other pests and reduce the dangers to health and the general nuisance occasioned by the same. The Contractor shall provide his staff and labour with suitable prophylactics for the prevention of malaria and take steps to prevent the formation of stagnant pools of water. He shall comply with all the regulations of the local health authorities in these respects and shall in particular arrange to spray thoroughly with approved insecticide all buildings erected on the Site. Such treatment shall be carried out at least once a year or as instructed by the Engineer. The Contractor shall warn his staff and labour of the dangers of bilharzia and wild animals.
Epidemics	**34.**	In the event of any outbreak of illness of an epidemic nature, the Contractor shall comply with and carry out such regulations, orders and requirements as may be made by the Government, or the local medical or sanitary authorities, for the purpose of dealing with and overcoming the same.
Burial of the Dead	**34.**	The Contractor shall make all necessary arrangements for the transport, to any place as required for burial, of any of his expatriate employees or members of their families who may die in (insert name of country). The Contractor shall also be responsible, to the extent required by the local regulations, for making any arrangements with regard to burial of any of his local employees who may die while engaged upon the Works.
Supply of Foodstuffs	**34.**	The Contractor shall arrange for the provision of a sufficient supply of suitable food at reasonable prices for all his staff, labour and Subcontractors, for the purposes of or in connection with the Contract.
Supply of Water	**34.**	The Contractor shall, so far as is reasonably practicable, having regard to local conditions, provide on the Site an adequate supply of drinking and other water for the use of his staff and labour.
Alcoholic Liquor or Drugs	**34.**	The Contractor shall not, otherwise than in accordance with the Statutes, Ordinances and Government Regulations or Orders for the time being in force, import, sell, give, barter or otherwise dispose of any alcoholic liquor or drugs, or permit or suffer any such importation, sale, gift, barter or disposal by his Subcontractors, agents, staff or labour.
Arms and Ammunition	**34.**	The Contractor shall not give, barter or otherwise dispose of to any person or persons, any arms or ammunition of any kind or permit or suffer the same as aforesaid.
Festivals and Religious Customs	**34.**	The Contractor shall in all dealings with his staff and labour have due regard to all recognised festivals, days of rest and religious or other customs.
Disorderly Conduct	**34.**	The Contractor shall at all times take all reasonable precautions to prevent any unlawful, riotous or disorderly conduct by or amongst his staff and labour and for the preservation of peace and protection of persons and property in the neighbourhood of the Works against the same.

Clause 35

Additional Sub-Clauses may be desirable to cover circumstances which require the maintenance of particular records or the provision of certain specific reports.

EXAMPLE SUB-CLAUSES (to be numbered, as appropriate)

Records of Safety and Health 35. *The Contractor shall maintain such records and make such reports concerning safety, health and welfare of persons and damage to property as the Engineer may from time to time prescribe.*

Reporting of Accidents 35. *The Contractor shall report to the Engineer details of any accident as soon as possible after its occurrence. In the case of any fatality or serious accident, the Contractor shall, in addition, notify the Engineer immediately by the quickest available means.*

Clause 40

For a Contract comprising dredging and some types of reclamation work the Clause may be varied.

Sub-Clause 40.1 – Suspension of Work

EXAMPLE
Delete paragraph (c) and renumber paragraph (d) as (c).

Sub-Clause 40.3 – Suspension Lasting more than 84 Days

EXAMPLE
In the first sentence delete the words ", (c) or (d)" and substitute "or (c)".

Clause 43

Sub-Clause 43.1 – Time for Completion

Where completion is stated to be by a date and not within a period of time, the Sub-Clause will require to be varied.

EXAMPLE
Delete the words, "within the time... such extended time" and substitute "by the date or dates stated in the Appendix to Tender for the whole of the Works or the Section (as the case may be) or such later date or dates".

Clause 45

For a Contract located in an isolated area, where environmental restrictions do not apply, or where a Contract comprises work, such as dredging and reclamation, that may require continuous working, the Clause may be varied.

EXAMPLE
Delete Sub-Clause 45.1 and substitute:

Working Hours 45.1 *Subject to any provision to the contrary contained in the Contract, the Contractor shall have the option to work continuously by day and by night and on locally recognised days of rest.*

The Contractor's option may be further extended by substituting, in place of the last three words:

holidays or days of rest.

Clause 47

Where it is desired to make provision for the payment of a bonus or bonuses for early completion, an additional Sub-Clause may be added.

In the case where a bonus is provided for early completion of the whole of the Works:

EXAMPLE SUB-CLAUSE

Bonus for 47.3
Completion
If the Contractor achieves completion of the Works prior to the time prescribed by Clause 43, the Employer shall pay to the Contractor a sum of (insert figure) for every day which shall elapse between the date stated in the Taking-Over Certificate in respect of the Works issued in accordance with Clause 48 and the time prescribed in Clause 43.

or

In the case where bonuses are provided for early completion of Sections of the Works and details, other than the dates, are given in the Specification:

EXAMPLE SUB-CLAUSE

Bonus for 47.3
Completion
Sections are required to be completed by the dates given in the Appendix to Tender in order that such Sections may be occupied and used by the Employer in advance of the completion of the whole of the Works.

Details of the work required to be executed to entitle the Contractor to bonus payments and the amount of the bonuses are stated in the Specification.

For the purposes of calculating bonus payments, the dates given in the Appendix to Tender for completion of Sections are fixed and, unless otherwise agreed, no adjustments of the dates by reason of granting an extension of time pursuant to Clause 44 or any other Clause of these Conditions will be allowed.

Issue of certificates by the Engineer that the Sections were satisfactory and complete by the dates given on the certificates shall, subject to Clause 60, entitle the Contractor to the bonus payments calculated in accordance with the Specification.

Clause 48

Where it can be foreseen that, when the whole of the Works have been substantially completed, the Contractor may be prevented by reasons beyond his control from carrying out the Tests on Completion, an additional Sub-Clause may be added.

EXAMPLE SUB-CLAUSE

Prevention 48.5
from Testing
If the Contractor is prevented from carrying out the Tests on Completion by a cause for which the Employer or the Engineer or other contractors employed by the Employer are responsible, the Employer shall be deemed to have taken over the Works on the date when the Tests on Completion would have been completed but for such prevention. The Engineer shall issue a Taking-Over Certificate accordingly. Provided always that the Works shall not be deemed to have been taken over if they are not substantially in accordance with the Contract.

If the Works are taken over under this Sub-Clause the Contractor shall nevertheless carry out the Tests on Completion during the Defects Liability Period. The Engineer shall require the Tests to be carried out by giving 14 days notice.

Any additional costs to which the Contractor may be put, in making the Tests on Completion during the Defects Liability Period, shall be added to the Contract Price.

15

Clause 49

For a Contract which includes a high proportion of Plant, an additional Sub-Clause may be necessary.

Extension of **49.5**
Defects Liability

EXAMPLE SUB-CLAUSE

The provisions of this Clause shall apply to all replacements or renewals of Plant carried out by the Contractor to remedy defects and damage as if the replacements and renewals had been taken over on the date they were completed. The Defects Liability Period for the Works shall be extended by a period equal to the period during which the Works cannot be used by reason of a defect or damage. If only part of the Works is affected the Defects Liability Period shall be extended only for that part. In neither case shall the Defects Liability Period extend beyond 2 years from the date of taking over.

When progress in respect of Plant has been suspended under Clause 40, the Contractor's obligations under this Clause shall not apply to any defects occurring more than 3 years after the Time for Completion established on the date of the Letter of Acceptance.

For a Contract comprising dredging work an additional Sub-Clause may be added.

No Remedying **49.5**
of Defects in
Dredging Work
after Completion

EXAMPLE SUB-CLAUSE

Notwithstanding Sub-Clause 49.2, the Contractor shall have no responsibility for the remedying of defects, shrinkages or other faults in respect of dredging work after the date stated in the Taking-Over Certificate.

Clause 50

For a Contract comprising dredging work and where the second Example Sub-Clause 49.5 has been adopted, an additional Sub-Clause should be added.

No Responsibility **50.2**
for Cost of
Searching of
Dredging Work

EXAMPLE SUB-CLAUSE

Notwithstanding Sub-Clause 50.1, the Contractor shall have no responsibility to bear the cost of searching for any defect, shrinkage or other fault in respect of dredging work after the date stated in the Taking-Over Certificate.

Clause 51

Sub-Clause 51.1 – Variations

For a Contract comprising dredging and some types of reclamation work the Sub-Clause may require to be varied.

EXAMPLE

Add final sentence as follows:

Provided also that the Contractor shall be under no obligation to execute any variation which cannot be executed by the Contractor's Equipment being used or to be used on the Works.

Clause 52

Where provision is made in the Contract for payment in foreign currency, this Clause may be varied.

Sub-Clause 52.1 – Valuation of Variations

EXAMPLE
Add final sentence as follows:

The agreement, fixing or determination of any rates or prices as aforesaid shall include any foreign currency and the proportion thereof.

Sub-Clause 52.2 –Power of Engineer to Fix Rates

Add to first paragraph final sentence as follows:

The agreement or <u>fixing of any rates or prices</u> as aforesaid shall include any foreign currency and the proportion thereof.

Sub-Clause 52.3 – Variations Exceeding 15 per cent

Add final sentence as follows:

The adjustment or fixing of any sum as aforesaid shall have due regard to any foreign currency included in the Effective Contract Price and the proportion thereof.

Where it is required to place some limitation on the range of items for which the rates and prices may be subject to review, the Clause may be varied.

Sub-Clause 52.2 – Power of Engineer to Fix Rates

EXAMPLE
At the end of the first paragraph add:

Provided further that no change in the rate or price for any item contained in the Contract shall be considered unless such item accounts for an amount more than 2 per cent of the Contract Price, and the actual quantity of work executed under the item exceeds or falls short of the quantity set out in the Bill of Quantities by more than 25 per cent.

Clause 54

Where vesting of Contractor's Equipment, Temporary Works and materials in the Employer is required, additional Sub-Clauses may be added.

EXAMPLE WORDING AND SUB-CLAUSES
Sub-Clauses 54.2 and 54.3 shall be renumbered as 54.3 and 54.4 and Sub-Clauses 54.4 to 54.8 shall be renumbered as 54.6 to 54.10. Add additional Sub-Clauses as follows:

Vesting 54.2 *All Contractor's Equipment, Temporary Works and materials owned by the Contractor, or by any company in which the Contractor has a controlling interest, shall, when on the Site, be deemed to be the property of the Employer. Provided always that the vesting of such property in the Employer shall not prejudice the right of the Contractor to the sole use of the said Contractor's Equipment, Temporary Works and materials for the purpose of the Works nor shall it affect the Contractor's responsibility to operate and maintain the same under the provisions of the Contract.*

Revesting and 54.5 Removal *Upon the removal, with the consent of the Engineer under Sub-Clauses 54.1, of any such Contractor's Equipment, Temporary Works or materials as have been deemed to have become the property of the Employer under Sub-Clause 54.2, the property therein shall be deemed to revest in the Contractor and, upon completion of the Works, the property in the remainder of such Contractor's Equipment, Temporary Works and materials shall, subject to Clause 63, be deemed to revest in the Contractor.*

Clause 60

Additional Sub-Clauses may be necessary to cover certain other matters relating to payments.

Where payments are to be made in various currencies in predetermined proportions and calculated at fixed rates of exchange the following 3 Sub-Clauses, which should be taken together, may be added:

EXAMPLE SUB-CLAUSES (to be numbered, as appropriate)

Currency of Account and Rates of Exchange

60. *The currency of account shall be the (insert name of currency) and for the purposes of the Contract conversion between (insert name of currency) and other currencies stated in the Appendix to Tender shall be made in accordance with the Table of Exchange Rates in the Appendix to Tender. Conversion between the currencies stated in such Table other than the (insert name of currency) shall be made at rates of exchange determined by use of the relative rates of exchange between such currencies and the (insert name of currency) set out therein.*

Payments to Contractor

60. *All payments to the Contractor by the Employer shall be made :*

(a) in the case of payment(s) under Sub-Clause(s) 70.2 and (insert number of any other applicable Clause), in (insert name of currency/ies);

(b) in the case of payments for certain provisional sum items excluded from the Appendix to Tender, in the currencies and proportions applicable to these items at the time when the Engineer gives instructions for the work covered by these items to be carried out; and

(c) in any other case, including Increase or Decrease of Costs under Sub-Clause 70.1, in the currencies and proportions stated in the Appendix to Tender as applicable to such payment provided that the proportions of currencies stated in the Appendix to Tender may from time to time upon the application of either party be varied as may be agreed.

Payments to Employer

60. *All payments to the Employer by the Contractor including payments made by way of deduction or set-off shall be made :*

(a) in the case of credit(s) under Sub-Clause(s) 70.2 and (insert number of any other applicable Clause) in (insert name of currency/ies);

(b) in the case of liquidated damages under Clause 47, in (insert name of currency/ies);

(c) in the case of reimbursement of any sum previously expended by the Employer, in the currency in which the sum was expended by the Employer; and

(d) in any other case, in such currency as may be agreed.

If the part payable in a particular currency of any sum payable to the Contractor is wholly or partly insufficient to satisfy by way of deduction or set-off a payment due to the Employer in that currency, in accordance with the provisions of this Sub-Clause, then the Employer may if he so desires make such deduction or set-off wholly or partly as the case may be from the balance of such sum payable in other currencies.

Where all payments are to be made in one currency the following Sub-Clause may be added:

EXAMPLE SUB-CLAUSE (to be numbered, as appropriate)

Currency of Account and Payments

60. *The currency of account shall be the (insert name of currency) and all payments made in accordance with the Contract shall be in (insert name of currency). Such (insert name of currency), other than for local costs, shall be fully convertible. The percentage of such payments attributed to local costs shall be as stated in the Appendix to Tender.*

Where place of payment is to be defined the following Sub-Clause may be added:

EXAMPLE SUB-CLAUSE (to be numbered, as appropriate)

Place of Payment 60. *Payments to the Contractor by the Employer shall be made into a bank account nominated by the Contractor in the country of the currency of payment. Where payment is to be made in more than one currency separate bank accounts shall be nominated by the Contractor in the country of each currency and payments shall be made by the Employer accordingly.*

Where provision is to be included for an advance payment the following Sub-Clause may be added:

EXAMPLE SUB-CLAUSE (to be numbered, as appropriate)

Advance Payment 60. *An advance payment of the amount stated in the Appendix to Tender shall, following the presentation by the Contractor to the Employer of an approved performance security in accordance with Sub-Clause 10.1 and a Guarantee in terms approved by the Employer for the full value of the advance payment, be certified by the Engineer for payment to the Contractor. Such Guarantee shall be progressively reduced by the amount repaid by the Contractor as indicated in Interim Payment Certificates of the Engineer issued in accordance with this Clause. The advance payment shall not be subject to retention. The advance payment shall be repaid by way of reduction in Interim Payment Certificates commencing with the next certificate issued after the total certified value of the Permanent Works and any other items in the Bill of Quantities (excluding the deduction of retention) exceeds (insert figure) per cent of the sum stated in the Letter of Acceptance. The amount of the reduction in each Interim Payment Certificate shall be one (insert fraction) of the difference between the total value of the Permanent Works and any other items in the Bill of Quantities (excluding the deduction of retention) due for certification in such Interim Payment Certificate and the said value in the last preceding Interim Payment Certificate until the advance payment has been repaid in full. Provided that upon the issue of a Taking-Over Certificate for the whole of the Works or upon the happening of any of the events specified in Sub-Clause 63.1 or termination under Clauses 65, 66 or 69, the whole of the balance then outstanding shall immediately become due and payable by the Contractor to the Employer.*

Clause 67

Where it is considered desirable to add to Sub-Clauses 67.3 provisions with respect to the number of arbitrators, the place of arbitration and the language of arbitration, the following paragraphs may be added to Sub-Clause 67.3:

EXAMPLE

The arbitral tribunal shall consist of ...... (a sole or three) arbitrator(s).

The place of arbitration shall be ......(city and country).

The language of the arbitration shall be.......

It is desirable that the place of arbitration be situated in a state, other than that of the Employer or the Contractor, which has a modern and liberal arbitration law and which has ratified a bilateral or multilateral convention (such as the 1958 New York Convention on the Recognition and Enforcement of Foreign Arbitral Awards), or both, that would facilitate the enforcement of an arbitral award in the states of the parties to the Contract.

In the absence of stipulations as to the three above mentioned matters, (number of arbitrators, place of arbitration and language of arbitration), the ICC will decide on the number of arbitrators (typically three in any substantial construction dispute) and on the place of arbitration. The arbitral tribunal will decide on the language of the arbitration if the parties cannot agree.

It may also be considered desirable in some cases for other parties to be joined into any arbitration between the Employer and the Contractor, thereby creating a multi-party arbitration. While this may be feasible, multi-party arbitration clauses require skillful draftmanship on a case-by-case basis. No satisfactory standard form of multi-party arbitration clause for international use has yet been developed.

Where it is decided that a settlement of dispute procedure, other than that of the International Chamber of Commerce (ICC), should be used the Clause may be varied.

Sub-Clause 67.3 – Arbitration

EXAMPLE

Following paragraph (b), delete the words "shall be finally settled... International Chamber of Commerce" and substitute "shall be finally settled under the UNCITRAL Arbitration Rules as administered by (insert name of administering authority)".

Where alternatives to the ICC are considered care should be taken to establish that the favoured alternative is appropriate for the circumstances of the Contract and that the wording of Clause 67 is checked and amended as may be necessary to avoid any ambiguity with the alternative. Care should be taken to define exactly how the arbitral tribunal is to be appointed and, where appropriate, an appointing authority should be designated.

Clause 68

Sub-Clause 68.2 – Notice to Employer and Engineer

For the purposes of this Sub-Clause the respective addresses are:

(a) The Employer (insert address)

(b) The Engineer (insert address)

The addresses should be inserted when the documents are being prepared prior to inviting tenders.

Clause 69

Sub-Clause 69.1 – Default of Employer

Where the Employer is a government it may be considered appropriate to vary the Sub-Clause.

EXAMPLE
Delete paragraph (c) and renumber paragraph (d) as (c).

Where the terms of the Sub-Clause, when read in conjunction with Sub-Clause 69.3, are in conflict with the law of the country the Sub-Clause may require to be varied.

EXAMPLE
Delete "or" at the end of paragraph (c) and delete paragraph (d).

Clause 70

Three alternative methods of dealing with price adjustment are given below.

The first alternative is suitable where a contract is of short duration and no price adjustment is to be made:

Sub-Clause 70.1—Increase or Decrease in Cost

EXAMPLE
Delete the text of the Sub-Clause and substitute

Subject to Sub-Clause 70.2, the Contract Price shall not be subject to any adjustment in respect of rise or fall in the cost of labour, materials or any other matters affecting the cost of execution of the Contract.

Sub-Clause 70.2—Subsequent Legislation

EXAMPLE
Delete the words ", other than under Sub-Clause 70.1, ".

The second alternative is suitable where price adjustment is to be made by establishing the difference in cost between the basic price and the current price of local labour and specified materials:

Sub-Clause 70.1—Increase or Decrease in Cost

EXAMPLE
Delete the text of the Sub-Clause and substitute

Adjustments to the Contract Price shall be made in respect of rise or fall in the cost of local labour and specified materials as set out in this Sub-Clause.
(a) Local Workmen

(i) For the purpose of this Sub-Clause:
"Local Workmen" means skilled, semi-skilled and unskilled workmen of all trades engaged by the Contractor on the Site for the purpose of or in connection with the Contract or engaged full time by the Contractor off the Site for the purpose of or in connection with the Contract (by way of illustration but not limitation: workmen engaged full time in any office, store, workshop or quarry);
"Basic Rate" means the applicable basic minimum wage rate prevailing on the date 28 days prior to the latest date for submission of tenders by reason of any National or State Statute, Ordinance, Decree or other Law or any regulations or bye-law of any local or other duly constituted authority, or in order to conform with practice amongst good employers generally in the area where the Works are to be carried out; and
"Current Rate" means the applicable basic minimum wage rate for Local Workmen prevailing on any date subsequent to the date 28 days prior to the latest date set for submission of tenders by reason of any National or State Statute, Ordinance, Decree or other Law or any regulation or bye-law of any local or other duly constituted authority, or in order to conform with practice amongst good employers generally in the area where the works are to be carried out.

(ii) The adjustment to the Contract Price under the terms of this Sub-Clause shall be calculated by multiplying the difference between the Basic and Current Rates for Local workmen by:

(a) the number of all hours actually worked, and

(b) in respect of those hours worked at overtime rates, by the product of the number of said hours and the percentage addition required by the law to be paid by the Contractor for overtime.

Such adjustment may be either an addition to or a deduction from the Contract Price.

(iii) No other adjustment of the Contract Price on account of fluctuation in the remuneration of Local Workmen shall be made.

(b) Specified Materials

(i) For the purpose of this Sub-Clause:
"Specified Materials" means the materials stated in Appendix (insert reference) to Tender required on the Site for the execution and completion of the Works;

"Basic Prices" means the current prices for the specified materials prevailing on the date 28 days prior to the latest date for submission of tenders; and

"Current Prices" means the current prices for the specified materials prevailing at any date subsequent to the date 28 days prior to the latest date for submission of tenders.

(ii) The adjustment to the Contract Price under the terms of this Sub-Clause shall be calculated by applying the difference between the Basic and Current Prices to the quantity of the appropriate Specified Material which is delivered to the Site during the period for which the particular Current Price is effective. Such adjustment may be either an addition to or a deduction from the Contract Price.

(iii) The Contractor shall use due diligence to ensure that excessive wastage of the Specified Materials shall not occur. Any Specified Materials removed from the Site shall be clearly identified in the records required under paragraph (d) of this Sub-Clause.

(iv) The provisions of this Sub-Clause shall apply to fuels used in Contractor's Equipment engaged on the Site for the purposes of executing the Works, including vehicles owned by the Contractor (or hired by him under long term arrangements under which the Contractor is obligated to supply fuel) engaged in transporting any staff, labour, Contractor's Equipment, Temporary Works, Plant or materials to and from the Site. Such fuels shall be clearly identified in the records required under paragraph (d) of this Sub-Clause. The provisions of this Sub-Clause shall not apply to any fuels sold or supplied to any employee of the Contractor or to any person for use in any motor vehicle not being used for the purposes of the Contract.

(v) The Contractor shall at all times have regard to suitable markets and shall, whenever buying materials a variation in the cost of which would give rise to an adjustment of the Contract Price under this Sub-Clause, be diligent to buy or procure the same at the most economical prices as are consistent with the due performance by the Contractor of his obligations under the Contract.

If at any time there shall have been any lack of diligence, default or negligence on the part of the Contractor, whether in observing the above requirements or otherwise, then, for the purposes of adjusting the Contract Price pursuant hereto, no account shall be taken of any increase in cost which may be attributable to such lack of diligence, default or negligence and the amount by which any cost would have been decreased but for such lack of diligence, default or negligence shall be deducted from the Contract Price.

(vi) No other adjustment to the Contract Price on account of fluctuation in the cost of materials shall be made.

(c) *Overheads and Profits Excluded*

In determining the amount of any adjustment to the Contract Price pursuant to this Sub-Clause no account shall be taken of any overheads or profits.

(d) *Notices and Records*

The Contractor shall forthwith, upon the happening of any event which may or may be likely to give rise to adjustment of the Contract Price pursuant to this Sub-Clause, give notice thereof to the Engineer and the Contractor shall keep such books, accounts and other documents and records as are necessary to enable adjustment under this Sub-Clause to be made and shall, at the request of the Engineer, furnish any invoices, accounts, documents or records so kept and such other information as the Engineer may require.

(e) *Adjustment after Date of Completion*

Adjustment to the Contract Price, after the due date for completion of the whole of the Works pursuant to Clause 43, or after the date of completion of the whole of the Works certified pursuant to Clause 48, shall be made in accordance with Current Rates or Current Prices, as applicable, ruling at the due date for completion or the date stated in the Taking-Over Certificate, whichever is the earlier.

(f) *Determination of Adjustment to Contract Price*

The amount of any adjustment to the Contract Price pursuant to this Sub-Clause shall be determined by the Engineer in accordance with the foregoing rules.

EXAMPLE APPENDIX TO TENDER
for use in conjunction with the second alternative.

SPECIFIED MATERIALS

MATERIAL	*UNIT*	*PRICE AND LOCATION*	*TRANSPORT TO SITE*	*PRICE DELIVERED TO SITE*	*REMARKS*
Bitumen					
Diesel					
Petrol					
Lubricants					
Cement					
Reinforcing Steel					
Explosives					

NOTES:

1. The Contractor shall provide copies of quotations to substantiate all prices included in the above table.

2. All subsequent price substantiation shall be from the same source as original unless otherwise agreed by the Engineer.

3. The Contractor shall submit full explanation and provide substantiating documentation for the mode of transport to Site he proposes. Only the proposed documented mode of transport shall qualify for price adjustment.

(Note: Materials stated in the Appendix to Tender should be those of which substantial quantities are involved.)

The third alternative is suitable where price adjustment is to be made through the application of indices in a formula:

Sub-Clause 70.1 – Increase or Decrease in Cost

EXAMPLE
Delete the text of the Sub-Clause and substitute

(a) Adjustments to the Contract Price in respect of rise and fall in the cost of labour and materials and other matters affecting the cost of execution of the Works shall be calculated for each monthly statement pursuant to Sub-Clause 60.1, the Statement at Completion pursuant to Sub-Clause 60.5 and the Final Statement pursuant to Sub-Clause 60.6 in accordance with the provisions of this Sub-Clause if there shall be any changes in the following Index figures compiled by (insert details of source of indices) and published by (insert details of publication):

(i) the Index of the cost of Labour in (insert name of country),

(ii) the Index of the cost of (insert other factor, as relevant), or

(iii) the Index of the cost of (insert other factor, as relevant).

(b) For the purpose of this Sub-Clause:

(i) "Base Index Figure" shall mean the index figure applicable on the date 28 days prior to the latest date for submission of tenders, and

(ii) "Current Index Figure" shall mean the index figure applicable on the last day of the period to which the particular statement relates.

Provided that in respect of any work the value of which is included in any such monthly statement (or Statement at Completion or Final Statement) and which was executed after the due date (or extended date) for completion of the whole of the Works, pursuant to Clause 43, the Current Index Figure shall be the index figure applicable on the aforesaid due date (or extended date) for completion of the whole of the Works.

(iii) "Effective Value" shall be the difference between:

(a) The amount which is due to the Contractor under the provisions of Sub-Clauses 60.2, 60.5 or 60.8 (before deducting retention and excluding repayment of the advance payment) less any amounts for:

work executed under nominated Subcontracts

materials and Plant on the Site, as referred to in Sub-Clause 60.1 (c)

dayworks, variations or any other items <u>based on actual cost</u> or current prices, and bonuses (if any)

adjustments under Clause 70,

and

(b) The amount calculated in accordance with (b) (iii) (a) of this Sub-Clause and included in the last preceding statement.

(c) The adjustment to the Contract Price shall be calculated by multiplying the Effective Value by a Price Fluctuation Factor which shall be the net sum of the products obtained by multiplying each of the proportions given in paragraph (d) of this Sub-Clause by the following fraction:

$$\frac{\text{Current Index Figure} - \text{Base Index Figure}}{\text{Base Index Figure}}$$

calculated using the relevant index figures.

(d) For the purpose of calculating the Price Fluctuation Factor, the proportions referred to in paragraph (c) of this Sub-Clause shall (irrespective of the actual constituents of the work) be as follows:

0. *in respect of labour (and supervision) costs subject to adjustment by reference to the Index referred to in (a) (i) of this Sub-Clause;*

0. *in respect of   by reference to the Index referred to in (a) (ii) of this Sub-Clause;*

0. *in respect of   by reference to the Index referred to in (a) (iii) of this Sub-Clause;*

0. *in respect of all other costs which shall not be subject to any adjustment;*

1.00 *Total*

(e) Where the value of an Index is not known at the time of calculation, the latest available value shall be used and any adjustment necessary shall be made in subsequent monthly statements.

(Note: The number of indices included under (a) of this Sub-Clause may be varied, if it is determined that a different number of factors should be separately identified, and in such case (d) of this Sub-Clause must be altered to be consistent.)

Clause 72

Sub-Clause 72.2 – Currency Proportions

Where it is decided that the rate or rates of exchange shall be established from a source other than the Central Bank of the country, the Sub-Clause may be varied.

EXAMPLE
Delete the words from "prevailing... " to the end of the sentence and substitute "stated in the Appendix to Tender".

Clause 73 onwards

Where circumstances require, additional Clauses may be added.

EXAMPLE CLAUSES (to be numbered, starting with Clause 73, as appropriate).

Where the law applicable to the Contract does not cover bribery, the following example Clause may be added.

Bribes   *.1*   *If the Contractor or any of his Subcontractors, agents or servants offers to give or agrees to offer or give to any person, any bribe, gift, gratuity or commission as an inducement or reward for doing or forbearing to do any action in relation to the Contract or any other contract with the Employer or for showing or forbearing to show favour or disfavour to any person in relation to the Contract or any other contract with the Employer, then the Employer may enter upon the Site and the Works and terminate the employment of the Contractor and the provisions of Clause 63 hereof shall apply as if such entry and termination had been made pursuant to that Clause.*

Where circumstances require that particular confidentiality is observed, the following example Clause may be added.

Details to be Confidential   *.1*   *The Contractor shall treat the details of the Contract as private and confidential, save in so far as may be necessary for the purposes thereof, and shall not publish or disclose the same or any particulars thereof in any trade or technical paper or elsewhere without the previous consent in writing of the Employer or the Engineer. If any dispute arises as to the necessity of any publication or disclosure for the purpose of the Contract the same shall be referred to the Employer whose determination shall be final.*

Where the Contract is being financed wholly or in part by an international financial institution whose rules or policies require a restriction on the use of the funds provided, the following example Clause may be added.

Expenditure Restricted   *.1*   *The Contractor shall not make any expenditures for the purpose of the Contract in the territories of any country which is not a member of (insert name of international financial institution) nor shall he make any expenditure for goods produced in or services supplied from such territories.*

Where the Contractor may be a joint venture, the following example Clause may be added.

Joint and Several Liability   *.1*   *If the Contractor is a joint venture of two or more persons, all such persons shall be jointly and severally bound to the Employer for the fulfilment of the terms of the Contract and shall designate one of such persons to act as leader with authority to bind the joint venture. The composition or the constitution of the joint venture shall not be altered without the prior consent of the Employer.*

PART II –
CONDITIONS OF PARTICULAR APPLICATION

Index   Clause

Index

Clause

EDITORIAL AMENDMENTS IN 1988

Following publication in 1987 of the Fourth Edition of the Conditions of Contract for Works of Civil Engineering Construction, a number of editorial amendments were agreed by FIDIC. The amendments have been incorporated during reprinting in 1988 and the list below clarifies the differences between the 1988 reprint and the original document.

Page **5**   Clause 9. The words "as stated in Sub-Clause 9.1 of Part 1 of these Conditions" have been added to the final line of the first paragraph.

Page **6**   Sub-Clause 12.2. A comma has been moved from after the word "words" to immediately before the word "other". The word "Site" has been capitalised.

Page **7**   Example performance guarantee. A comma previously appeared between the words "and" and "complete" in the third line of the paragraph beginning "Whereas" .
The fifth line of the paragraph beginning "Now the Condition . . ." previously read ". . . default by the Contract . . ."

Page **12**   Sub-Clause 21.3. (b) (ii). A full stop has been inserted following "50".

Page **13**   Sub-Clause 34. Repatriation of Labour. A comma has been inserted between the words "country)" and "shall".

Page **14**   Sub-Clause 34. Epidemics. The word "Contractor" has been capitalised in the first line.
Sub-Clause 34. Alcoholic Liquor or Drugs. The word "Contractor" has been capitalised in the first line.

Page **15**   Sub-Clause 40.3. This was previously incorrectly listed as 40.2.

Page **17**   Sub-Clause 49.5. The last line of the first paragraph previously read " . . . extend beyond 730 days".

Page **20**   Sub-Clause 67.3. The word "a" previously appeared before the bracket on the penultimate line of the Example.

Page **21**   Sub-Clause 70.2. A comma has been moved from after the word "words" to immediately before the word "other".

FURTHER AMENDMENTS IN 1992

The following amendments have been made to the 1988 reprint of the Fourth Edition. In addition, some minor changes in the use of punctuation marks (commas, semicolons, colons and stops), as well as the use of the words "or" and "and" have been introduced to attain uniformity in the style of all Clauses. These minor changes which improve the style, but which have no effect on the meaning of Clauses, have not been listed below.

Contents

The words "Index" and "Editorial Amendments" have been added at the bottom of the page.

Page   **1**   INTRODUCTION. The words ", subject to minor modifications" have been added, and the word " equally" changed to read "also".

Page   **3**   Sub-Clause 1.1. In the last sentence, the words "for example the name of an International Financing Institution (IFI)" have been deleted.

Page   **4**   Clause 9. In the first paragraph the words "of Part I" have been added. In the second paragraph "1" has been corrected to read "I".

Page   **5**   Clause 12. Sub-Clause 12.2. In the title the word "Adverse" has been changed to read "Not Foreseeable" (also amended in the Contents and the Index).

Page   **10**   Sub-Clause 21.1, sub-para (a). The words "(the term "cost" in this context shall include profit)" have been added.

Page   **13**   Example Sub-Clause for Supply of Foodstuffs. The words "staff and labour, or his Subcontractors" have been changed to read " staff, labour and Subcontractors"

Page   **19**   Example Sub-Clause for Advance Payment. The words "interim certificate" have been changed to read "Interim Payment Certificate", in both the singular and plural.

Clause 67. The first four paragraphs of the commentary have been added.

Page   **24**   Sub-Clause 70.1. In the formula, the word "Based" has been corrected to read "Base".

Page   **25**   Example Clause for Bribes. The word "Sub-contractors" has been corrected to read "Subcontractors".

Example Clause for Details to be Confidential. In the sixth line, the words "the decision of" have been deleted. In the seventh line, the word "award" has been changed to read "determination"

Example Clause for Expediture Restricted. In the commentary and text, the leading capital letters on the words "International Financing Institutions" have been changed to small letters. In the commentary, the word "Articles" has been changed to read "rules or policies". In the third line, the word "not" has been corrected to read "nor".

EDITORIAL AMENDMENTS (1988). In the last item, the words "Line 21" have been corrected to read "Page 21".

5. Alphabetische Vokabelliste typischer Adverbien, Adjektive und Konjunktionen der FIDIC-Bedingungen
5. Wordlist of typical Adverbs, Adjectives and Conjunctions appearing in the FIDIC-Conditions (English/German)

Diese Liste enthält Vokabeln, die in den Bedingungen wiederholt vorkommen. Der Leser sollte sie sich zweckmäßigerweise vorab einprägen. Die an erster Stelle stehenden deutschen Bedeutungen entsprechen dem Textzusammenhang. Weitere Bedeutungen sind nur der Vollständigkeit halber zum weiteren Spracherwerb angegeben.

accordingly	entsprechend
aforesaid	oben erwähnt, oben genannt, besagt
as far as ... is, (are) concerned	was ... betrifft
as such	als solcher
as to	bezüglich, im Hinblick auf, was ... (an)betrifft
consequent thereon	als Folge von
consistent (with)	im Einklang stehend, übereinstimmend, vereinbar (mit)
foregoing	voriger, vorgehend, vorangehend, früher(e, es, er)
forthwith	sofort, gleich, unverzüglich
from time to time	von Zeit zu Zeit
further	weiterhin, weiter, überdies
hereafter	= hereinafter
hereby	hierdurch, dadurch
herein	hierin
hereinafter	nachstehend, im folgenden (erwähnt), unten (angeführt)
hereof	hiervon
hereunder = hereinafter	
hereupon	hierauf, darauf(hin)
herewith	hiermit, hierdurch
howsoever = however	
in accordance with	in Übereinstimmung mit
incidental thereto	dabei entstehend, damit verbunden
in respect of (to), (with respect to)	bezüglich, hinsichtlich, im Hinblick auf
in so far as	insofern, insoweit (als)
in witness where of ...	zu Urkund dessen ...
likely	wahrscheinlich, voraussichtlich
nevertheless	nichtsdestoweniger, dessenungeachtet, dennoch
notwithstanding	ungeachtet, unbeschadet, dennoch
other than	außer, anders als
otherwise	sonst, anderenfalls, anders, sonstig
prior	vorherig, vor
properly	richtig, angemessen
provided further	weiterhin vorausgesetzt

provided that	vorausgesetzt, daß
pursuant to	gemäß, (Dativ) entsprechend
said	(vor)erwähnt, besagt
save as	außer wie
save insofar as	außer insofern als
save that	abgesehen davon, daß; nur daß
sole	alleinig
subject to	abhängig von, vorbehaltlich
subsequently	anschließend, in der Folge
thereabout	etwa da, daherum, in der Nähe
thereafter	danach, nachher/demgemäß
thereby	dadurch, auf diese Weise/dabei, daran, davon/nahe dabei
therefor	dafür
therefore	darum, deswegen, deshalb, daher, demgemäß, folglich, also
therefrom	davon, daraus, daher
therein	darin/in dieser Hinsicht
thereinafter	(weiter)unten, nachstehend, später
thereof	davon/dessen, deren
thereon	darüber, daran, darauf
thereto	dazu, daran, dafür/außerdem, noch dazu
thereunder	darunter, gemäß dem Vertrag
thereupon	daraufhin, danach, darauf (örtlich)
therewith	damit
to the intend that	in der Absicht, daß; damit
unless	es sei denn, daß, wenn ... nicht
	am Satzanfang: sofern ... nicht
whatever	was (auch immer), alles was, welche (r,s) ... auch (immer)
whatsoever = whatever	
whenever	jedesmal, wenn
whereas	wohingegen, während, in Anbetracht dessen, daß ..., wo...doch
	(Beginn einer typisch englischen Vertragsklausel)
whereby	wodurch, wovon, womit, durch welche(n, s)
wherein	worin, in welche(m, n, s, r,)
whereof	wovon, woraus
whereon	worauf, auf dem (der, die)
wheresoever = wherever	wo (auch) immer, egal oder einerlei wo
whereupon	worauf, wonach, daraufhin
whether ... or not ...	ob... oder nicht
while	während
whomsoever	wen, (welche, n) auch immer
with respect to	im Hinblick auf, bezüglich

6. Übersetzung der Randbemerkungen des Teils I der FIDIC-Bedingungen in die deutsche Sprache
6. Translation into German of the Marginal Notes Part I of the FIDIC-Conditions

Begriffsbestimmungen und Auslegung

Ingenieur und Vertreter des Ingenieurs

Abtretung und Weitervergabe

Vertragsunterlagen

Allgemeine Verpflichtungen

7. Verzeichnis der Vokabeln der FIDIC-Bedingungen in der Reihenfolge des Auftretens (Englisch/Deutsch)

Vorbemerkung:

Die Vokabeln in diesem Abschnitt sind wie folgt bezeichnet:
I F 1: Teil I, Foreword, laufende Nummer 1 der Vokabel innerhalb des Vorworts.
I 1. 1 1: Teil I, Klausel 1.1, laufende Nummer 1 der Vokabel innerhalb der Klausel.
II 1 1: Teil II, Seitennummer, laufende Nummer 1 der Vokabel jeder Seite. Die Vokabeln der »editorial amendments« sind unter Seite 26 aufgeführt.

Sollten Vokabeln, die bereits früher aufgeführt sind, nicht mehr im Gedächtnis sein, so kann im alphabetischen Verzeichnis nachgeschlagen werden (Abschnitt 8).

Die Großschreibung im Englischen bestimmter Ausdrücke der FIDIC-Bedingungen wurde im Verzeichnis beibehalten. Es sind nur die deutschen Bedeutungen aufgeführt, die im Zusammenhang mit den FIDIC-Bedingungen stehen. Für alle weiteren erforderlichen Vokabeln dürfte ein einfaches englisch/deutsches Wörterbuch ausreichen.

Die deutschen Grammatikbezeichnungen in den Vokabelverzeichnissen sind nur für das jeweilige Haupteintragswort angegeben, sie sollen Lesern mit anderer Muttersprache als Deutsch eine Hilfe sein.

Bei Formengleichheit von Adjektiv und Adverb im Deutschen ist nur die der englischen Form entsprechende Abkürzung aufgeführt. Bei den englischen Wörtern ist nur für die Verben eine grammatikalische Wortbezeichnung angegeben. Es bedeuten:

adj	Adjektiv
adv	Adverb
conj	Konjunktion
f	weiblich
fpl	weiblich plural
m	männlich
mpl	männlich plural
n	sächlich
npl	sächlich plural
prep	Präposition
vi	intransitives Verbum
vrefl	reflexives Verbum
vt	transitives Verbum

7. Wordlist in order of appearance of the FIDIC-Conditions (English/German)

Preliminary Note:

The words in this chapter are marked as follows:

I F 1: Part I, Foreword, consecutive number in the foreword
I 1. 1 1: Part I, Clause 1.1, consecutive number 1 in the Clause
II 1 1: Part II, page number, consecutive number on each page. The vocabulary of the »editorial amendments« are listed under page 26.

Words which have appeared earlier and are not remembered can be looked up in the alphabetical list (chapter 8).

The capitalisation of certain words in the FIDIC-Conditions has been maintained. Only those German meanings are listed which relate to the FIDIC-Conditions. Further words can be obtained from any normal dictionary.

The German grammatical abbreviations in the wordlists refer to the main entry, they are meant to assist readers whose mothertongue is not German.

When adjective and adverb have equal forms in German only the abbreviation corresponding to the English entry is given. Only verbs are designated by the English grammatical abbreviation.

Abbreviations:

adj	adjective
adv	adverb
conj	conjunction
f	feminine
fpl	feminine plural
m	masculine
mpl	masculine plural
n	neuter
npl	neuter plural
prep	preposition
vi	verb intransitive
vrefl	verb reflexive
vt	verb transitive

Vorwort:

I F 1   **Conditions of Contract** Vertragsbedingungen *fpl*

I F 2   **Works of Civil Engineering Construction** Ingenieurbauarbeiten *fpl*, Ingenieurbauleistungen *fpl*

I F 3   **Fédération Internationale des Ingénieurs-Conseils (FIDIC)** Internationale Vereinigung der Beratenden Ingenieure (FIDIC) *f*

I F 4   **recommend** *vt* empfehlen *vt*, vorschlagen *vt*

I F 5   **purpose** Zweck *m*

I F 6   **invite tenders** *vt* auffordern zur Angebotsabgabe *vt*

I F 7   **Conditions** Bedingungen *fpl (eines Vertrages)*, Klauseln *fpl (eines Vertrages)*

I F 8   **minor modifications** geringfügige Änderungen *fpl*

I F 9   **suitable** brauchbar *adj*, geeignet *adj*, angemessen *adj*

I F 10   **domestic contracts** inländische Bauverträge *mpl (Gegensatz: Contracts on international basis)*

I F 11   **translation** Übersetzung *f (z. B. eines Textes)*

I F 12   **recognise** *vt* erkennen *vt*, anerkennen *vt*

I F 13   **Clause** Klausel *f (eines Vertrages)*, Absatz *m (eines Vertrages)*

I F 14   **applicable** anwendbar *adj*

I F 15   **vary** *vt, vi* abändern *vt*, verändern *vt*, variieren *vi, vt*

I F 16   **take account of** *vt* berücksichtigen *vt*

I F 17   **circumstances** Umstände *mpl*

I F 18   **locality of the Works** Ort der (Bau)arbeiten *m*

I F 19   **General Conditions** allgemeine Bedingungen *fpl*

I F 20   **facilitate** *vt* erleichtern *vt*

I F 21   **inclusion** Einbeziehung *f*, Einschluß *m*

I F 22   **contract documents** Vertragsdokumente *fpl*, Vertragsunterlagen *fpl*

I F 23   **Conditions of Particular Application** Bedingungen zur besonderen Anwendung *fpl*

I F 24   **link with** *vt* verbinden mit *vt*

I F 25   **comprise** *vt* enthalten *vt*, einschließen *vt*, umfassen *vt*

I F 26   **govern** *vt* bestimmen *vt*, regeln *vt*

I F 27   **obligation** Verpflichtung *f*

I F 28   **draft** *vt* abfassen *vt (z. B. Schriftstück)*, entwerfen *vt (z. B. Text)*

I F 29   **dredging** Naßbaggern *n*

I F 30   **reclamation work** Landgewinnungsarbeit(en) *f (pl)*

I F 31   **involve** *vt* einbeziehen *vt*, einschließen *vt*

I F 32   **consideration** Berücksichtigung *f*, Überlegung *f*, Erwägung *f*

I F 33   **preparation** Vorbereitung *f*, Abfassung *f (eines Textes)*

I F 34   **explanatory** erläuternd *adj*, erklärend *adj*

I F 35   **example clause** Beispielklausel *f*

I F 36   **guideline** Richtlinie *f*

I F 37   **anticipate** *vt* erwarten *vt*, vorhersehen *vt*

I F 38   **include** *vt* einschließen *vt*, umfassen *vt*

I F 39	**provision** Bestimmung *f,* Bedingung *f,* Vorschrift *f*
I F 40	**refer to** *vt, vi* hinweisen auf *vt,* verweisen auf *vt,* sich beziehen auf *vrefl*
I F 41	**edition** Ausgabe *f (z. B. einer Schriftenreihe)*
I F 42	**tendering procedure** Ausschreibungsverfahren *n*
I F 43	**insurance** Versicherung *f*
I F 44	**suggestion** Vorschlag *m*
I F 45	**mandatory** Bevollmächtigter *m*
I F 46	**participation** Beteiligung *f,* Mitwirkung *f*

Teil I:

I 1.1 1	**definition** Begriffsbestimmung *f,* Erklärung *f,* Definition *f*
I 1.1 2	**interpretation** Auslegung *f,* Interpretation *f*
I 1.1 3	**contract** Vertrag *m*
I 1.1 4	**as hereinafter defined** wie im folgenden festgelegt
I 1.1 5	**expression** Ausdruck *m*
I 1.1 6	**meaning** Bedeutung *f*
I 1.1 7	**assign to** *vt* zuteilen *vt,* zuweisen *vt*
I 1.1 8	**context** Zusammenhang *m,* Kontext *m*
I 1.1 9	**require** *vt, vi* benötigen *vt,* erfordern *vt*
I 1.1 10	**Employer** Auftraggeber *m,* Bauherr *m*
I 1.1 11	**legal successor in title** Rechtsnachfolger *m*
I 1.1 12	**consent** Einwilligung *f,* Zustimmung *f*
I 1.1 13	**assignee** Abtretungsempfänger *m,* Bevollmächtigter *m,* Rechtsnachfolger *m,* Zessionar *m*
I 1.1 14	**Contractor** Bauunternehmer *m,* Auftragnehmer *m,* Unternehmer *m*
I 1.1 15	**Tender** Angebot *n*
I 1.1 16	**accept** *vt* annehmen *vt*
I 1.1 17	**Subcontractor** Subunternehmer *m,* Nachunternehmer *m*
I 1.1 18	**Engineer** Bauleiter des Auftraggebers *m (mit gewisser Schiedsrichterfunktion gemäß FIDIC-Vertrag),* Ingenieur *m (mit Funktionen gemäß FIDIC-Vertrag)*
I 1.1 19	**appoint** *vt* beauftragen *vt,* ernennen *vt,* einsetzen *vt*
I 1.1 20	**Engineer's Representative** Vertreter des Bauleiters des Auftraggebers *m (gemäß den FIDIC-Bedingungen)*
I 1.1 21	**Specification** technische Beschreibung *f,* technische Vertragsbedingung *f (etwa VOB Teil C entsprechend)*
I 1.1 22	**Bill of Quantities** Leistungsverzeichnis *n*
I 1.1 23	**priced** mit Preisangabe *f,* mit Preisen versehen *mpl*
I 1.1 24	**execution** Ausführung *f,* Durchführung *f*
I 1.1 25	**completion** Fertigstellung *f*
I 1.1 26	**remedy** *vt* abstellen *vt (Mißstand),* heilen *vt (auch juristisch),* abhelfen *vt (einer Sache),* beheben *vt (Mangel),* beseitigen *vt (Mangel)*
I 1.1 27	**in accordance with** in Übereinstimmung mit *f*
I 1.1 28	**Letter of Acceptance** Annahmeerklärung *f (des Auftraggebers bezüglich des Angebots)*

I 1.1 29   **Contract Agreement** Vertragsvereinbarung *f*

I 1.1 30   **Appendix to Tender** Anhang zum Angebot *m*

I 1.1 31   **annex** *vt* anfügen *vt*, beifügen *vt*

I 1.1 32   **Commencement Date** Anfangszeitpunkt *m (Datum des Erhalts der Mitteilung des »Engineers« zum Baubeginn)*, Baubeginn *m*

I 1.1 33   **receive** *vt* erhalten *vt (bekommen)*

I 1.1 34   **commence** *vt* beginnen *vt, vi*

I 1.1 35   **issue** *vt* herausgeben *vt*, ausgeben *vt*, erteilen *vt*

I 1.1 36   **pursuant to** gemäß *adv*, übereinstimmend mit *adv*

I 1.1 37   **Time for Completion** Ausführungsfrist *f*, Fertigstellungszeit *f*, Vertragsfrist *f*

I 1.1 38   **pass** *vt* bestehen *vt (z. B. Test)*

I 1.1 39   **state** *vt* festlegen *vt*, festsetzen *vt*, darlegen *vt*

I 1.1 40   **extend** *vt, vi* fortsetzen *vt*, verlängern *vt*, ausdehnen, sich *vrefl*

I 1.1 41   **calculate** *vt* berechnen *vt*

I 1.1 42   **Tests on Completion** Prüfungen bei Fertigstellung *fpl (vor der Abnahme der Arbeiten)*

I 1.1 43   **specify** *vt* genau beschreiben *vt*, spezifizieren *vt*

I 1.1 44   **agree** *vt, vi* übereinkommen *vi*, vereinbaren *vt*

I 1.1 45   **take over** *vt* abnehmen *vt*, übernehmen *vt*

I 1.1 46   **Taking-Over Certificate** Abnahmebescheinigung *f*

I 1.1 47   **Contract Price** Vertragspreis *m*

I 1.1 48   **payable** zahlbar *adj*, zu zahlen

I 1.1 49   **Retention Money** Einbehaltungsgeld *n*, Einbehalt von Geld *m*, einbehaltener Betrag *m*

I 1.1 50   **aggregate of all monies** Gesamtbetrag *m*, Gesamtsumme *f*

I 1.1 51   **retain** *vt* zurückbehalten *vt*, einbehalten *vt*, zurückhalten *vt*

I 1.1 52   **Interim Payment Certificate** Zwischenzahlungsbescheinigung *f*

I 1.1 53   **Final Payment Certificate** Schlußzahlungsbescheinigung *f*

I 1.1 54   **Permanent Works** verbleibende Bauten *mpl (Gegensatz: Temporary Works)*

I 1.1 55   **Temporary Works** zeitweilige Bauten *mpl*, Hilfsbauwerke *npl*

I 1.1 56   **Plant** *(Contrary to the earlier editions in the fourth edition the word means machinery, apparatus and the like intended to form or form part of the Permanent Works. In the earlier editions plant meant Contractor's Equipment.)* maschinelle Einrichtungen *fpl (Im Gegensatz zu früheren Auflagen bedeutet das Wort »Plant« in der vierten Auflage der FIDIC-Bedingungen die fest einzubauenden maschinellen Anlagen und nicht die Baugeräte des Auftragnehmers.)*

I 1.1 57   **the like** derartig(es) *adj*

I 1.1 58   **intended** bestimmt *adj*, beabsichtigt *adj*

I 1.1 59   **Contractor's Equipment** *(term does not include Temporary Works)* Baugeräte des Auftragnehmers *npl (ohne Hilfsbauwerke)*

I 1.1 60   **appliance** Vorrichtung *f*, Gerät *n*, Mittel *n*, Hilfsmittel *n*

I 1.1 61   **Section** Teil *m*, Abschnitt *m (im Vertrag als solcher ausdrücklich festgelegt)*

I 1.1 62   **specifically** ausdrücklich *adv*, spezifisch *adv*

I 1.1 63	**identify** *vt* ausweisen *vt*, feststellen *vt*	
I 1.1 64	**Site** Baustelle *f (u.U. weitere Flächen, die im Vertrag als zur Baustelle gehörig festgelegt sind)*	
I 1.1 65	**provide** *vt* liefern *vt*, zur Verfügung stellen *vt*	
I 1.1 66	**designate** *vt* kennzeichnen *vt*, bezeichnen *vt*, bestimmen *vt*	
I 1.1 67	**cost** *(Does not include any allowance for profit.)* Kosten *fpl (Die Definitionen für Kosten und Aufwand decken sich nicht in USA, GB und Europa!)*, Unkosten *fpl*	
I 1.1 68	**expenditure** Aufwand *m (Die Definitionen für Aufwand und Kosten decken sich nicht in den USA, GB und Europa!)*, Ausgabe *f*, Ausgaben *fpl*	
I 1.1 69	**properly** *adv* angemessen *adv*, richtig *adv*, zweckmäßig *adv*	
I 1.1 70	**incur** *vt* eingehen *vt (z. B. Verpflichtungen)*, auf sich laden *vrefl*, auf sich nehmen *vrefl*	
I 1.1 71	**overhead(s)** Gemeinkosten *fpl*	
I 1.1 72	**charge** Forderung *f*, Belastung *f (finanzieller Art)*	
I 1.1 73	**allocable** *adj* zuteilbar *adj*, zuweisbar *adj* *zurechenbar*	
I 1.1 74	**allowance for profit** Ansatz für Gewinn *m*, Zuschlag für Gewinn *mf*	
I 1.1 75	**foreign currency** Devisen *fpl*, ausländische Währung *f*	
I 1.1 76	**facsimile transmission** Fernkopieren *n*	
I 1.2 1	**heading** Überschrift *f*	
I 1.2 2	**marginal notes** Randbezeichnungen *fpl*	
I 1.2 3	**construction of the contract** Auslegung des Vertrages *f*	
I 1.2 4	**deem** *vt* erachten für *vt*, betrachten als *vt*	
I 1.2 5	**take into consideration** *vt*, berücksichtigen *vt*, in Betracht ziehen *vt*	
I 1.3 1	**import** *vt* bedeuten *vt*, angehen *vt*, betreffen *vt*	
I 1.3 2	**corporation** *(This term has different meanings in the USA.)* Körperschaft *f*, Gesellschaft *f*	
I 1.3 3	**legal capacity** Geschäftsfähigkeit *f*, Rechtsfähigkeit *f*	
I 1.4 1	**vice versa** umgekehrt *adv*, wechselseitig *adv*	
I 1.5 1	**notice** Mitteilung *f*, Nachricht *f*, Benachrichtigung *f*	
I 1.5 2	**approval** Genehmigung *f*, Zustimmung *f*, Anerkennung *f*, Zulassung *f (besonders technisch)*	
I 1.5 3	**certificate** Bescheinigung *f*, Zertifikat *n*	
I 1.5 4	**determination** Bestimmung *f*, Entscheidung *f*, Festsetzung *f*	
I 1.5 5	**construe** *vt* deuten *vt*, auslegen *vt*	
I 1.5 6	**accordingly** entsprechend *adv*, demgemäß *adv*, folglich *adv*	
I 1.5 7	**withhold** *vt* zurück(be)halten *vt*, vorenthalten *vt*	
I 1.5 8	**delay** *vt* verschieben *vt*, verzögern *vt*	
I 2.1 1	**duty** Pflicht *f*, Aufgabe *f*	
I 2.1 2	**exercise** *vt* ausüben *vt*	
I 2.1 3	**imply** *vt* beinhalten *(stillschweigend) vt*, mitenthalten *vt*, stillschweigend voraussetzen *vt*	
I 2.1 4	**provided** vorausgesetzt *conj*	
I 2.1 5	**terms of appointment** Bedingungen der Beauftragung *f*	

I 2.1 6	**appointment** Beauftragung *f*, Einsetzung *f*, Bestellung *f*	
I 2.1 7	**obtain** *vt* erhalten *vt*, erlangen *vt*, bekommen *vt*	
I 2.1 8	**particulars** Einzelheiten *fpl*, nähere Angaben *fpl*	
I 2.1 9	**requirement** Erfordernis *n*, Bedingung *f*, Forderung *f*, Auflage *f*	
I 2.1 10	**further** weiterhin *adv*	
I 2.1 11	**requisite** erforderlich *adj*, notwendig *adj*	
I 2.1 12	**expressly** ausdrücklich *adv*	
I 2.1 13	**relieve of** *vt* entbinden von *vt*, entlasten von *vt*	
I 2.2 1	**responsible** verantwortlich *adj*	
I 2.2 2	**delegate** *vt* delegieren *vt*, übertragen *vt*	
I 2.3 1	**vest in s.o.** *vt* übertragen, jemandem *vt*, verleihen, jemandem *vt*	
I 2.3 2	**revoke** *vt* widerrufen *vt*, zurücknehmen *vt*	
I 2.3 3	**delegation** Übertragung *f*, Bevollmächtigung *f*	
I 2.3 4	**take effect** *vt* Gültigkeit erlangen *vt*	
I 2.3 5	**deliver** *vt* übergeben *vt*, aushändigen *vt*	
I 2.3 6	**communication** Mitteilung *f*, Nachricht *f*, Benachrichtigung *f*	
I 2.3 7	**failure to disapprove work** Versäumnis, Leistungen zurückzuweisen *n*, Unterlassung, Leistungen zurückzuweisen *f*	
I 2.3 8	**prejudice** *vt* beeinträchtigen *vt*, beeinflussen *vt*	
I 2.3 9	**rectification** Nachbesserung *f*, Richtigstellung *f*, Nachbearbeitung *f*, Mängelbeseitigung *f*	
I 2.3 10	**confirm** bestätigen *vt*	
I 2.3 11	**reverse** *vt* rückgängig machen *vt*, aufheben *vt*	
I 2.3 12	**contents** sg = pl Inhalt *m*	
I 2.4 1	**scope of authority** Bereich der Befugnis *m*, Umfang der Befugnis *m*	
I 2.4 2	**save in so far as** abgesehen von Fällen, in denen ..., außer in Fällen, in denen ...	
I 2.4 3	**enable** *vt* ermächtigen *vt*, befähigen *vt*	
I 2.4 4	**secure** *vt* sichern *vt*, schützen *vt*, sicherstellen *vt*	
I 2.4 5	**acceptance** Abnahme *f*, Entgegennahme *f*	
I 2.4 6	**workmanship** Ausführung in bezug auf Qualität der Arbeit *f*, handwerkliches Fachkönnen *n*, Handwerksarbeit *f*	
I 2.4 7	**instruction** Anordnung *f*, Anweisung *f* (Befehl)	
I 2.5 1	**consider** *vt* betrachten als *vt*, halten für *vt*, ansehen als *vt*	
I 2.5 2	**orally** mündlich *adv*	
I 2.5 3	**comply with** *vt* nachkommen *vt* (z. B. Befehl), erfüllen *vt*, sich halten an *vi* (z. B. Anweisung)	
I 2.5 4	**confirmation** Bestätigung *f*	
I 2.5 5	**whether ... or** sei es ... oder *conj*	
I 2.5 6	**contradict** *vt* widersprechen *vt*	
I 2.5 7	**equally** ebenso *adv*	
I 2.5 8	**apply to instructions** *vt* Anwendung finden auf Anweisungen *vt*	
I 2.6 1	**discretion** Entscheidungsfreiheit *f*, Ermessen *n*	
I 2.6 2	**decision** Entscheidung *f*	

I 2.6 3	**opinion** Meinung *f*, Ansicht *f*	
I 2.6 4	**satisfaction** Befriedigung *f*, Zufriedenheit *f*	
I 2.6 5	**determine** *vt* bestimmen *vt*, festlegen *vt*, festsetzen *vt*	
I 2.6 6	**value** Wert *m*	
I 2.6 7	**affect** *vt* beeinträchtigen *vt*	
I 2.6 8	**impartially** gerecht *adv*, unparteiisch *adv*	
I 2.6 9	**regard** Beachtung *f*, Rücksicht *f*	
I 2.6 10	**action** Handlung *f*	
I 2.6 11	**open up** *vt* wieder aufnehmen *vt (z. B. Verfahren)*	
I 2.6 12	**review** *vt* durchsehen *vt*, überprüfen *vt*, nachprüfen *vt*	
I 3.1 1	**assignment** Abtretung *f*, Übertragung *f*, Zession *f*	
I 3.1 2	**subcontracting** Weitervergabe *f*	
I 3.1 3	**prior consent** vorherige Zustimmung *f*	
I 3.1 4	**notwithstanding** ungeachtet *prep*, unbeschadet *prep*	
I 3.1 5	**sole** alleinig *adj*	
I 3.1 6	**benefit** Vorrecht *n*, Nutzen *m*, Vorteil *m*	
I 3.1 7	**charge in favour of** Pfandbelastung zugunsten *f*, Zahlungsversprechen zugunsten *n*	
I 3.1 8	**due** fällig *adj*, sofort zahlbar *adj*	
I 3.1 9	**insurer** Versicherer *m*, Assekurant *m*	
I 3.1 10	**discharge** *vt* begleichen *vt*, bezahlen *vt*, erfüllen *vt*	
I 3.1 11	**loss** Verlust *m*	
I 3.1 12	**liability** Haftpflicht *f*, Verpflichtung *f*, Haftung *f*	
I 3.1 13	**relief** Rechtsschutz *m*, Recht, vor Gericht zu gehen *n*	
I 3.1 14	**liable** haftbar *adj*, verantwortlich *adj*	
I 4.1 1	**default** Nichterfüllung *f*, Versäumnis *n*	
I 4.1 2	**neglect** Nachlässigkeit *f*, Unterlassung *f*	
I 4.1 3	**purchase** Kauf *m*	
I 4.1 4	**agent** Beauftragter *m*, Vertreter des Auftragnehmers *m (auf der Baustelle)*, Bauleiter des Auftragnehmers *m*	
I 4.1 5	**standard** Norm *f*, Anforderung *f*	
I 4.2 1	**in the event of** im Fall, daß *conj*	
I 4.2 2	**undertake an obligation** *vt* Verpflichtung übernehmen *vt*, verpflichten, sich *vrefl*	
I 4.2 3	**in respect of** hinsichtlich *prep*	
I 4.2 4	**execute** *vt* ausführen *vt*	
I 4.2 5	**supply** *vt* bereitstellen *vt*, liefern *vt*	
I 4.2 6	**continuing** fortlaufend *adj*	
I 4.2 7	**exceeding** überschreitend *adj*, übersteigend *adj*	
I 4.2 8	**Defects Liability Period** Gewährleistungsfrist *f*, Mängelhaftungszeitraum *m*, Baumängelhaftungszeitraum *m*	
I 4.2 9	**expiration** Ende *n (zeitlich)*, Erlöschen *n (zeitlich)*, Verfall *m (zeitlich)*, Ablauf *m (einer Frist)*	
I 4.2 10	**request** Ersuchen *n*, Verlangen *n*, Bitte *f*	

I 8.1 2   **care** Sorgfalt *f*, Fürsorge *f*

I 8.1 3   **diligence** Eifer *m*, Fleiß *m*, Sorgfalt *f*

I 8.1 4   **design** *vt* auslegen *vt (z. B technische Anlagen)*, bemessen *vt*, entwerfen *vt*, planen *vt*

I 8.1 5   **superintendence** Aufsicht *f*, Oberaufsicht *f*, Leitung *f*

I 8.1 6   **design** Entwurf und Berechnung *m f*, Konstruktion *f* (*"design« bedeutet im Englischen nicht nur die Gestaltung!*), technische Bearbeitung *f*, Planung *f*

I 8.1 7   **inferred from the Contract** abzuleiten aus dem Vertrag *m*

I 8.2 1   **stability** Beständigkeit *f*, Stabilität *f*, Standsicherheit *f*

I 8.2 2   **Site operations** Baustellentätigkeiten *fpl*, Arbeitsvorgänge auf der Baustelle *mpl*

I 9.1 1   **call upon s.o.** *vt* auffordern, jemanden *vt*, ersuchen, jemanden *vt*

I 9.1 2   **modification** Bauvertragsänderung *f*, Leistungsänderung *f (gegenüber der ursprünglichen vertraglichen Leistung)*, Änderung *f*, Abwandlung *f*, Bauausführungsänderung *f*

I 10.1 1   **performance security** Ausführungsbürgschaft *f*

I 10.1 2   **receipt** Empfang *m*, Erhalt *m*

I 10.1 3   **security** Sicherheit *f*, Bürgschaft *f*

I 10.1 4   **subject to** *adj* vorbehaltlich *adj*

I 10.2 1   **validity** Gültigkeit *f*

I 10.2 2   **valid** gültig *adj*, rechtsgültig *adj*

I 10.2 3   **claim** Forderung *f*, Rechtsanspruch *m*, Reklamation *f*, Anspruch *m*

I 11.1 1   **inspection of site** Baustellenbesichtigung *f (vor Angebotsabgabe)*

I 11.1 2   **submission** Einreichung *f*, Vorlage *f*, Unterbreitung *f*

I 11.1 3   **data** Daten *fpl*, Angaben *fpl*

I 11.1 4   **hydrological** hydrologisch *adj*

I 11.1 5   **sub-surface conditions** Untergrundverhältnisse *npl*

I 11.1 6   **on behalf of the Employer** im Namen des Auftraggebers *m*

I 11.1 7   **investigation** Untersuchung *f*, Nachforschung *f*

I 11.1 8   **relevant to** anwendbar auf *adj*, erheblich für *adj*, sachdienlich für *adj*, rechtserheblich für *adj*

I 11.1 9   **surroundings** Umgebung *f*, Umgegend *f*

I 11.1 10   **considerations of cost** Kostenerwägungen *fpl*, Kostenüberlegungen *fpl*, Kostengesichtspunkte *mpl*

I 11.1 11   **means of access** Zugangsmöglichkeiten *fpl*

I 11.1 12   **accommodation** Unterkunft *f*, Unterbringung *f*

I 11.1 13   **contingencies** mögliche Ereignisse *npl*, Unvorhergesehenes *n*, unvorhergesehene Ereignisse *npl*, Eventualverbindlichkeiten *fpl*

I 11.1 14   **mention** *vt* erwähnen *vt*

I 11.1 15   **influence** *vt* beeinflussen *vt*

I 11.1 16   **examination** Untersuchung *f*

I 11.1 17   **aforementioned** oben erwähnt *adj*, oben genannt *adj*

I 12.1 1   **sufficiency** Angemessenheit *f*, Vollständigkeit *f*, Zulänglichkeit *f*

I 12.1 2   **Provisional Sum** provisorische Summe *f (Position in englischen Bauverträgen)*

für noch nicht genau festgelegte Leistungen wie z. B. Untervergabe,
manchmal auch für Baustelleneinrichtung usw.), vorläufiger Betrag *m*

I 12.2 1   **encounter physical obstructions** *vt* naturbedingte Hindernisse antreffen *vt*, auf naturbedingte Hindernisse treffen *vt*

I 12.2 2   **encounter** *vt* stoßen auf *vt*, antreffen *vt*

I 12.2 3   **foreseeable** voraussehbar *adj*

I 12.2 4   **experienced** erfahren *adj*

I 12.2 5   **forthwith** sogleich *adv*, unverzüglich *adv*

I 12.2 6   **connection** Verbindung *f*

I 12.2 7   **measure** Maßnahme *f*

I 12.2 8   **in the absence of** in Ermangelung von *f*

I 13.1 1   **comply with instructions** *vt* Anweisungen befolgen *vt*

I 13.1 2   **adhere to instructions** *vt* Anweisungen befolgen *vt*, an Anweisungen halten, sich *vrefl*

I 13.1 3   **concern** *vt* betreffen *vt*

I 14.1 1   **prescribe** *vt* verordnen *vt*, vorschreiben *vt*

I 14.1 2   **arrangements** Vorkehrungen *fpl*

I 14.1 3   **propose** *vt* vorschlagen *vt*

I 14.1 4   **adopt methods** *vt* Methoden anwenden *vt*, Methoden sich zu eigen machen *vrefl*

I 14.2 1   **progress** Fortschritt *m*

I 14.2 2   **conform to** *vt* übereinstimmen mit *vt*

I 14.3 1   **cash flow estimate** vorläufiger Zahlungsplan *m*

I 14.3 2   **entitled** berechtigt *adj*

I 14.3 3   **subsequently** anschließend *adv*, nachfolgend *adv*

I 14.4 1   **description** Beschreibung *f*

I 14.4 3   **revised** überprüft *adj*, verbessert *adj*

I 15.1 1   **withdraw** *vt* zurücknehmen *vt*, zurückziehen *vt*

I 15.1 2   **practicable** durchführbar *adj*, möglich *adj*

I 15.1 3   **not ... on the Works in any capacity** in keiner anderen Funktion auf der Baustelle *f*

I 15.1 4   **replace** *vt* ersetzen *vt*

I 16.1 1   **employee** Arbeitnehmer *m*, Angestellter *m*

I 16.1 2   **skilled** erfahren *adj*, Fachkenntnisse besitzend *adj*

I 16.1 3   **calling** Beruf *m*, Beschäftigung *f*

I 16.1 4   **foreman** Polier *m*, Vorarbeiter *m*

I 16.1 5   **semi-skilled labour** sg = pl angelernte Arbeitskräfte *fpl*

I 16.2 1   **be at liberty to** *vi* berechtigt sein zu *vi*

I 16.2 2   **object to** *vt* Einspruch erheben gegen *vt*, etwas dagegen haben *vt*

I 16.2 3   **misconduct o.s.** *vrefl* eines Fehlverhaltens schuldig machen, sich *vrefl*, schlecht betragen, sich *vrefl*

I 16.2 4   **negligent** nachlässig *adj*, unachtsam *adj*

I 16.2 5   **undesirable** unerwünscht *adj*

I 16.2 6   **remove** *vt* entfernen *vt*

I 17.1 1	**setting-out** Abstecken *n*, Absteckung *f*
I 17.1 2	**level of reference** Höhenangabe *f*
I 17.1 3	**alignment** Fluchten *n*, Einfluchten *n*, Ausrichtung *f*, Flucht *f*
I 17.1 4	**checking** Nachprüfung *f*, Überprüfung *f*
I 17.1 5	**bench-mark** Höhenfestpunkt *m*, Festpunkt *m*, Fixpunkt *m*
I 17.1 6	**sight-rail** Visiergerüst *n*, Visiertafel *f*
I 17.1 7	**peg** Pflock *m*, Absteckpflock *m*
I 18.1 1	**borehole** Bohrloch *n*
I 18.1 2	**excavation** Aushub *m*, Ausschachtung *f*
I 19.1 1	**avoidance** Vermeidung *f*
I 19.1 2	**fencing** Einzäunung *f*, Umzäunung *f*
I 19.1 3	**environment** Umwelt *f*, Umfeld *n*, Umgebung *f*
I 19.1 4	**nuisance** Ärgernis *n*, Belästigung *f*
I 19.1 5	**pollution** Verunreinigung *f*, Verschmutzung *f*
I 19.1 6	**damage to property** Sachschaden *m*, Vermögensschaden *m*
I 19.2 1	**employ** *vt* einsetzen *vt*, beschäftigen *vt*, verwenden *vt*
I 20.1 1	**care of Works** Erhaltung der Bauleistungen *f*
I 20.1 2	**cease to** *vt* aufhören zu *vt*
I 20.1 3	**incorporation in** Eingliederung in *f*, Aufnahme in *f* (*z. B. Klausel in Vertrag*)
I 20.2 1	**rectify loss or damage** *vt* Verluste oder Schaden beseitigen *vt*
I 20.2 2	**occasion** *vt* veranlassen *vt*, verursachen *vt*
I 20.3 1	**Employer's Risks** (*Term introduced in the fourth edition of the conditions*) Bauherrnrisiken *npl*, Auftraggeberwagnissse *npl*
I 20.4 1	**hostility** Feindschaft *f*, Feindseligkeit *f*
I 20.4 2	**foreign** ausländisch *adj*, fremd *adj*
I 20.4 3	**insurrection** Aufruhr *m*, Aufstand *m*
I 20.4 4	**usurp** *vt* aneignen, sich *vrefl (widerrechtlich)*, an sich reißen *vt*
I 20.4 5	**civil war** Bürgerkrieg *m*
I 20.4 6	**ionising radiations** ionisierende Strahlungen *fpl*
I 20.4 7	**contamination** Verunreinigung *f*, Verschmutzung *f*
I 20.4 8	**nuclear waste** radioaktiver Abfall *m*, Atommüll *m*
I 20.4 9	**fuel** Brennstoff *m*, Kraftstoff *m*
I 20.4 10	**combustion** Verbrennung *f*
I 20.4 11	**toxic** giftig *adj*, toxisch *adj*
I 20.4 12	**explosive** Explosivstoff *m*, Sprengstoff *m*
I 20.4 13	**hazardous properties** gefährliche Eigenschaften *fpl*
I 20.4 14	**nuclear assembly** kerntechnische Einheit *f*
I 20.4 15	**component** Bestandteil *m*, Teil *m, n*
I 20.4 16	**pressure wave** Druckwelle *f*
I 20.4 17	**device** Vorrichtung *f*
I 20.4 18	**sonic speed** Schallgeschwindigkeit *f*
I 20.4 19	**riot** Zusammenrottung *f*, Aufruhr *m*
I 20.4 20	**commotion** Tumult *m*, Unruhen *fpl*
I 20.4 21	**disorder** Krawall *m*, Ruhestörung *f*

I 20.4 22 **solely** einzig und allein *adv*, ausschließlich *adv*

I 20.4 23 **restricted to** beschränkt auf *adj*

I 20.4 24 **precaution** Vorkehrung *f*, Vorsichtsmaßnahme *f*

I 21.1 1 **insure** *vt* versichern *vt (z. B. Bauleistungen)*

I 21.1 2 **replacement cost(s)** Wiederbeschaffungskosten *f*

I 21.1 3 **incidental to** dabei entstehend *adj*, verbunden mit *adj*

I 21.1 4 **professional fees** Honorare für Freiberufler *npl (z. B. Beratende Ingenieure)*

I 21.1 5 **demolish** *vt* abbrechen *vt*, abreißen *vt*, niederreißen *vt*

I 21.1 6 **debris** Trümmer *npl*, Schutt *m*, Bruchstücke *npl*,

I 21.2 1 **scope** Umfang *m*, Bereich *m*, Gebiet *n*

I 21.2 2 **in the joint names of** gesamtschuldnerisch *adv*, gemeinsam *adv*

I 21.2 3 **cover** *vt* abdecken *vt (versicherbare Risiken)*

I 21.4 1 **exclusion** Ausschluß *m*

I 22.1 1 **indemnify** *vt* entschädigen *vt*, Schadenersatz leisten *vt*, Schadloshaltung zusagen *vt*

I 22.1 2 **injury** Personenschaden *m*, Verletzung *f*

I 22.1 3 **exception** Ausnahme *f*

I 22.1 4 **expense(s)** Aufwand *m (Die Definitionen für Aufwand und Kosten decken sich nicht in den USA, GB und Europa!)*, Ausgabe *f*, Ausgaben *fpl*

I 22.1 5 **proceeding** Prozeß *m*, Verfahren *n*, Gerichtsverfahren *n*

I 22.1 6 **damages** Entschädigung *f*, Schadenersatz *m*

I 22.2 1 **unavoidable result** unvermeidbares Ergebnis *n*

I 22.2 2 **contribute to** *vt* beisteuern zu *vt*, beitragen zu *vt*

I 22.2 3 **just and equitable** recht und billig *adj*

I 23.1 1 **third party insurance** Haftpflichtversicherung *f*

I 23.1 2 **Employer's Property** Eigentum des Auftraggebers *n*

I 23.2 1 **Minimum Amount of Insurance** Mindestdeckungssumme *f*

I 23.2 2 **at least** wenigstens *adv*, zumindest *adv*

I 23.3 1 **cross liabilities** wechselseitige Haftpflicht *f*

I 23.3 2 **policy** Police *f*, Versicherungsschein *m*

I 23.3 3 **insured** Versicherter *m*, Versicherungsnehmer *m*

I 24.1 1 **accident** Unfall *m*

I 24.1 2 **compensation** Schadenersatz *m*, Abfindung *f*, Bezahlung *f*, Entschädigung *f*

I 24.1 3 **employment** Anstellung *f*, Beschäftigung *f*, Arbeitsverhältnis *n*

I 24.2 1 **current premium** laufende Versicherungsprämie *f*

I 25.1 1 **evidence** Beweismittel *n*, Beweis *m*, Nachweis *m*

I 25.1 2 **prior to** vor *adv* (zeitlich)

I 25.2 1 **ensure** *vt* gewährleisten *vt*, sicherstellen *vt*, garantieren *vt*

I 25.3 1 **effect** *vt* abschließen *vt (z. B. Versicherung)*

I 25.3 2 **in force** geltend *adj*, gültig *adj*

I 25.3 3 **deduct** *vt* abziehen *vt (Summe)*, abrechnen *vt (i.S. von abziehen)*

I 25.3 4 **recover** *vt* wiedererlangen *vt*, eintreiben *vt*

I 25.3 5 **debt** Schuld *f*

I 25.4 1 **compliance with policy conditions** Einhaltung der Bedingungen der

Versicherungspolicen *f*

I 25.4 2   **impose** *vt* aufbürden *vt*, auferlegen *vt*

I 26.1 1   **Statute** Gesetz *n*, Statut *n*

I 26.1 2   **Ordinance** Satzung *f*, Verordnung *f*

I 26.1 3   **regulation** Bestimmung *f*, Durchführungsverordnung *f*, Rechtsverordnung *f*

I 26.1 4   **bye-law** Statut *n*, Gemeindeverordnung *f*, Satzung *f*

I 26.1 5   **duly** ordnungsgemäß *adv*

I 26.1 6   **public body** öffentlich-rechtliche Körperschaft *f*

I 26.1 7   **authority** Autorität *f*, Behörde *f*, Ermächtigung *f*, Vollmacht *f*, Befugnis *f*

I 26.1 8   **company** Gesellschaft *f*, Kapitalgesellschaft *f*

I 26.1 9   **penalty** Vertragsstrafe *f*, Geldstrafe *f*, Strafe *f*, Pönale *f*

I 26.1 10   **breach of provisions** Verletzung von Bestimmungen *f*, Verstoß gegen Bestimmungen *m*

I 26.1 11   **planning permission** Baugenehmigung *f*

I 26.1 12   **zoning permission** Baunutzungsgenehmigung *f*

I 26.1 13   **proceed** *vi* voranschreiten *vi*, vorwärtsgehen *vi*, fortfahren *vi*, weitergehen *vi*

I 27.1 1   **fossil** Fossil *n*, Versteinerung *f*

I 27.1 2   **coin** Münze *f*

I 27.1 3   **acquaint** *vt* in Kenntnis setzen *vt*

I 28.1 1   **save harmless from** *vt* bewahren vor *vt*

I 28.1 2   **infringement of patent rights** Verletzung von Patentrechten *f*

I 28.1 3   **trademark** Schutzmarke *f*, Warenzeichen *n*

I 28.2 1   **royalty** Lizenz *f*, Lizenzgebühr *f*

I 28.2 2   **tonnage** Lastgebühr *f*, Schiffszoll *m*

I 29.1 1   **interference with traffic** Beeinträchtigung des Verkehrs *f*

I 29.1 2   **convenience of the public** Bedürfnisse der Öffentlichkeit *npl*, Annehmlichkeiten der Öffentlichkeit *fpl*

I 29.1 3   **access** Zufahrt *f*, Zugang *m*

I 29.1 4   **possession** Besitz *m*

I 30.1 1   **in particular** insbesondere *adv*

I 30.1 2   **restrict** *vt* beschränken *vt*, einschränken *vt*

I 30.1 3   **distribute** *vt* verteilen *vt*

I 30.1 4   **load** Last *f*, Belastung *f*

I 30.1 5   **inevitably** unvermeidlich *adv*

I 30.2 1   **strengthen** *vt* stärken *vt*, verstärken *vt*

I 30.2 2   **alter** *vt* ändern *vt*, verändern *vt*

I 30.2 3   **improve** *vt* verbessern *vt*

I 30.2 4   **negotiate** *vt*, *vi* verhandeln *vt*, *vi*

I 30.3 1   **haulier** Frachtführer *m*

I 30.3 2   **settlement** Klärung *f*, Regelung *f*

I 30.3 3   **in relation thereto** in Beziehung dazu *f*

I 30.4 1   **waterborne traffic** Wasserverkehr *m*

I 30.4 2   **lock** Schleuse *f*, Schleusenkammer *f*

I 30.4 3 **dock** Anlegeplatz *m*, Dock *n*, Hafenbecken *n*
I 30.4 4 **sea wall** Küstenschutzmauer *f*, Deich *m*, Hafendamm *m*, Kaimauer *f*
I 30.4 5 **craft** *sg = pl* Schiff(e) *n*, *(pl)* Flugzeug(e) *n*, *(pl)*
I 31.1 1 **opportunities for other contractors** Erleichterungen für andere Auftragnehmer *fpl*
I 31.1 2 **ancillary to the Works** Bauarbeiten dienend *adj*, Bauarbeiten ergänzend *adj*
I 31.2 1 **facilities** Einrichtungen *fpl*
I 31.2 2 **permit** *vt* erlauben *vt*, zulassen *vt*, gestatten *vt*
I 32.1 1 **obstruction** Behinderung *f*, Hindernis *n*
I 32.1 2 **store** *vt* einlagern *vt*, lagern *vt*
I 32.1 3 **surplus materials** Überschußmaterial(ien) *n*, *(pl)*
I 32.1 4 **wreckage** Trümmer *npl*, Trümmerhaufen *m*
I 32.1 5 **rubbish** Abfall *m*, (Bau)schutt *m*
I 33.1 1 **clearance of site on completion** Baustellenräumung nach Fertigstellung *f*
I 33.1 2 **clear away** *vt* entfernen *vt*, wegräumen *vt*
I 33.1 3 **workmanlike** fachgemäß *adj adv*, fachgerecht *adj adv*
I 34.1 1 **labour** Arbeitskräfte *fpl*, Arbeit *f*
I 34.1 2 **staff** Belegschaft *f*, Mitarbeiterstab *m*, Personal *n*
I 34.1 3 **house** *vt* unterbringen *vt (z. B. in einer Wohnung)*, aufnehmen *vt*
I 35.1 1 **return** Aufstellung *f (z. B. in Form einer Liste)*, Bericht *m*
I 36.1 1 **manufacture** Fertigung *f*, Herstellung *f*, Fabrikation *f*
I 36.1 2 **fabrication** Fertigung *f*, Herstellung *f*, Fabrikation *f*
I 36.1 3 **measuring** Messen *n*, Vermessen *n*, Aufmessen *n*
I 36.1 4 **samples of materials** Materialproben *fpl*
I 36.2 1 **intend** *vt* beabsichtigen *vt*
I 36.3 1 **particularise** *vt* ausführlich angeben *vt*, einzeln aufführen *vt*
I 36.3 2 **partially** teilweise *adv*
I 36.4 1 **tests not provided for** nicht vorgesehene Prüfungen *fpl (laut Vertrag)*
I 37.1 1 **inspection of operations** Inspektion der Arbeitsvorgänge *f*, Gütekontrolle der Arbeitsvorgänge *f*
I 37.1 2 **afford facility for** *vt* Gelegenheit schaffen für *vt*
I 37.2 1 **workshop** Werkstatt *f*, Werkhalle *f*
I 37.2 2 **release from** *vt* entlassen aus *vt*, befreien von *vt*
I 37.3 1 **attend the test** *vt, vi* anwesend sein beim Test *vi (z. B. Materialprüfung)*
I 37.3 2 **duly certified** ordnungsgemäß beglaubigt *adj*, ordnungsgemäß bestätigt *adj*
I 37.3 3 **test readings** Testergebnisse *npl*
I 37.3 4 **accurate** exakt *adj*, genau *adj*, richtig *adj*
I 37.4 1 **rejection** Zurückweisung *f*, Abnahmeverweigerung *f*, Nichtabnahme *f*
I 37.4 2 **reject materials** *vt* Material(ien) zurückweisen *vt*, Material(ien) nicht abnehmen *vt*
I 37.4 3 **repetition** Wiederholung *f*
I 37.4 4 **recoverable** eintreibbar *adj (z. B. Kosten)*, zurückzuverlangen *adj (z. B. Kosten)*
I 37.5 1 **independent** unabhängig *adj*

I 45.1 2   **provision to the contrary** gegenteilige Bestimmung *f*
I 45.1 3   **recognised day of rest** anerkannter Ruhetag *m*, gesetzlicher Feiertag *m*
I 45.1 4   **customary** gebräuchlich *adj*, üblich *adj*
I 45.1 5   **multiple shifts** Mehrschichtbetrieb *m*
I 46.1 1   **rate of progress of the works** Arbeitsfortschritt *m*
I 46.1 2   **expedite** *vt* beschleunigen *vt (z. B. Bauarbeiten)*
I 46.1 3   **seek** *vt* erbitten *vt*, ersuchen *vt*
I 46.1 4   **involve in additional costs** *vt* zusätzliche Kosten verursachen *vt*
I 47.1 1   **liquidated damages** im voraus der Höhe nach bestimmter Schadenersatz *m*,
         pauschalierter Schadenersatz *m*, vertraglich festgesetzte Schadenssumme *f*
I 47.1 2   **elapse** *vi* vergehen *vi*, verstreichen *vi (z. B. Zeit)*
I 47.1 3   **without prejudice to** unbeschadet *prep*, ohne Schaden für *m*
I 47.1 4   **recovery** Eintreibung *f*, Beitreibung *f*, Erstattung *f*
I 47.2 1   **reduction** Verringerung *f*, Minderung *f*
I 47.2 2   **remainder of the Works** Rest der Bauleistungen *m*, übrige Bauleistungen *fpl*
I 47.2 3   **absence** Fehlen *n (z. B. von Vertragsbestimmungen)*, Abwesenheit *f*
I 48.1 1   **written undertaking** schriftliche Verpflichtung *f*
I 48.1 2   **delivery** Überbringung *f*, Zusendung *f*, Lieferung *f*, Übergabe *f*
I 48.1 3   **substantially** im wesentlichen *adv*, weitgehend *adv*
I 48.2 1   **taking over of Sections** Abnahme von Abschnitten *f*, Übernahme von
         Abschnitten *f*
I 48.2 2   **occupy** *vt* besitzen *vt*, in Besitz nehmen *vt*, belegen *vt (Gebäude)*
I 48.2 3   **temporary measure** zeitweilige Maßnahme *f*
I 48.3 1   **substantial completion** wesentliche Fertigstellung *f*
I 48.4 1   **surface** Oberfläche *f*
I 48.4 2   **reinstatement** Wiederherstellung *f*
I 48.4 3   **unless** sofern nicht *conj*, wenn nicht *conj*, außer wenn *conj*
I 49.1 1   **Defects Liability** Mängelhaftung *f*, Gewährleistung *f*
I 49.2 1   **outstanding work** ausstehende Arbeiten *fpl*
I 49.2 2   **fair wear and tear** normale Abnutzung *f*
I 49.2 3   **amendment** Berichtigung *f*, Verbesserung *f*, Nachtrag *m*
I 49.2 4   **shrinkage** Schrumpfung *f*, Schwinden *n*, Schrumpfen *n*
I 49.2 5   **fault** Fehler *m*, Mangel *m*
I 49.3 1   **necessity** Notwendigkeit *f*
I 49.3 2   **implied** stillschweigend mitinbegriffen *adj*, sinngemäß beinhaltend *adj*
I 49.4 1   **monies** Gelder *npl*, Beträge *mpl*
I 50.1 1   **search** *vt* suchen *vt*
I 51.1 1   **alterations** Änderungen *fpl*
I 51.1 2   **additions** Zusätze *fpl*
I 51.1 3   **increase** *vt* erhöhen *vt (z. B. Mengen)*, vergrößern *vt*, vermehren *vt*
I 51.1 3   **variation** Bauvertragsänderung *f*, Leistungsänderung *f (gegenüber der*
         ursprünglichen vertraglichen Leistung), Änderung *f*, Abwandlung *f*,
         Bauausführungsänderung *f*
I 51.1 4   **appropriate** passend *adj*, angemessen *adj*

I 51.1 5   **decrease** *vt* vermindern *vt*, verringern *vt*
I 51.1 6   **omit** *vt* auslassen *vt*, weglassen *vt*
I 51.1 7   **sequence** Abfolge *f*, Folge *f*, Reihenfolge *f*
I 51.1 8   **vitiate** *vt* ungültig machen *vt*, aufheben *vt*
I 51.1 9   **invalidate** *vt* außer Kraft setzen *vt*, unwirksam machen *vt*
I 51.1 10 **attributable to** beizumessen(d) *adj*, zuzuschreiben(d) *adj*
I 52.1 1   **value** *vt* bewerten *vt*, einschätzen *vt*, Preis bestimmen *vt*
I 52.1 2   **rate** Preis *m*, Ansatz *m*
I 52.1 3   **valuation** Bewertung *f*, Wertbestimmung *f*
I 52.1 4   **disagreement** Meinungsverschiedenheit *f*, Nichtübereinstimmung *f*
I 52.1 5   **provisional** einstweilig *adj*, vorläufig *adj*
I 52.1 6   **on-account payment** Abschlagszahlung *f*, Zwischenzahlung *f*
I 52.2 1   **power** Befugnis *f*
I 52.2 2   **relative to** bezüglich *prep*
I 52.2 3   **rendered inappropriate** unangemessen gemacht
I 52.2 4   **inapplicable** unanwendbar *adj (Preise)*
I 52.2 5   **claim** *vt* fordern *vt (z. B. zusätzliche Bezahlung)*, beanspruchen *vt*
I 52.3 1   **adjustment** Angleichung *f*, Anpassung *f*, Korrektur *f*
I 52.3 2   **measurement** Aufmaß *n*, Messen *n*, Vermessung *f*
I 52.3 3   **daywork** Stundenlohnarbeit(en) *f (pl)*, Tagelohnarbeit(en) *f (pl)*
I 52.3 4   **deduction** Abzug *m (Betrag)*
I 52.3 5   **be in excess of s.th.** *vi* etwas überschreiten *vt (z. B. Prozentsatz)*, etwas übersteigen *vt (z. B. Prozentsatz)*
I 52.3 6   **excluding** ausgenommen *prep*
I 52.3 7   **overhead costs** Gemeinkosten *fpl*
I 52.3 8   **Effective Contract Price** wirksamer Auftragswert *m (nach FIDIC Auftragswert des Vertrages ohne »Provisional Sums« und Ansatz für Stundenlohnarbeiten)*
I 52.4 1   **daywork schedule** Stundenlohn(preis)verzeichnis *n*
I 52.4 2   **affix** *vt* beifügen *vt*, hinzufügen *vt*
I 52.4 3   **furnish** *vt* liefern *vt*, verschaffen *vt*
I 52.4 4   **voucher** Beleg *m*, Bescheinigung *f*, Zahlungsbeleg *m*
I 52.4 5   **quotation** Angebot *n*, Kostenanschlag *m*, Preisangebot *n*
I 52.4 6   **in duplicate** in doppelter Ausfertigung *f*
I 52.4 7   **statement** Aufstellung *f*, Darlegung *f*
I 52.4 8   **punctually** pünktlich *adv*
I 52.4 9   **impracticable** unausführbar *adj*, undurchführbar *adj*, unbrauchbar *adj*
I 52.4 10 **authorise** *vt* billigen *vt*, genehmigen *vt*
I 53.1 1   **procedure** Verfahren *n*, Vorgehen *n*
I 53.1 2   **intention** Absicht *f*, Vorsatz *m*
I 53.2 1   **contemporary records** gleichzeitig *(mit dem Ereignis)* aufgestellte Aufzeichnungen *fpl*
I 53.2 2   **admit** *vt* anerkennen *vt*
I 53.3 1   **substantiation** Begründung *f*, Glaubhaftmachung *f*

I 53.3 2	**accumulated** angesammelt *adj (z. B. Beträge)*, zusammengerechnet *adj*
I 53.3 3	**final account** Schlußberechnung *f*
I 53.4 1	**entitlement** Anspruch *m*, Berechtigung *f*
I 53.4 2	**arbitrator** Schiedsrichter *m*
I 53.4 3	**assess** *vt* bewerten *vt*, festsetzen *vt*, schätzen *vt*
I 53.4 4	**verify** *vt* beweisen *vt*, bestätigen *vt*
I 53.5 1	**insufficient** unzulänglich *adj*, unzureichend *adj*
I 53.5 2	**substantiate** *vt* begründen *vt*, glaubhaft machen *vt*
I 54.1 1	**exclusively** ausschließlich *adv*
I 54.1 2	**vehicle** Fahrzeug *n*, Beförderungsmittel *n*
I 54.1 3	**engaged in** beschäftigt mit *adj*
I 54.3 1	**endeavour** Bemühung *f*, Anstrengung *f*
I 54.3 2	**clearance through customs** Zollabfertigung *f*
I 54.4 1	**re-export** Wiederausfuhr *f*
I 54.4 2	**procure** *vt* beschaffen *vt*, besorgen *vt*
I 54.5 1	**hire** *vt* mieten *vt (Baugeräte)*
I 54.5 2	**availability** Verfügbarkeit *f*
I 54.5 3	**hire purchase** Mietkauf *m*, Abzahlungskauf *m*
I 54.5 4	**save that** abgesehen davon, daß *conj*, nur, daß *conj*
I 54.5 5	**hire charges** Mietkosten *fpl (Baugeräte)*
I 54.7 1	**subcontract** Nachunternehmervertrag *m*, Subunternehmervertrag *m*
I 54.7 2	**incorporate in** *vt* aufnehmen in *vt*, einfügen in *vt*
I 55.1 1	**quantity** Masse *f*, Menge *f*
I 55.1 2	**estimated** überschläglich ermittelt *adj*, geschätzt *adj*
I 56.1 1	**ascertain** *vt* ermitteln *vt*, feststellen *vt*
I 56.1 2	**lodge notice** *vt*, Benachrichtigung einreichen *vt*
I 56.1 3	**confirm** *vt* bestätigen *vt*
I 57.1 1	**method of measurement** Aufmaßverfahren *n*
I 57.1 2	**net** netto *adj adv*
I 57.1 3	**local custom** ortsüblicher Brauch *m*
I 57.2 1	**breakdown of lumpsum items** Aufgliederung der Pauschalpositionen *f*, Aufschlüsselung der Pauschalpreise *f*
I 57.2 2	**lump sum** Pauschalsumme *f*
I 57.2 3	**item** Position *f (im Leistungsverzeichnis)*
I 58.1 1	**relate to** *vi* sich beziehen auf *vrefl*
I 58.2 1	**use of sums** Verwendung der Beträge *f*
I 58.2 2	**equal** entsprechend *adj*, gleich *adj*
I 58.2 3	**nominated Subcontractor** benannter Nachunternehmer *m*, benannter Subunternehmer *m*
I 58.3 1	**production of vouchers** Vorlage von Belegen *f*
I 58.3 2	**invoice** Rechnung *f*, Warenrechnung *f*, Abrechnung *f*
I 59.1 1	**merchant** Großhändler *m*, Kaufmann *m*
I 59.1 2	**tradesman** Handwerker *m*, Einzelhändler *m*, Händler *m*
I 59.1 3	**by virtue of** kraft *prep*, aufgrund von *prep*

I 59.2 1   **raise objection** *vt* Einwand vorbringen *vt*, Einspruch erheben *vt*

I 59.2 2   **decline to enter into a contract** *vt* ablehnen, einen Vertrag abzuschließen *vt*

I 59.2 3   **negligence** Unachtsamkeit *f*, Fahrlässigkeit *f*

I 59.2 4   **misuse** Mißbrauch *m*

I 59.5 1   **certification of payments** Bestätigung der Bauleistungsabrechnungen *f (durch den »Engineer« zur Zahlung durch den Auftraggeber)*

I 59.5 2   **demand** *vt* fordern *vt*, verlangen *vt*

I 59.5 3   **retentions** Einbehalte *mpl (von den Zwischenrechnungen)*

I 59.5 4   **proof** Beweis *m*, Nachweis *m*

I 59.5 5   **withholding** Vorenthalten *n*, Zurück(be)halten *n*

I 59.5 6   **set-off** *vt* gegenrechnen *vt*, aufrechnen *vt*

I 60.1 1   **monthly statements** monatliche Zwischenrechnungen *fpl*

I 60.1 2   **invoice value** Rechnungswert *m*

I 60.3 1   **balance** Guthaben *n*, Kontostand *m*, Restbetrag *m*, Saldo *m*

I 60.3 2   **remain** *vi* verbleiben *vi (i. S. von noch übrig sein)*

I 60.4 1   **Interim Payment Certificate** Zwischenbescheinigung *f (für Zahlungen)*, Zwischenzahlungsbeschleunigung

I 60.5 1   **Statement at Completion** Aufstellung bei Fertigstellung *f*, Fertigstellungsmeldung *f (mit vorläufiger Schlußrechnung)*

I 60.6 1   **draft final statement** Entwurf der Schluß(ab)rechnung *m*, Entwurf der endgültigen Aufstellung *m*

I 60.6 2   **Final Statement** endgültige Aufstellung *f (für die Zahlungsanweisung durch den »Engineer«)*, Schlußabrechnung *f*

I 60.7 1   **written discharge** schriftliche, rechtswirksame Bestätigung *f*

I 60.8 1   **Final Payment Certificate** Schlußzahlungsbescheinigung *f*

I 60.9 1   **cessation** Aufhören *n*, Beendigung *f*

I 60.10 1   **time for payment** Zahlungsfrist *f*

I 60.10 2   **interest** Zins *m*, Zinsen *mpl*

I 61.1 1   **Defects Liability Certificate** Bescheinigung am Ende der Gewährleistungsfrist(en) *f (pl)*, Gewährleistungsbescheinigung *f*

I 62.1 1   **condition precedent to** Anfangsbedingung für *f*, aufschiebende Bedingung für *f*

I 62.2 1   **unfulfilled obligations** nicht erfüllte Verpflichtungen *fpl*

I 62.2 2   **unperformed** unerfüllt *adj*, ungetan *adj*

I 63.1 1   **remedy** Rechtsmittel *n*, Rechtsschutz *m*, Rechtsbehelf *m*, Abhilfe *f*

I 63.1 2   **voluntary** freiwillig *adj*, vorsätzlich *adj*

I 63.1 3   **involuntary** unabsichtlich *adj*, unfreiwillig *adj*

I 63.1 4   **bankruptcy** Konkurs *m*, Zahlungseinstellung *f*

I 63.1 5   **dissolution** Auflösung *f (z. B. einer Firma)*, Annullierung *f*

I 63.1 6   **amalgamation** Fusion *f*, Zusammenschluß *m*

I 63.1 7   **insolvent** insolvent *adj*, zahlungsunfähig *adj*

I 63.1 8   **creditor** Gläubiger *m*

I 63.1 9   **committee of inspection of creditors** Gläubigerausschuß zur Aufsicht *m*

I 63.1 10   **receiver** Konkursverwalter *m*, Zwangsverwalter *m*

I 63.1 11   **administrator** Nachlaßverwalter *m*, Verwalter *m*

I 63.1 12	**trustee** Treuhänder *m*, Vermögensverwalter *m*	

I 63.1 12 **trustee** Treuhänder *m*, Vermögensverwalter *m*
I 63.1 13 **liquidator** Abwickler *m*, Liquidator *m*
I 63.1 14 **assets** Betriebsvermögen *n*, Vermögen *n*, Vermögenswerte *mpl*, Aktiva *npl*
I 63.1 15 **contravene** *vt* verstoßen gegen *vt*, zuwiderhandeln *vt*
I 63.1 16 **levy an execution** *vt* Zwangsvollstreckung durchführen *vt*
I 63.1 17 **repudiate the contract** *vt* Vertrag für unverbindlich erklären *vt*
I 63.1 18 **despite** trotz *prep*, ungeachtet *prep*
I 63.1 19 **persistently** beharrlich *adv*, nachhaltig *adv*
I 63.1 20 **flagrantly** eklatant *adv*, offenkundig *adv*
I 63.2 1 **ex parte** seitens einer Partei *adv*, einseitig *adv*
I 63.2 2 **enquiry** Nachforschung *f*, Prüfung *f*, Ermittlung *f*
I 63.2 3 **accrue to** *vi* zustehen *vi*, zufallen *vi*, zukommen *vi*
I 63.2 4 **termination** Beendigung *f*, Kündigung *f*
I 63.4 1 **prohibit** *vt* untersagen *vt*, verbieten *vt*
I 63.4 2 **assign** *vt* abtreten *vt*, übereignen *vt*
I 64.1 1 **remedial work** Abhilfemaßnahmen *fpl*, Nachbesserungsarbeiten *fpl*
I 64.1 2 **urgent** dringend *adj*, eilig *adj*
I 64.1 3 **occurrence** Auftreten *n* (*z. B. eines Notfalls*)
I 64.1 4 **emergency** Notfall *m*, Notlage *f*, Notstand *m*
I 65.1 1 **Special Risks** besondere Risiken *npl* (*Definition nach Klausel 65.2 der FIDIC-Bedingungen, nicht ganz identisch mit »Employer's Risk«, vgl. Klausel 20.4*)
I 65.1 2 **indemnity** Entschädigung *f*, Schadenersatz *m*
I 65.3 1 **in transit to the Site** auf dem Transport zur Baustelle *m*
I 65.3 2 **sustain destruction** *vt* Zerstörung erleiden *vt*
I 65.3 3 **fair market value** üblicher Marktwert *m*
I 65.4.1 **impact** Anprall *m*, Aufprall *m*, Einschlag *m*
I 65.4 2 **shell** Granate *f*, Sprenggeschoß *n*
I 65.4 3 **grenade** Gewehrgranate *f*, Handgranate *f*
I 65.4 4 **projectile** Geschoß *n*, Projektil *n*
I 65.4 5 **missile** Geschoß *n*, Flugkörper *m*
I 65.5 1 **repay** *vt* zurückzahlen *vt*
I 65.6 1 **currency** Laufzeit *f* (*eines Vertrages*), Gültigkeitsdauer *f*, Währung *f*
I 65.6 2 **materially** beträchtlich *adv*, erheblich *adv*, einschlägig *adv*
I 65.6 3 **antecedent** vorausgegangen *adj*, vorangehend *adj*, vorhergehend *adj*
I 65.8 1 **preliminary items** Positionen im Leistungsverzeichnis für Baustelleneinrichtung oder ähnliches *fpl*
I 65.8 2 **repatriation** Heimführung *f*, Repatriierung *f*, Rückführung in die Heimat *f*
I 65.8 3 **advance** Anzahlung *f*, Vorauszahlung *f*
I 66.1 1 **Release from Performance** Verzicht auf Vertragserfüllung *m*
I 66.1 2 **unlawful** rechtswidrig *adj*, ungesetzlich *adj*
I 67.1 1 **settlement of disputes** Beilegung von Streitigkeiten *f*
I 67.1 2 **repudation** Unverbindlichkeitserklärung *f* (*z. B. bezüglich eines Vertrages*), Nichtanerkennung *f*
I 67.1 3 **amicable settlement** gütliche Beilegung *f*, Vergleich *m*

I 67.1 4	**arbitral award** Schiedsspruch *m*
I 67.1 5	**arbitration** Schieds(gerichts)verfahren *n*, Schiedsgerichtsbarkeit *f*
I 67.1 6	**establish the entitlement** *vt* Berechtigung begründen *vt*, Berechtigung nachweisen *vt*
I 67.1 7	**binding** bindend *adj*, verbindlich *adj*, verpflichtend *adj*
I 67.2 1	**attempt** Versuch *m*
I 67.3 1	**conciliation** Schlichtung *f*, Vermittlung *f*
I 67.3 2	**Chamber of Commerce** Handelskammer *f*
I 67.3 3	**neither party** keine (von beiden) Parteien
I 67.3 4	**disqualify s.o. from being called as a witness** *vt* Zeugenfähigkeit absprechen, jemandem *vt*, Zeugenfähigkeit nehmen, jemandem *vt*
I 67.3 5	**conduct** *vt* betreiben *vt*, führen *vt* *(z. B. Schiedsgerichtsverfahren)*
I 68.1 1	**principal place of business** Hauptverwaltungssitz *m*
I 69.1 1	**Default of the Employer** Leistungsverzug des Auftraggebers *m* *(vor allem Zahlungsverzug nach Klausel 69.1 der FIDIC-Bedingungen)*
I 69.1 2	**expiry** Ablauf *m*
I 69.1 3	**interfere with** *vt* beeinträchtigen *vt*, eingreifen in *vt*, stören *vt*
I 69.1 4	**scheme of reconstruction** Sanierungsplan *m*
I 69.1 5	**economic** wirtschaftlich *adj*
I 69.1 6	**reason** Grund *m*
I 69.2 1	**despatch** Schnelligkeit *f*, schnelle Erledigung *f*
I 69.4 1	**suspend** *vt* unterbrechen *vt*
I 69.5 1	**resumption** Wiederaufnahme *f (z. B. der Arbeiten)*
I 69.5 2	**lapse** *vi* erlöschen *vi*, verfallen *vi*
I 70.1 1	**legislation** Gesetzgebung *f*
I 70.2 1	**subsequent** nachträglich *adj*
I 70.2 2	**Decree** Erlaß *m*, Verfügung *f*
I 71.1 1	**rate of exchange** Wechselkurs *m*
I 71.1 2	**currency restriction** Devisenbeschränkung *f*, Devisenbewirtschaftung *f*
I 71.1 3	**reimburse to** *vt* zurückzahlen *vt*, erstatten *vt*, vergüten *vt* (Geldbetrag)
I 72.2 1	**proportion** Anteil *m*, Verhältnis *n*
I 72.2 2	**prevail** *vi* allgemein gelten *vi*, vorherrschen *vi*, herrschen *vi*
I 72.3 1	**set forth** *vt* erklären *vt*, darlegen *vt*
I 72.3 2	**utilise** *vt* benutzen *vt*, verwenden *vt*, ausnutzen *vt*
I 72.3 3	**reference** Bezug *m*, Empfehlung *f*, Hinweis *m*
I 72.3 4	**wording** Formulierung *f*, Wortlaut *m*
I 72.3 5	**supplement** *vt* ergänzen *vt*

Teil II:

II 1 1	**application** Verwendung *f*, Gebrauch *m*, Anwendung *f*
II 1 2	**aid** *vt* helfen *vt*
II 1 3	**task** Aufgabe *f*
II 1 4	**option** Alternative *f*, Möglichkeit *f*
II 1 5	**indicate** *vt* anzeigen *vt*

II 1 6	**aide-memoire** Denkschrift *f*, Gedächtnisstütze *f*
II 2 1	**dredger** Naßbagger *m*, Schwimmbagger *m*
II 2 2	**operate a dredger** *vt* Naßbagger einsetzen *vt*
II 2 3	**fashion** Art und Weise *f*, Methode *f*
II 2 4	**over-riding** überwiegend *adj*, vorrangig *adj*
II 2 5	**relating to** in bezug auf *prep*
II 2 6	**instance** Einzelfall *m*
II 2 7	**adopted changes** gewählte Änderungen *fpl*
II 2 8	**unaltered** unverändert *adj*
II 3 1	**essential** erforderlich *adj*, unentbehrlich *adj*
II 3 2	**limit** Grenze *f*, Preisgrenze *f*, Obergrenze *f*
II 3 3	**monetary** geldlich *adj*, finanziell *adj*
II 3 4	**adjoining property** angrenzendes Eigentum *n (nicht auf Grundstücke beschränkt)*, benachbarte Besitztümer *npl*
II 3 5	**abate** *vt* vermindern *vt*, verringern *vt*
II 3 6	**reduce** *vt* herabsetzen *vt*, reduzieren *vt*, vermindern *vt*
II 4 1	**delete** *vt* streichen *vt* (z. B. Textstelle), auslöschen *vt*
II 4 2	**substitute** *vt* ersetzen *vt*
II 4 3	**order of precedence of documents** Rangfolge der Geltung der (Vertrags)dokumente *f*
II 4 4	**under seal** gesiegelt *adj (etwa: notariell beglaubigt)*
II 4 5	**denominate** benennen *vt*, bezeichnen *vt*
II 5 1	**source** Quelle *f*, Ursprung *m*
II 5 2	**bank guarantee** Bankbürgschaft *f*, Bankgarantie *f*
II 5 3	**bulk of the data** Menge der Daten *f*, Umfang der Daten *m*
II 5 4	**advisable** ratsam *adj*
II 5 5	**hydrographic and sub-seabed conditions** hydrographische und Meeresuntergrundverhältnisse *npl*
II 5 6	**consistency** Übereinstimmung *f*, Vereinbarkeit *f*
II 6 1	**guarantor** Bürge *m*, Garantiegeber *m*
II 6 2	**successor** Nachfolger *m*, Rechtsnachfolger *m*
II 6 3	**assign** *(see: assignee)*
II 6 4	**jointly und severally** gemeinsam und einzeln *adv*
II 6 5	**conformity** Übereinstimmung *f*
II 6 6	**null and void** null und nichtig *adj*
II 6 7	**stipulation** Bedingung *f*, Vereinbarung *f*, Vertragsklausel *f*
II 6 8	**purport** Tenor *m*, Sinn *m*
II 6 9	**forbearance** Unterlassung *f*
II 6 10	**forgiveness** Erlassung *f*, Vergebung *f*
II 6 11	**in the capacity of** in der Eigenschaft als *f*
II 7 1	**surety bond for performance** Erfüllungsbürgschaftsurkunde *f*
II 7 2	**know all men by these presents** hiermit jedermann kund und zu wissen
II 7 3	**principal** Hauptschuldner *m*, Versprechensgeber *m*
II 7 4	**legal title** rechtliche Legitimation *f*

II 7 5	**obligee** Versprechensempfänger *m*, Forderungsberechtigter *m*
II 7 6	**faithfully** genau *adv*, gewissenhaft *adv*
II 7 7	**bid** Angebot *n*
II 7 8	**bidder** Anbieter *m*, Bieter *m*
II 7 9	**funds** Gelder *npl*, Geldmittel *npl*, Kapital *n*
II 7 10	**surety** Bürge *m*, Bürgschaft *f*
II 7 11	**bond** Bürgschaft *f*, Haftung *f (auch i. S. von Haftung an etwas)*
II 8 1	**suit** Antrag *m*, Rechtsstreit *m*
II 8 2	**heir** Erbe *m*
II 9 1	**be fluent in a particular language** *vi* eine spezielle Sprache beherrschen *vt*
II 9 2	**language ability** Sprachkenntnis(se) *f (pl)*
II 9 3	**interpreter** Dolmetscher(in) *m f*
II 9 4	**superintend** *vt* beaufsichtigen *vt*, überwachen *vt*
II 9 5	**working knowledge of a language** praktisch anwendbare Kenntnisse in einer Sprache *fpl*
II 9 6	**encourage** *vt* ermutigen *vt*, anhalten *vt (z. B. zu einer Handlung)*
II 9 7	**extent** Ausmaß *n*, Umfang *m (z. B. einer Handlung)*
II 9 8	**exploratory excavation** Aushub für Untersuchungszwecke *m*, Aufschließungsaushub *m*, Schürfen *n*
II 9 9	**recreation area** Erholungsgebiet *n*
II 9 10	**soluble** lösbar *adj*, löslich *adj*
II 9 11	**sediment** schichtige Ablagerung *f*, Sediment *n*
II 9 12	**for instance** zum Beispiel *n*
II 10 1	**deductible** abzugsfähig *adj (z. B. Geldbetrag)*, absetzbar *adj (von der Steuer)*
II 10 2	**preferable** vorzuziehen *adj*, wünschenswert *adj*
II 10 3	**preclude from** *vt* hindern an *vt*
II 10 4	**take out insurance** *vt* Versicherung abschließen *vt*
II 10 5	**tender stage** Ausschreibungsstadium *n*
II 10 6	**policy deductibles** Versicherungsselbstbeteiligung *f*, Selbstbeteiligung *f*, Versicherungsselbstbehalt *m*
II 10 7	**plant for incorporation** maschinelle Einrichtung(en) zum Einbau *f*
II 10 8	**replacement** Ersatz *m*, Wiederbeschaffung *f*
II 11 1	**terms of insurances** Bedingungen der Versicherungen *fpl (wie sie in den Ausschreibungsunterlagen gefordert werden)*
II 11 2	**premium** Prämie *f*, Versicherungsprämie *f*
II 11 3	**dumping** Abkippen *n*, Schüttentleerung *f*
II 11 4	**levy** *vt, vi* erheben *vt*, auferlegen *vt*
II 12 1	**rent** Miete *f*
II 12 2	**expatriate employee** ausländischer Angestellter *m*, *ausländischer Arbeitnehmer m*
II 12 3	**recruitment** Anwerbung *f*, Einstellung *f*
II 12 4	**provision of power** Energieversorgung *f*
II 12 5	**communal buildings** Gemeinschaftsgebäude *npl*
II 12 6	**refuse collection** Müllabfuhr *f*
II 12 7	**rate of pay** Lohnsatz *m*

II 12 8	**labour legislation** arbeitsrechtliche Gesetzgebung *f*
II 12 9	**maintenance of records** Führen und Aufbewahren von Aufzeichnungen *n*
II 12 10	**wage** Arbeitslohn *m*, Lohn *m*
II 12 11	**trade** Handwerk *n*, Baugewerbe *n*, Handel *m*
II 12 12	**recruit** *vt* anwerben *vt*, einstellen *vt*
II 12 13	**amongst** unter *prep (einer Personengruppe)*, zwischen *(einer Personengruppe) prep*
II 12 14	**domicile** Wohnort *m*, Wohnsitz *m*
II 12 15	**amenities** nützliche Anlagen *fpl*, Wohnkomfort *m*, gesellschaftliche Einrichtungen *fpl (z. B. Einkaufsmöglichkeiten)*
II 12 16	**supply** Versorgung *f*, Lieferung *f*
II 12 17	**sanitation** sanitäre Einrichtungen *fpl*, Gesundheitmaßnahmen *fpl*
II 12 18	**cookhouse** Kochstelle *f*, Küchengebäude *n*
II 12 19	**fire prevention** Brandverhütung *f*, Feuerverhütung *f*, Feuerschutz *m*
II 12 20	**fire-fighting equipment** Brandbekämpfungsausrüstung *f*, Löschausrüstung *f*
II 12 21	**air conditioning** Klimaregelung *f*, Klimatisierung *f*
II 12 22	**cooker** Kocher *m*, Kochgerät *n*
II 12 23	**refrigerator** Kühlschrank *m*
II 12 24	**furniture** Möbel *sg = pl npl*
II 12 25	**reinstate to its original condition** *vt* wiederherrichten in ursprünglichem Zustand *vt*
II 12 26	**accident prevention** Unfallverhütung *f*, Arbeitssicherheit *f*
II 12 27	**accident prevention officer** Sicherheitsbeauftragter *m*, Sicherheitsingenieur *m*
II 13 1	**collaboration** Zusammenarbeit *f*
II 13 2	**health authority** Gesundheitsbehörde *f*
II 13 3	**first aid equipment and stores** Ausrüstung und Vorräte für Erste Hilfe *f*, *m*
II 13 4	**sick bay** Lazarett *n*, Krankenrevier *n*
II 13 5	**welfare** Wohlergehen *n*, Wohlfahrt *f*
II 13 6	**ambulance** Krankenwagen *m*
II 13 7	**insect nuisance** Insektenplage *f*
II 13 8	**pest** Schädling *m*
II 13 9	**prophylactic** Prophylaktikum *n*, vorbeugende Maßnahme *f*
II 13 10	**formation** Entstehung *f*
II 13 11	**stagnant** stehend *adj*, stillstehend *adj*
II 13 12	**spray** *vt* sprühen *vt*, versprühen *vt*, besprühen *vt*
II 13 13	**thoroughly** gänzlich *adv*, völlig *adv*, vollkommen *adv*
II 13 14	**insecticide** Insektenvernichtungsmittel *n*, Insektizid *n*
II 13 15	**erect** *vt* montieren *vt*, bauen *vt*, errichten *vt*
II 13 16	**bilharzia** Bilharziose *f*
II 13 17	**burial** Begräbnis *n*, Beisetzung *f*, Beerdigung *f*
II 13 18	**barter** *vt* tauschen *vt*, eintauschen *vt*
II 13 19	**suffer** *vt, vi* dulden *vt*, erlauben *vt*, gestatten *vt*
II 13 20	**ammunition** Munition *f*
II 13 21	**dealings with his staff** Umgang mit seinem Personal *m*

II 13 22	**riotous** aufrührerisch *adj*, ausschweifend *adj*
II 13 23	**disorderly** *adj* gesetzwidrig *adj*, ordnungswidrig *adj*
II 13 24	**conduct** Verhalten *n*, Betragen *n*
II 13 25	**neighbourhood** Nachbarschaft *f*, Umgebung *f*
II 14 1	**fatality** tödlicher Unfall *m*, Todesopfer *n*
II 14 2	**environmental restrictions** Beschränkungen wegen der Umgebung *fpl (der Baustelle)*
II 15 1	**bonus for early completion** Prämie für vorzeitige Fertigstellung *f*, Beschleunigungsvergütung *f*
II 15 2	**granting an extension of time** Bewilligen einer (Bau)zeitverlängerung *n*
II 16 1	**renewal** Erneuerung *f*
II 16 2	**beyond** über hinaus *prep (Zeitraum)*
II 17 1	**range of items** Bereich der Positionen *m (des Leistungsverzeichnisses)*
II 17 2	**vesting of Contractor's Equipment** Übereignung der Geräte des Auftragnehmers *f*
II 17 3	**revest the property in the Contractor** *vt*, Eigentum zurückübertragen an Auftragnehmer *vt*
II 17 4	**remainder** Rest *m*, Restbestand *m*
II 18 1	**predetermined** vorher festgesetzt *adj*, vorher bestimmt *adj*
II 18 2	**currency of account** Abrechnungswährung *f*
II 18 3	**conversion** Umrechnung *f*, Umwechslung *f*
II 18 4	**Table of Exchange Rates** Wechselkurstabelle *f*
II 18 5	**increase of costs** Kostensteigerung *f*, Kostenerhöhung *f*
II 18 6	**decrease of costs** Kostenverringerung *f*, Kostenverminderung *f*
II 18 7	**reimbursement** Erstattung *f*, Rückerstattung *f*, Rückzahlung *f*
II 18 8	**convertible** konvertierbar *adj*, umwandelbar *adj*
II 19 1	**bank account** Bankkonto *n*
II 19 2	**advance payment** Vorauszahlung *f*, Vorschußzahlung *f*
II 19 3	**presentation** Einreichung *f*, Vorlage *f*, Unterbreitung *f*
II 19 4	**progressively** fortschreitend *adv*, schrittweise *adv*
II 20 1	**International Chamber of Commerce** (ICC) Internationale Handelskammer *f*
II 20 2	**UNCITRAL Arbitration Rules** UNCITRAL – Schiedsgerichtsordnung *f* *(UNCITRAL = United Nations Commission on International Trade Law)*
II 20 3	**amend, to** *vt* berichtigen *vt*, verbessern *vt*
II 21 1	**price adjustment** Preisangleichung *f*
II 21 2	**skilled workman** Facharbeiter *m (in England teilweise ohne Lehre)*, gelernter Arbeiter *m*
II 21 3	**semi-skilled workman** angelernter Arbeiter *m*
II 21 4	**unskilled workman** ungelernter Arbeiter *m*, Hilfsarbeiter *m*
II 21 5	**by way of illustration** als Beispiel *n*
II 21 6	**quarry** Steinbruch *m*
II 21 7	**basic rate** *(basic minimum wage rate 28 days prior to the latest day for submission of tenders)* Grundlohn *m*, (zur Berechnung bei Preisfluktuation) *m*

II 21 8	**current rate** *(basic minimum wage rate on any date subsequent to the date 28 days prior to the latest date for submission of tenders)* derzeitiger (Mindest)lohnsatz *m* (zur Berechnung bei Preisfluktuation)
II 21 9	**overtime rate** Überstundenlohnsatz *m*
II 21 10	**remuneration** Entlohnung *f*, Vergütung *f (z. B. durch Geldbeträge)*, Honorar *n*
II 21 11	**basic prices** *(prices for specified materials on the date 28 days prior to the latest date for submission of tenders)* Grundpreise *mpl (zur Berechnung bei Preisfluktuation)*
II 21 12	**current prices** *(prices for specified materials at any date subsequent to the date 28 days prior to the latest date for submission of tenders)* derzeitige Preise *mpl (zur Berechnung bei Preisfluktuationen)*
II 22 1	**due diligence** erforderliche Sorgfalt *f*
II 22 2	**wastage** Verlust *m*, Verschwendung *f*
II 22 3	**long term arrangement** langfristige Vereinbarung *f*
II 22 4	**lack of diligence** Mangel an Sorgfalt *m*
II 22 5	**fluctuation** Fluktuation *f*, Schwankung *f*
II 23 1	**lubricants** Schmierstoffe *mpl*, Schmiermittel sg=pl *npl*
II 23 2	**reinforcing** Bewehrung *f*
II 23 3	**explanation** Erläuterung *f*, Aufklärung *f*
II 23 4	**mode of transport** Transportmethode *f*, Transportweise *f*
II 23 5	**substantial quantities** wesentliche Mengen *fpl*
II 24 1	**irrespective of** ohne Rücksicht auf *f*, unabhängig von *adj*
II 24 2	**constituents** Bestandteile *mpl*
II 24 3	**be subject to any adjustment** *vi* einer Anpassung unterworfen sein *vi*
II 25 1	**bribery** Bestechung *f*
II 25 2	**bribe** Bestechungsgeld *n*, Schmiergeld *n*
II 25 3	**gratuity** Zuwendung *f*, Geldgeschenk *n*
II 25 4	**commission** Provision *f*, Kommission *f*
II 25 5	**inducement** Anreiz *m*, Beweggrund *m*
II 25 6	**reward** Entgelt *n*, Belohnung *f*
II 25 7	**forbearing** Unterlassen *n*, Vermeiden *n*
II 25 8	**favour** Gunst *f*, Wohlwollen *n*
II 25 9	**disfavour** Mißbilligung *f*, Ungnade *f*
II 25 10	**confidential** *adj* vertraulich *adj*
II 25 11	**disclosure** Enthüllung *f*, Offenlegung *f*
II 25 12	**disclose** *vt* offenlegen *vt (z. B. vertrauliche Angelegenheiten)*
II 25 13	**joint venture** Arbeitsgemeinschaft *f (nach jeweiligem Rechtssystem)*, ARGE = Arbeitsgemeinschaft *f*
II 25 14	**composition of the joint venture** Zusammensetzung der Arbeitsgemeinschaft *f*
II 25 15	**editorial amendments** redaktionelle Berichtigungen *fpl*
II 25 16	**clarify** *vt* klären *vt*, erklären *vt*
II 25 17	**capitalise** *vt* großschreiben *vt (mit großen Anfangsbuchstaben)*
II 25 18	**full stop** Punkt *m (am Ende eines Satzes)*
II 25 19	**penultimate line** vorletzte Zeile *f*
II 25 20	**further amendments** weitere Berücksichtigungen *fpl*
II 25 21	**colon** Doppelpunkt *m*

8. Alphabetische Vokabelliste der FIDIC-Bedingungen (Englisch/Deutsch)
8. Wordlist in alphabetical order of the FIDIC-Conditions (English/German)

abate *vt* vermindern *vt,* verringern *vt*

absence Fehlen *n (z. B. von Vertragsbestimmungen),* Abwesenheit *f*

accept *vt* annehmen *vt*

acceptance Abnahme *f,* Entgegennahme *f*

access Zufahrt *f,* Zugang *m*

accident Unfall *m*

accident prevention Unfallverhütung *f,* Arbeitssicherheit *f*

accident prevention officer Sicherheitsbeauftragter *m,* Sicherheitsingenieur *m*

accommodation Unterkunft *f,* Unterbringung *f*

accordingly entsprechend *adv,* demgemäß *adv,* folglich *adv*

accrue to *vi* zustehen *vi,* zufallen *vi,* zukommen *vi*

accumulated angesammelt *adj (z. B. Beträge),* zusammengerechnet *adj*

accurate exakt *adj,* genau *adj,* richtig *adj*

acquaint *vt* in Kenntnis setzen *vt*

action Handlung *f*

additions Zusätze *fpl*

adequacy Gemäßheit *f,* Angemessenheit *f*

adequate angemessen *adj*

adhere to instructions *vt* Anweisungen befolgen *vt,* an Anweisungen halten, sich *vrefl*

adjoining property angrenzendes Eigentum *n (nicht auf Grundstücke beschränkt),* benachbarte Besitztümer *npl*

adjust *vt* abstimmen *vt (Konten),* angleichen *vt,* anpassen *vt*

adjustment Angleichung *f,* Anpassung *f,* Korrektur *f*

administrator Nachlaßverwalter *m,* Verwalter *m*

admit *vt* anerkennen *vt*

adopt methods *vt* Methoden anwenden *vt,* Methoden sich zu eigen machen *vrefl*

adopted changes gewählte Änderungen *fpl*

advance Anzahlung *f,* Vorauszahlung *f*

advance payment Vorauszahlung *f,* Vorschußzahlung *f*

adverse ungünstig *adj,* widrig *adj*

advisable ratsam *adj*

affect *vt* beeinträchtigen *vt*

affix *vt* beifügen *vt,* hinzufügen *vt*

afford facility for *vt* Gelegenheit schaffen für *vt*

aforementioned oben erwähnt *adj,* oben genannt *adj*

agent Beauftragter *m,* Vertreter des Auftragnehmers *m (auf der Baustelle),* Bauleiter des

Auftragnehmers *m*

aggregate of all monies Gesamtbetrag *m*, Gesamtsumme *f*

agree *vt, vi* übereinkommen *vi*, vereinbaren *vt*

aid *vt* helfen *vt*

aide-memoire Denkschrift *f*, Gedächtnisstütze *f*

air conditioning Klimaregelung *f*, Klimatisierung *f*

alignment Fluchten *n*, Einfluchten *n*, Ausrichtung *f*, Flucht *f*

allocable *adj* zuteilbar *adj*, zuweisbar *adj*

allowance for profit Ansatz für Gewinn *m*, Zuschlag für Gewinn *m*

alter *vt* ändern *vt*, verändern *vt*

alterations Änderungen *fpl*

amalgamation Fusion *f*, Zusammenschluß *m*

ambiguity Mehrdeutigkeit *f*, Zweideutigkeit *f*, Doppelsinn *m*

ambulance Krankenwagen *m*

amend *vt* berichtigen *vt*, verbessern *vt*

amendment Berichtigung *f*, Verbesserung *f*, Nachtrag *m*

amenities nützliche Anlagen *fpl*, Wohnkomfort *m*, gesellschaftliche Einrichtungen *fpl*
   (*z. B. Einkaufsmöglichkeiten*)

amicable settlement gütliche Beilegung *f*, Vergleich *m*

ammunition Munition *f*

amongst unter *prep (einer Personengruppe)*, zwischen *prep (einer Personengruppe)*

amount Geldsumme *f*, Betrag *m*, Summe *f*

ancillary to the Works Bauarbeiten dienend *adj*, Bauarbeiten ergänzend *adj*

annex *vt* anfügen *vt*, beifügen *vt*

antecedent vorausgegangen *adj*, vorangehend *adj*, vorhergehend *adj*

anticipate *vt* erwarten *vt*, vorhersehen *vt*

appendix Anhang *m*

Appendix to Tender Anhang zum Angebot *m*

appliance Vorrichtung *f*, Gerät *n*, Mittel *n*, Hilfsmittel *n*

applicable anwendbar *adj*

application Verwendung *f*, Gebrauch *m*, Anwendung *f*

apply to instructions *vt* Anwendung finden auf Anweisungen *vt*

appoint *vt* beauftragen *vt*, ernennen *vt*, einsetzen *vt*

appointment Beauftragung *f*, Einsetzung *f*, Bestellung *f*

appropriate passend *adj*, angemessen *adj*

approval Genehmigung *f*, Zustimmung *f*, Anerkennung *f*, Zulassung *f* (*besonders technisch*)

arbitral award Schiedsspruch *m*

arbitration Schieds(gerichts)verfahren *n*, Schiedsgerichtsbarkeit *f*

arbitrator Schiedsrichter *m*

arrangements Vorkehrungen *fpl*

as hereinafter defined wie im folgenden festgelegt

ascertain *vt* ermitteln *vt*, feststellen *vt*

assembly Aufstellung *f*, Zusammensetzung *f*, Zusammenstellung *f*, Zusammenbau *m*

assess *vt* bewerten *vt*, festsetzen *vt*, schätzen *f*
assets Betriebsvermögen *n*, Vermögen *n*, Vermögenswerte *mpl*, Aktiva *npl*
assign *(see: assignee)*
assign *vt* abtreten *vt*, übereignen *vt*
assign to *vt* zuteilen *vt*, zuweisen *vt*
assignee Abtretungsempfänger *m*, Bevollmächtigter *m*, Rechtsnachfolger *m*, Zessionar *m*
assignment Abtretung *f*, Übertragung *f*, Zession *f*
at least wenigstens *adv*, zumindest *adv*
attempt Versuch *m*
attend the test *vt*, *vi* anwesend sein beim Test *vi (z. B. Materialprüfung)*
attributable to beizumessen(d) *adj*, zuzuschreiben(d) *adj*
authorise *vt* billigen *vt*, genehmigen *vt*
authority Autorität *f*, Behörde *f*, Ermächtigung *f*, Vollmacht *f*, Befugnis *f*
availability Verfügbarkeit *f*
available verfügbar *adj*, erhältlich *adj*
avoidance Vermeidung *f*
balance Guthaben *n*, Kontostand *m*, Restbetrag *m*, Saldo *m*
bank account Bankkonto *n*
bank guarantee Bankbürgschaft *f*, Bankgarantie *f*
bankruptcy Konkurs *m*, Zahlungseinstellung *f*
barter *vt* tauschen *vt*, eintauschen *vt*
basic prices *(prices for specified materials on the date 28 days prior to the latest date for submission of tenders)* Grundpreise *mpl (zur Berechnung bei Preisfluktuation)*
basic rate *(basic minimum wage rate 28 days prior to the latest day for submission of tenders)* Grundlohn *m* (zur Berechnung bei Preisfluktuation)
be at liberty to *vi* berechtigt sein zu *vi*
be fluent in a particular language *vi* eine spezielle Sprache beherrschen *vt*
be in excess of s.th. *vi* etwas überschreiten *vt (z. B. Prozentsatz)*, etwas übersteigen *vt (z. B. Prozentsatz)*
be subject to any adjustment *vi* einer Anpassung unterworfen sein *vi*
bench-mark Höhenfestpunkt *m*, Festpunkt *m*, Fixpunkt *m*
benefit Vorrecht *n*, Nutzen *m*, Vorteil *m*
beyond über hinaus *prep (Zeitraum)*
bid Angebot *n*
bidder Anbieter *m*, Bieter *m*
bilharzia Bilharziose *f*
bill Rechnung *f*, Warenrechnung *f*, Abrechnung *f*
Bill of Quantities Leistungsverzeichnis *n*
binding bindend *adj*, verbindlich *adj*, verpflichtend *adj*
bond Bürgschaft *f*, Haftung *f (auch i. S. von Haftung an etwas)*
boning rod Visiergerüst *n*, Visiertafel *f*
bonus for early completion Prämie für vorzeitige Fertigstellung *f*, Beschleunigungsvergütung *f*
borehole Bohrloch *n*

breach of provisions Verletzung von Bestimmungen *f*, Verstoß gegen Bestimmungen *m*

breakdown of lumpsum items Aufgliederung der Pauschalpositionen *f*, Aufschlüsselung der Pauschalpreise *f*

bribe Bestechungsgeld *n*, Schmiergeld *n*

bribery Bestechung *f*

bulk of the data Menge der Daten *f*, Umfang der Daten *m*

burial Begräbnis *n*, Beisetzung *f*, Beerdigung *f*

by these presents hiermit *adv*, hierdurch *adv*

by virtue of kraft *prep*, aufgrund von *prep*

by way of illustration als Beispiel *n*

bye-law Statut *n*, Gemeindeverordnung *f*, Satzung *f*

calculate *vt* berechnen *vt*

calculation Berechnung *f*

call upon s.o. *vt* auffordern, jemanden *vt*, ersuchen, jemanden *vt*

calling Beruf *m*, Beschäftigung *f*

capitalise *vt* großschreiben *vt* *(mit großen Anfangsbuchstaben)*

care Sorgfalt *f*, Fürsorge *f*

care of Works Erhaltung der Bauleistungen *f*

cash flow estimate vorläufiger Zahlungsplan *m*

cease to *vt* aufhören zu *vt*

certificate Bescheinigung *f*, Zertifikat *n*

certification of payments Bestätigung der Bauleistungsabrechnungen *f (durch den »Engineer« zur Zahlung durch den Auftraggeber)*

cessation Aufhören *n*, Beendigung *f*

Chamber of Commerce Handelskammer *f*

charge Forderung *f*, Belastung *f (finanzieller Art)*

charge in favour of Pfandbelastung zugunsten *f*, Zahlungsversprechen zugunsten *n*

checking Nachprüfung *f*, Überprüfung *f*

circumstances Umstände *mpl*

civil war Bürgerkrieg *m*

claim Forderung *f*, Rechtsanspruch *m*, Reklamation *f*, Anspruch *m*

claim *vt* fordern *vt (z. B. zusätzliche Bezahlung)*, beanspruchen *vt*

clarify *vt* klären *vt*, erklären *vt*

Clause Klausel *f (eines Vertrages)*, Absatz *m (eines Vertrages)*

clear away *vt* entfernen *vt*, wegräumen *vt*

clearance of site on completion Baustellenräumung nach Fertigstellung *f*

clearance through customs Zollabfertigung *f*

coin Münze *f*

collaboration Zusammenarbeit *f*

colon Doppelpunkt *m*

combustion Verbrennung *f*

commence *vt* beginnen *vt*, *vi*

commencement Beginn *m*

Commencement Date Anfangszeitpunkt *m (Datum des Erhalts der Mitteilung des »Engineers« zum Baubeginn)*, Baubeginn *m*

commission Provision *f*, Kommission *f*
committee of inspection of creditors Gläubigerausschuß zur Aufsicht *m*
commotion Tumult *m*, Unruhen *fpl*
communal buildings Gemeinschaftsgebäude *npl*
communication Mitteilung *f*, Nachricht *f*, Benachrichtigung *f*
company Gesellschaft *f*, Kapitalgesellschaft *f*
compensation Schadenersatz *m*, Abfindung *f*, Bezahlung *f*, Entschädigung *f*
compile *vt* zusammentragen *vt (z. B. Material)*, kompilieren *vt*
completion Fertigstellung *f*
compliance Beachtung *f*, Befolgung *f*, Einhaltung *f*
compliance with policy conditions Einhaltung der Bedingungen der
    Versicherungspolicen *f*
comply with nachkommen *vt (z. B. Befehl)*, erfüllen *vt*
comply with instructions *vt* Anweisungen befolgen *vt*
component Bestandteil *m*, Teil *m, n*
composition of the joint venture Zusammensetzung der Arbeitsgemeinschaft *f*
comprise *vt* enthalten *vt*, einschließen *vt*, umfassen *vt*
concern *vt* betreffen *vt*
conciliation Schlichtung *f*, Vermittlung *f*
condition precedent to Anfangsbedingung für *f*, aufschiebende Bedingung für *f*
Conditions Bedingungen *fpl (eines Vertrages)*, Klauseln *fpl (eines Vertrages)*
Conditions of Contract Vertragsbedingungen *fpl*
Conditions of Particular Application Bedingungen zur besonderen Anwendung *fpl*
conduct Verhalten *n*, Betragen *n*
conduct *vt* betreiben *vt*, führen *vt (z. B. Schiedsgerichtsverfahren)*
confidential *adj* vertraulich *adj*
confidentiality Vertraulichkeit *f*
confirm *vt* bestätigen *vt*
confirmation Bestätigung *f*
conform to *vt* übereinstimmen mit *vt*
conformity Übereinstimmung *f*
connection Verbindung *f*
consent Einwilligung *f*, Zustimmung *f*
consequent thereon folgend daraus *adv*
consider *vt* betrachten als *vt*, halten für *vt*, ansehen als *vt*
consider as *vt* betrachten als *vt*
consideration Berücksichtigung *f*, Überlegung *f*, Erwägung *f*
considerations of cost Kostenerwägungen *fpl*, Kostenüberlegungen *fpl*,
    Kostengesichtspunkte *mpl*
consistency Übereinstimmung *f*, Vereinbarkeit *f*
constituents Bestandteile *mpl*
construction of the contract Auslegung des Vertrages *f*
construe *vt* deuten *vt*, auslegen *vt*
consultation Beratung *f*, Rücksprache *f*, Konsultation *f*

contamination Verunreinigung *f*, Verschmutzung *f*

contemporary records gleichzeitig *(mit dem Ereignis)* aufgestellte Aufzeichnungen *fpl*

contents *sg* = *pl* Inhalt *m*

context Zusammenhang *m*, Kontext *m*

contingencies mögliche Ereignisse *npl*, Unvorhergesehenes *n*, unvorhergesehene Ereignisse *npl*, Eventualverbindlichkeiten *fpl*

continuing fortlaufend *adj*

contract Vertrag *m*

Contract Agreement Vertragsvereinbarung *f*

contract documents Vertragsdokumente *fpl*, Vertragsunterlagen *fpl*

Contract Price Vertragspreis *m*

Contractor Bauunternehmer *m*, Auftragnehmer *m*, Unternehmer *m*

Contractor's Equipment *(term does not include Temporary Works)* Baugeräte des Auftragnehmers *npl (ohne Hilfsbauwerke)*

contradict *vt* widersprechen *vt*

contravene *vt* verstoßen gegen *vt*, zuwiderhandeln *vt*

contribute to *vt* beisteuern zu *vt*, beitragen zu *vt*

convenience of the public Bedürfnisse der Öffentlichkeit *npl*, Annehmlichkeiten der Öffentlichkeit *fpl*

conversion Umrechnung *f*, Umwechslung *f*

convertible konvertierbar *adj*, umwandelbar *adj*

cooker Kocher *m*, Kochgerät *n*

cookhouse Kochstelle *f*, Küchengebäude *n*

corporation *(This term has different meanings in the USA.)* Körperschaft *f*, Gesellschaft *f*

cost *(Does not include any allowance for profit.)* Kosten *fpl (Die Definitionen für Kosten und Aufwand decken sich nicht in USA, GB und Europa!)*, Unkosten *fpl*

cover *vt* abdecken *vt (versicherbare Risiken)*

cover up *vt* abdecken *vt*, verbergen *vt*, verdecken *vt*

craft *sg* = pl Schiff(e) *n (pl)*, Flugzeug(e) *n (pl)*

creditor Gläubiger *m*

cross liabilities wechselseitige Haftpflicht *f*

currency Laufzeit *f (eines Vertrages)*, Gültigkeitsdauer *f*, Währung *f*

currency of account Abrechnungswährung *f*

currency restriction Devisenbeschränkung *f*, Devisenbewirtschaftung *f*

current *adj* derzeitig *adj*, gegenwärtig *adj*

current premium laufende Versicherungsprämie *f*

current prices *(prices for specified materials at any date subsequent to the date 28 days prior to the latest date for submission of tenders)* derzeitige Preise *mpl (zur Berechnung bei Preisfluktuation)*

current rate *(basic minimum wage rate on any date subsequent to the date 28 days prior to the latest date for submission of tenders)* derzeitiger (Mindest)lohnsatz *m (zur Berechnung bei Preisfluktuationen)*

custody Obhut *f*, Verwahrung *f*

customary gebräuchlich *adj*, üblich *adj*

damage to property Sachschaden *m*, Vermögensschaden *m*

damages Entschädigung *f*, Schadenersatz *m*

data Daten *fpl*, Angaben *fpl*

daywork Stundenlohnarbeit(en) *f (pl)*, Tagelohnarbeit(en) *f (pl)*

daywork schedule Stundenlohn(preis)verzeichnis *n*

dealings with his staff Umgang mit seinem Personal *m*

debris Trümmer *npl*, Schutt *m*, Bruchstücke *npl*

debt Schuld *f*

decision Entscheidung *f*

decline *vt, vi* verfallen *vi (in Verfall geraten)*, sinken *vi (Preise)*, zurückgehen *vi (sich verschlechtern)*, ablehnen *vt (höflich)*

decline to enter into a contract *vt, vi* ablehnen, einen Vertrag abzuschließen *vt*

decrease Verminderung *f*

decrease *vt* vermindern *vt*, verringern *vt*

decrease of costs Kostenverringerung *f*, Kostenverminderung *f*

Decree Erlaß *m*, Verfügung *f*

deduct *vt* abziehen *vt (Summe)*, abrechnen *vt (i. S. von abziehen)*

deductible abzugsfähig *adj (z. B. Geldbetrag)*, absetzbar *adj (von der Steuer)*

deduction Abzug *m (Betrag)*

deem *vt* erachten für *vt*, betrachten als *vt*

default Nichterfüllung *f*, Versäumnis *n*

Default of the Employer Leistungsverzug des Auftraggebers *m (vor allem Zahlungsverzug nach Klausel 69.1 der FIDIC-Bedingungen)*

Defects Liability Mängelhaftung *f*, Gewährleistung *f*

Defects Liability Certificate Bescheinigung am Ende der Gewährleistungsfrist(en) *f (pl)*, Gewährleistungsbescheinigung *f*

Defects Liability Period Gewährleistungsfrist *f*, Mängelhaftungszeitraum *m*, Baumängelhaftungszeitraum *m*

definition Begriffsbestimmung *f*, Erklärung *f*, Definition *f*

delay Verzögerung *f*, Verzug *m*

delay *vt* verschieben *vt*, verzögern *vt*

delegate *vt* delegieren *vt*, übertragen *vt*

delegation Übertragung *f*, Bevollmächtigung *f*

delete *vt* streichen *vt (z. B. Textstelle)*, auslöschen *vt*

deliver *vt* übergeben *vt*, aushändigen *vt*

delivery Überbringung *f*, Zusendung *f*, Lieferung *f*, Übergabe *f*

demand *vt* fordern *vt*, verlangen *vt*

demolish *vt* abbrechen *vt*, abreißen *vt*, niederreißen *vt*

denominate benennen *vt*, bezeichnen *vt*

description Beschreibung *f*

design Entwurf und Berechnung *m f*, Konstruktion *f (»design« bedeutet im Englischen nicht nur die Gestaltung!)*, technische Bearbeitung *f*, Planung *f*

design *vt* auslegen *vt (z. B. technische Anlagen)*, bemessen *vt*, entwerfen *vt*, planen *vt*

designate bezeichnen *vt*, bestimmen *vt vt* 2. *vt* kennzeichnen *vt*, bezeichnen *vt*

despatch Schnelligkeit *f*, schnelle Erledigung *f*

despite trotz *prep*, ungeachtet *prep*

determination Bestimmung *f*, Entscheidung *f*, Festsetzung *f*

determine *vt* bestimmen *vt*, festlegen *vt*, festsetzen *vt*

device Vorrichtung *f*

diligence Eifer *m*, Fleiß *m*, Sorgfalt *f*

diligent sorgfältig *adj*, eifrig *adj*

disagreement Meinungsverschiedenheit *f*, Nichtübereinstimmung *f*

discharge *vt* begleichen *vt*, bezahlen *vt*, erfüllen *vt*

disclose *vt* offenlegen *vt (z. B. vertrauliche Angelegenheiten)*

disclosure Enthüllung *f*, Offenlegung *f*

discrepancy Widerspruch *m (z. B. in Vertragsdokumenten)*, Diskrepanz *f*

discretion Entscheidungsfreiheit *f*, Ermessen *n*

disfavour Mißbilligung *f*, Ungnade *f*

dislocation Erschütterung *f*, Störung *f*

dismantle *vt* abbauen *vt*, demontieren *vt*, auseinandernehmen *vt*, abmontieren *vt*

disorder Krawall *m*, Ruhestörung *f*

disorderly *adj* gesetzwidrig *adj*, ordnungswidrig *adj*

dispatch rasche Erledigung *f*, Schnelligkeit *f (des Arbeitsablaufs)*

dispose of *vt* abgeben *vt (z. B. Alkohol)*, verfügen über *vt*

disqualify s.o. from being called as a witness *vt* Zeugenfähigkeit absprechen, jemandem *vt*, Zeugenfähigkeit nehmen, jemandem *vt*

disrupt *vt* unterbrechen *vt*

disruption of progress Unterbrechung des Baufortschrittes *f*

dissolution Auflösung *f (z. B. einer Firma)*, Annullierung *f*

distribute *vt* verteilen *vt*

dock Anlegeplatz *m*, Dock *n*, Hafenbecken *n*

documents Unterlagen *fpl*

domestic contracts inländische Bauverträge *mpl (Gegensatz: Contracts on international basis)*

domicile Wohnort *m*, Wohnsitz *m*

draft *vt* abfassen *vt (z. B. Schriftstück)*, entwerfen *vt (z. B. Text)*

draft final statement Entwurf der Schluß(ab)rechnung *m*, Entwurf der endgültigen Aufstellung *m*

draw up *vt (report)* aufsetzen *vt (Bericht)*, abfassen *vt (Bericht)*, ausfertigen *vt (Dokument)*

dredger Naßbagger *m*, Schwimmbagger *m*

dredging Naßbaggern *n*

due fällig *adj*, sofort zahlbar *adj*

due diligence erforderliche Sorgfalt *f*

duly ordnungsgemäß *adv*

duly certified ordnungsgemäß beglaubigt *adj*, ordnungsgemäß bestätigt *adj*

dumping Abkippen *n*, Schüttentleerung *f*

duration Dauer *f*, Laufzeit *f*

duty Pflicht *f*, Aufgabe *f*

economic wirtschaftlich *adj*

edition Ausgabe *f (z. B. einer Schriftenreihe)*

editorial amendments redaktionelle Berichtigungen *fpl*

effect *vt* abschließen *vt (z. B. Versicherung)*

effect delegation *vt* Bevollmächtigung veranlassen *vt*

Effective Contract Price wirksamer Auftragswert *m (nach FIDIC Auftragswert des Vertrages ohne »Provisional Sums« und Ansatz für Stundenlohnarbeiten)*

effective value Effektivwert *m*

elapse *vi* vergehen *vi*, verstreichen *vi (z. B. Zeit)*

elect erwählen *vt*, sich entscheiden für *vrefl*

emergency Notfall *m*, Notlage *f*, Notstand *m*

employ *vt* einsetzen *vt*, beschäftigen *vt*, verwenden *vt*

employee Arbeitnehmer *m*, Angestellter *m*

Employer Auftraggeber *m*, Bauherr *m*

Employer's Property Eigentum des Auftraggebers *n*

Employer's Risks *(Term introduced in the fourth edition of the conditions)* Bauherrnrisiken *npl*, Auftraggeberwagnissse *npl*

employment Anstellung *f*, Beschäftigung *f*, Arbeitsverhältnis *n*

enable *vt* ermächtigen *vt*, befähigen *vt*

encounter *vt* stoßen auf *vt*, antreffen *vt*

encounter physical obstructions, to *vt* naturbedingte Hindernisse antreffen *vt*, auf naturbedingte Hindernisse treffen *vi*

encourage *vt* ermutigen *vt*, anhalten *vt (z. B. zu einer Handlung)*

endeavour Bemühung *f*, Anstrengung *f*

engaged in beschäftigt mit *adj*

Engineer Bauleiter des Auftraggebers *m (mit gewisser Schiedsrichterfunktion gemäß FIDIC-Vertrag)*, Ingenieur *m (mit Funktionen gemäß FIDIC-Vertrag)*

Engineer's Representative Vertreter des Bauleiters des Auftraggebers *m (gemäß den FIDIC-Bedingungen)*

enquiry Nachforschung *f*, Prüfung *f*, Ermittlung *f*

ensure *vt* gewährleisten *vt*, sicherstellen *vt*, garantieren *vt*

entitled berechtigt *adj*

entitlement Anspruch *m*, Berechtigung *f*

environment Umwelt *f*, Umfeld *n*, Umgebung *f*

environmental restrictions Beschränkungen wegen der Umgebung *fpl (der Baustelle)*

equal entsprechend *adj*, gleich *adj*

equally ebenso *adv*

erect *vt* montieren *vt*, bauen *vt*, errichten *vt*

essential erforderlich *adj*, unentbehrlich *adj*

establish the entitlement, to *vt* Berechtigung begründen *vt*, Berechtigung nachweisen *vt*

estimated überschläglich ermittelt *adj*, geschätzt *adj*

event Ereignis *n*, Vorfall *m*

event of default Fall von Vertragsverletzung *f*, Fall von Vertragsbruch *m*

evidence Beweismittel *n*, Beweis *m*, Nachweis *m*

ex parte seitens einer Partei *adv*, einseitig *adv*

examination Untersuchung *f*

example clause Beispielklausel *f*

excavation Aushub *m*, Ausschachtung *f*

exceed *vt* überschreiten *vt*, übersteigen *vt*

exceeding überschreitend *(Prozentsatz)*, übersteigend *(Prozentsatz)*

exception Ausnahme *f*

excluding ausgenommen *prep*

exclusion Ausschluß *m*

exclusively ausschließlich *adv*

execute *vt* ausführen *vt*

execution Ausführung *f*, Durchführung *f*

exercise *vt* ausüben *vt*

expatriate employee ausländischer Angestellter *m,* ausländischer Arbeitnehmer *m*

expedite *vt* beschleunigen *vt (z. B. Bauarbeiten)*

expedition Eile *f*, Beschleunigung *f*

expenditure Aufwand *m (Die Definitionen für Aufwand und Kosten decken sich nicht in den USA, GB und Europa!)*, Ausgabe *f*, Ausgaben *fpl*

expense(s) Aufwand *m (Die Definitionen für Aufwand und Kosten decken sich nicht in den USA, GB und Europa!)*, Ausgabe *f*, Ausgaben *fpl*

experienced erfahren *adj*

expiration Ende *n (zeitlich)*, Erlöschen *n (zeitlich)*, Verfall *m (zeitlich)*, Ablauf *m (einer Frist)*

expiry *(see: expiration)*

explanation Erläuterung *f*, Aufklärung *f*

explanatory erläuternd *adj*, erklärend *adj*

exploratory excavation Aushub für Untersuchungszwecke *m*, Aufschließungsaushub *m*, Schürfen *n*

explosive Explosivstoff *m*, Sprengstoff *m*

expression Ausdruck *m*

expressly ausdrücklich *adv*

extend *vt, vi* fortsetzen *vt*, verlängern *vt*, ausdehnen, sich *vrefl*

extension of time Terminverlängerung *f*, Fristverlängerung *f*

extent Ausmaß *n*, Umfang *m (z. B. einer Handlung)*

fabrication Fertigung *f*, Herstellung *f*, Fabrikation *f*

facilitate *vt* erleichtern *vt*

facilities Einrichtungen *fpl*

facsimile transmission Fernkopieren *n*

failure Unterlassung *f*, Versäumnis *n*

failure to disapprove work Versäumnis, Leistungen zurückzuweisen *n*, Unterlassung, Leistungen zurückzuweisen *f*

fair market value üblicher Marktwert *m*

fair wear and tear normale Abnutzung *f*

fairly gerechterweise *adv*
faithfully genau *adv*, gewissenhaft *adv*
fashion Art und Weise *f*, Methode *f*
fatality tödlicher Unfall *m*, Todesopfer *n*
fault Fehler *m*, Mangel *m*
favour Gunst *f*, Wohlwollen *n*
Fédération Internationale des Ingénieurs-Conseils (FIDIC) Internationale Vereinigung der Beratenden Ingenieure *(FIDIC) f*
fencing Einzäunung *f*, Umzäunung *f*
final account Schlußberechnung *f*
Final Payment Certificate Schlußzahlungsbescheinigung *f*
Final Statement endgültige Aufstellung *f (für die Zahlungsanweisung durch den »Engineer«)*, Schlußabrechnung *f*
fire prevention Brandverhütung *f*, Feuerverhütung *f*, Feuerschutz *m*
fire-fighting equipment Brandbekämpfungsausrüstung *f*, Löschausrüstung *f*
first aid equipment and stores Ausrüstung und Vorräte für Erste Hilfe *f, n*
flagrantly eklatant *adv*, offenkundig *adv*
fluctuation Fluktuation *f*, Schwankung *f*
for instance zum Beispiel *n*
forbearance Unterlassung *f*
forbearing Unterlassen *n*, Vermeiden *n*
foreign ausländisch *adj*, fremd *adj*
foreign currency Devisen *fpl*, ausländische Währung *f*
foreman Polier *m*, Vorarbeiter *m*
foreseeable voraussehbar *adj*
forgiveness Erlassung *f*, Vergebung *f*
formation Entstehung *f*
forms of tender and agreement Angebots- und Vertragsformulare *npl*
forthwith sogleich *adv*, unverzüglich *adv*
fossil Fossil *n*, Versteinerung *f*
foundation Gründung *f*, Fundament *n*, Gründungssohle *f*
free of charge kostenlos *adv*, gebührenfrei *adv*, unentgeltlich *adv*
fuel Brennstoff *m*, Kraftstoff *m*
full stop Punkt *m (am Ende eines Satzes)*
funds Gelder *npl*, Geldmittel *npl*, Kapital *n*
furnish *vt* liefern *vt*, verschaffen *vt*
furniture Möbel *sg = pl npl*
further weiterhin *adv*
General Conditions allgemeine Bedingungen *fpl*
gift Geschenk *n*, Gabe *f*
govern *vt* bestimmen *vt*, regeln *vt*
grant *vt* bewilligen *vt*, gewähren *vt*
granting an extension of time Bewilligen einer (Bau)zeitverlängerung *n*
gratuity Zuwendung *f*, Geldgeschenk *n*

grenade Gewehrgranate *f*, Handgranate *f*

guarantor Bürge *m*, Garantiegeber *m*

guideline Richtlinie *f*

haulier Frachtführer *m*

hazardous properties gefährliche Eigenschaften *fpl*

heading Überschrift *f*

health authority Gesundheitsbehörde *f*

heir Erbe *m*

hire *vt* mieten *vt (Baugeräte)*

hire charges Mietkosten *fpl (Baugeräte)*

hire purchase Mietkauf *m*, Abzahlungskauf *m*

hostility Feindschaft *f*, Feindseligkeit *f*

house *vt* unterbringen *vt (z. B. in einer Wohnung)*, aufnehmen *vt*

hydrographic and sub-seabed conditions hydrographische und Meeresuntergrundverhältnisse *npl*

hydrological hydrologisch *adj*

identify *vt* ausweisen *vt*, feststellen *vt*

IFI *(International Financing Institution)* Internationales Finanzierungsinstitut *n*

impact Anprall *m*, Aufprall *m*, Einschlag *m*

impartially gerecht *adv*, unparteiisch *adv*

impediment Behinderung *f*, Hindernis *n*

implied stillschweigend mitinbegriffen *adj*, sinngemäß beinhaltend *adj*

imply *vt* beinhalten *(stillschweigend)* *vt*, mitenthalten *vt*, stillschweigend voraussetzen *vt*

import *vt* bedeuten *vt*, angehen *vt*, betreffen *vt*

impose *vt* aufbürden *vt*, auferlegen *vt*

impracticable unausführbar *adj*, undurchführbar *adj*, unbrauchbar *adj*

improper work mangelhafte Bauleistung(en) *f*, *(pl)*

improve *vt* verbessern *vt*

in accordance with in Übereinstimmung mit *f*

in duplicate in doppelter Ausfertigung *f*

in force geltend *adj*, gültig *adj*

in particular insbesondere *adv*

in relation thereto in Beziehung dazu *f*

in respect of hinsichtlich *prep*

in the absence of in Ermangelung von *f*

in the capacity of in der Eigenschaft als *f*

in the event of im Fall, daß *conj*

in the joint names of gesamtschuldnerisch *adv*, gemeinsam *adv*

in transit to the Site auf dem Transport zur Baustelle *m*

inability Unfähigkeit *f*, Unvermögen *n*

inapplicable unanwendbar *adj (Preise)*

incidental thereto daraus ergebend *adj*, damit verbunden *adj*

incidental to dabei entstehend *adj*, verbunden mit *adj*

include *vt* einschließen *vt*, umfassen *vt*

inclusion Einbeziehung *f*, Einschluß *m*

incorporate in *vt* aufnehmen in *vt*, einfügen in *vt*

incorporation in Eingliederung in *f*, Aufnahme in *f (z. B. Klausel in Vertrag)*

increase *vi* erhöhen *vt (z. B. Mengen)*, vergrößern *vt*, vermehren *vt*

increase of costs Kostensteigerung *f*, Kostenerhöhung *f*

incur *vt* eingehen *vt (z. B. Verpflichtungen)*, auf sich laden *vrefl*, auf sich nehmen *vrefl*

indemnifications Entschädigung *f*, Schadenersatz *m*

indemnify *vt* entschädigen *vt*, Schadenersatz leisten *vt*, Schadloshaltung zusagen *vt* *s.o. again*

indemnity Entschädigung *f*, Schadenersatz *m* *loss*

independent unabhängig *adj*

index figure Indexzahl *f*

index of the cost of labour Lohnkostenindex *m*

indicate *vt* anzeigen *vt*

indirect costs Gemeinkosten *fpl*

inducement Anreiz *m*, Beweggrund *m*

inevitably unvermeidlich *adv*

infer from *vt* ableiten aus *vt (folgern)*, folgern aus *vt*, schließen aus *vt*

inferred from the Contract abzuleiten aus dem Vertrag *m*

influence *vt* beeinflussen *vt*

infringement of patent rights Verletzung von Patentrechten *f*

injury Personenschaden *m*, Verletzung *f*

insect nuisance Insektenplage *f*

insecticide Insektenvernichtungsmittel *n*, Insektizid *n*

insolvent insolvent *adj*, zahlungsunfähig *adj*

inspection of operations Inspektion der Arbeitsvorgänge *f*, Gütekontrolle der Arbeitsvorgänge *f*

inspection of site Baustellenbesichtigung *f (vor Angebotsabgabe)*

instance Einzelfall *m*

instruction Anordnung *f*, Anweisung *f (Befehl)*

insufficient unzulänglich *adj*, unzureichend *adj*

insurance Versicherung *f*

insure *vt* versichern *vt (z. B. Bauleistungen)*

insured Versicherter *m*, Versicherungsnehmer *m*

insurer Versicherer *m*, Assekurant *m*

insurrection Aufruhr *m*, Aufstand *m*

intend *vt* beabsichtigen *vt*

intended bestimmt *adj*, beabsichtigt *adj*

intention Absicht *f*, Vorsatz *m*

interest Zins *m*, Zinsen *mpl*

interfere with *vt* beeinträchtigen *vt*, eingreifen in *vt*, stören *vt*

interference with traffic Beeinträchtigung des Verkehrs *f*

interim einstweilig *adj*, vorläufig *adj*

Interim Payment Certificate Zwischenzahlungsbescheinigung *f*

interim payment Abschlagszahlung *f*, Zwischenzahlung *f*

International Chamber of Commerce *(ICC)* Internationale Handelskammer *f*
interpret *vt* auslegen *vt*
interpretation Auslegung *f*, Interpretation *f*
interpreter Dolmetscher(in) *m f*
invalidate *vt* außer Kraft setzen *vt*, unwirksam machen *vt*
investigation Untersuchung *f*, Nachforschung *f*
invite tenders *vt* auffordern zur Angebotsabgabe *vt*
invoice Rechnung *f*, Warenrechnung *f*, Abrechnung *f*
invoice value Rechnungswert *m*
involuntary unabsichtlich *adj*, unfreiwillig *adj*
involve *vt* einbeziehen *vt*, einschließen *vt*
involve in additional costs *vt* zusätzliche Kosten verursachen *vt*
ionising radiations ionisierende Strahlungen *fpl*
irrespective of ohne Rücksicht auf *f*, unabhängig von *adj*
issue Ausgabe *f (z. B. eines Zertifikats)*
issue *vt* herausgeben *vt*, ausgeben *vt*, erteilen *vt*
item Position *f (im Leistungsverzeichnis)*
joint venture Arbeitsgemeinschaft *f (nach jeweiligem Rechtssystem),* ARGE =
    Arbeitsgemeinschaft *f*
jointly und severally gemeinsam und einzeln *adv*
just and equitable recht und billig *adj*
know all men by these presents hiermit jedermann kund und zu wissen
labour Arbeitskräfte *fpl*, Arbeit *f*
labour legislation arbeitsrechtliche Gesetzgebung *f*
lack of diligence Mangel an Sorgfalt *m*
language ability Sprachkenntnis(se) *f (pl)*
lapse *vi* erlöschen *vi*, verfallen *vi*
legal capacity Geschäftsfähigkeit *f*, Rechtsfähigkeit *f*
legal successor in title Rechtsnachfolger *m*
legal title rechtliche Legitimation *f*
legislation Gesetzgebung *f*
Letter of Acceptance Annahmeerklärung *f (des Auftraggebers bezüglich des Angebots)*
level of reference Höhenangabe *f*
levy *vt*, *vi* erheben *vt*, auferlegen *vt*
levy an execution *vt* Zwangsvollstreckung durchführen *vt*
liability Haftpflicht *f*, Verpflichtung *f*, Haftung *f*
liable haftbar *adj*, verantwortlich *adj*
limit Grenze *f*, Preisgrenze *f*, Obergrenze *f*
link with *vt* verbinden mit *vt*
liquidated damages im voraus der Höhe nach bestimmter Schadenersatz *m*,
    pauschalierter Schadenersatz *m*, vertraglich festgesetzte Schadenssumme *f*
liquidator Abwickler *m*, Liquidator *m*
load Last *f*, Belastung *f*
local custom ortsüblicher Brauch *m*

locality of the Works Ort der (Bau)arbeiten *m*

lock Schleuse *f*, Schleusenkammer *f*

lodge notice *vt* Benachrichtigung einreichen *vt*

long-term arrangement langfristige Vereinbarung *f*

loss Verlust *m*

lubricants Schmierstoffe *mpl*, Schmiermittel *sg=pl npl*

lump sum Pauschalsumme *f*

maintain *vt* unterhalten *vt*, aufrechterhalten *vt (z. B. Betrieb)*, erhalten *vt*

maintenance manual Wartungshandbuch *n*

maintenance of records Führen und Aufbewahren von Aufzeichnungen *n*

mandatory Bevollmächtigter *m*

manner Art und Weise *f*

manufacture Fertigung *f*, Herstellung *f*, Fabrikation *f*

marginal notes Randbezeichnungen *fpl*

materially beträchtlich *adv*, erheblich *adv*, einschlägig *adv*

meaning Bedeutung *f*

means of access Zugangsmöglichkeiten *fpl*

measure Maßnahme *f*

measurement Aufmaß *n*, Messen *n*, Vermessung *f*

measuring Messen *n*, Vermessen *n*, Aufmessen *n*

mention *vt* erwähnen *vt*

merchant Großhändler *m*, Kaufmann *m*

method of measurement Aufmaßverfahren *n*

Minimum Amount of Insurance Mindestdeckungssumme *f*

minor modifications geringfügige Änderungen *fpl*

misconduct o.s. *vrefl* sich eines Fehlverhaltens schuldig machen *vrefl*, sich schlecht betragen *vrefl*

missile Geschoß *n*, Flugkörper *m*

misuse Mißbrauch *m*

mode of transport Transportmethode *f*, Transportweise *f*

modification Bauvertragsänderung *f*, Leistungsänderung *f (gegenüber der ursprünglichen vertraglichen Leistung)*, Änderung *f*, Abwandlung *f*, Bauausführungsänderung *f*

monetary geldlich *adj*, fnaziell *adj*

monies Gelder *npl*, Beträge *mpl*

monthly statements monatliche Zwischenrechnungen *fpl*

multiple shifts Mehrschichtbetrieb *m*

mutually gegenseitig *adv*, wechselseitig *adv*

nature of extra work Art der zusätzlichen Bauleistungen *f*

necessity Notwendigkeit *f*

neglect Nachlässigkeit *f*, Unterlassung *f*

negligence Unachtsamkeit *f*, Fahrlässigkeit *f*

negligent nachlässig *adj*, unachtsam *adj*

negotiate *vt*, *vi* verhandeln *vt*, *vi*

neighbourhood Nachbarschaft *f*, Umgebung *f*

neither party keine *(von beiden)* Parteien *pl*

net netto *adj adv*

nominated Subcontractor benannter Nachunternehmer *m*, benannter Subunternehmer *m*

notice Mitteilung *f*, Nachricht *f*, Benachrichtigung *f*

notification Benachrichtigung *f*, Mitteilung *f*

not ... on the Works in any capacity zu keiner anderen Funktion auf der Baustelle *f*

notwithstanding ungeachtet *prep*, unbeschadet *prep*

nuclear assembly kerntechnische Einheit *f*

nuclear waste radioaktiver Abfall *m*, Atommüll *m*

nuisance Ärgernis *n*, Belästigung *f*

null and void null und nichtig *adj*

object to *vt* Einspruch erheben gegen *vt*, etwas dagegen haben *vt*

obligation Verpflichtung *f*

obligee Versprechensempfänger *m*, Forderungsberechtigter *m*

obstruction Behinderung *f*, Hindernis *n*

obtain *vt* erhalten *vt*, erlangen *vt*, bekommen *vt*

occasion *vt* veranlassen *vt*, verursachen *vt*

occupy *vt* besitzen *vt*, in Besitz nehmen *vt*, belegen *vt* *(Gebäude)*

occurrence Auftreten *n* *(z. B. eines Notfalls)*

omission Auslassung *f (von Bauleistungen)*, Wegfall *m (von Bauleistungen)*, Teilkündigung *f*

omit *vt* auslassen *vt*, weglassen *vt*

on behalf of the Employer im Namen des Auftraggebers *m*

on-account payment Abschlagszahlung *f*, Zwischenzahlung *f*

open up *vt* wieder aufnehmen *vt* *(z. B. Verfahren)*

opening Durchbruch *m*, Öffnung *f*

operate *vt* bedienen *vt*, betreiben *vt*

operate a dredger *vt* Naßbagger einsetzen *vt*

opinion Meinung *f*, Ansicht *f*

opportunities for other contractors Erleichterungen für andere Auftragnehmer *fpl*

option Alternative *f*, Möglichkeit *f*

orally mündlich *adv*

order of precedence of documents Rangfolge der Geltung der (Vertrags)dokumente *f*

Ordinance Satzung *f*, Verordnung *f*

outstanding work ausstehende Arbeiten *fpl*

overhead(s) Gemeinkosten *fpl*

overhead costs Gemeinkosten *fpl*

over-riding überwiegend *adj*, vorrangig *adj*

overtime rate Überstundenlohnsatz *m*

partially teilweise *adv*

participation Beteiligung *f*, Mitwirkung *f*

particularise *vt* ausführlich angeben *vt*, einzeln aufführen *vt*

particulars Einzelheiten *fpl*, nähere Angaben *fpl*

pass *vt* bestehen *vt (z. B. Test)*
payable zahlbar *adj*, zu zahlen
peg Pflock *m*, Absteckpflock *m*
penalty Vertragsstrafe *f*, Geldstrafe *f*, Strafe *f*, Pönale *f*
penultimate line vorletzte Zeile *f*
performance Durchführung *f*, Leistung *f*
performance security Ausführungsbürgschaft *f*
Permanent Works verbleibende Bauten *mpl (Gegensatz: Temporary Works)*
permission Erlaubnis *f*, Genehmigung *f*
permit *vt* erlauben *vt*, zulassen *vt*, gestatten *vt*
persistently beharrlich *adv*, nachhaltig *adv*
personnel Belegschaft *f*, Mitarbeiterstab *m*, Personal *n*
pest Schädling *m*
planning permission Baugenehmigung *f*
Plant *(Contrary to the earlier editions in the fourth edition the word means machinery, apparatus and the like intended to form or form part of the Permanent Works. In the earlier editions plant meant Contractor's Equipment)* maschinelle Einrichtungen *fpl (Im Gegensatz zu früheren Auflagen bedeutet das Wort »Plant« in der vierten Auflage der FIDIC-Bedingungen die fest einzubauenden maschinellen Anlagen und nicht die Baugeräte des Auftragnehmers)*
plant for incorporation maschinelle Einrichtung(en) zum Einbau *f*
policy Police *f*, Versicherungsschein *m*
policy deductibles Versicherungsselbstbeteiligung *f*, Selbstbeteiligung *f*, Versicherungsselbstbehalt *m*
pollution Verunreinigung *f*, Verschmutzung *f*
portion Anteil *m*, Teil *m*
possession Besitz *m*
possession of site Inbesitznahme der Baustelle *f*
power Befugnis *f*
practicable durchführbar *adj*, möglich *adj*
precaution Vorkehrung *f*, Vorsichtsmaßnahme *f*
preclude from *vt* hindern an *vt*
predetermined vorher festgesetzt *adj*, vorher bestimmt *adj*
preferable vorzuziehen *adj*, wünschenswert *adj*
prejudice *vt* beeinträchtigen *vt*, beeinflussen *vt*
preliminary items Positionen im Leistungsverzeichnis für Baustelleneinrichtung oder ähnliches *fpl (siehe auch »preliminaries«)*
premium Prämie *f*, Versicherungsprämie *f*
preparation Vorbereitung *f*, Abfassung *f (eines Textes)*
prescribe *vt* verordnen *vt*, vorschreiben *vt*
presentation Einreichung *f*, Vorlage *f*, Unterbreitung *f*
pressure wave Druckwelle *f*
prevail *vi* allgemein gelten *vi*, vorherrschen *vi*, herrschen *vi*
prevention Verhinderung *f*

previous vorherig *adj*
price adjustment Preisangleichung *f*
price fluctuation factor Preisgleitfaktor *m*
priced mit Preisangabe *f*, mit Preisen versehen *mpl*
principal Hauptschuldner *m*, Versprechensgeber *m*
principal place of business Hauptverwaltungssitz *m*
prior consent vorherige Zustimmung *f*
prior to vor *adv (zeitlich)*
priority Vorrang *m*
procedure Verfahren *n*, Vorgehen *n*
proceed *vi* voranschreiten *vi*, vorwärtsgehen *vi*, fortfahren *vi*, weitergehen *vi*
proceeding Prozeß *m*, Verfahren *n*, Gerichtsverfahren *n*
procure *vt* beschaffen *vt*, besorgen *vt*
production Fertigung *f*, Herstellung *f*, Fabrikation *f*
production of vouchers Vorlage von Belegen *f*
professional fees Honorare für Freiberufler *npl (z. B. Beratende Ingenieure)*
progress Fortschritt *m*
progress payment Abschlagszahlung *f*, Zwischenzahlung *f*
progressively fortschreitend *adv*, schrittweise *adv*
prohibit *vt* untersagen *vt*, verbieten *vt*
projectile Geschoß *n*, Projektil *n*
proof Beweis *m*, Nachweis *m*
proper ordnungsgemäß *adj*, exakt *adj*, genau *adj*
properly *adv* angemessen *adv*, richtig *adv*, zweckmäßig *adv*
prophylactic Prophylaktikum *n*, vorbeugende Maßnahme *f*
proportion Anteil *m*, Verhältnis *n*
proposal Vorschlag *m*
propose *vt* vorschlagen *vt*
provide *vt* liefern *vt*, zur Verfügung stellen *vt*
provided vorausgesetzt *conj*
provision Bestimmung *f*, Bedingung *f*, Vorschrift *f*
provision of power Energieversorgung *f*
provision to the contrary gegenteilige Bestimmung *f*
provisional einstweilig *adj*, vorläufig *adj*
Provisional Sum provisorische Summe *f (Position in englischen Bauverträgen für noch nicht genau festgelegte Leistungen wie z. B. Untervergabe, manchmal auch für Baustelleneinrichtung usw.)*, vorläufiger Betrag *m*
public body öffentlich-rechtliche Körperschaft *f*
punctually pünktlich *adv*
purchase Kauf *m*
purport Tenor *m*, Sinn *m*
purpose Zweck *m*
pursuant to gemäß *adv*, übereinstimmend mit *adv*
quantity Masse *f*, Menge *f*

quarry Steinbruch *m*

quotation Angebot *n*, Kostenanschlag *m*, Preisangebot *n*

raise objection *vt* Einwand vorbringen *vt*, Einspruch erheben *vt*

range of items Bereich der Positionen *m (des Leistungsverzeichnisses)*

rate Preis *m*, Ansatz *m*

rate of exchange Wechselkurs *m*

rate of pay Lohnsatz *m*

rate of progress of the works Arbeitsfortschritt *m*

reassemble *vt* wieder zusammenbauen *vt*

receipt Empfang *m*, Erhalt *m*

receive *vt* erhalten *vt (bekommen)*

receiver Konkursverwalter *m*, Zwangsverwalter *m*

reclamation work Landgewinnungsarbeit(en) *f (pl)*

recognise *vt* erkennen *vt*, anerkennen *vt*

recognised day of rest anerkannter Ruhetag *m*, gesetzlicher Feiertag *m*

recommend *vt* empfehlen *vt*, vorschlagen *vt*

record Unterlage *f*, Beleg *m*, Aufzeichnung *f*, Bericht *m (schriftlich)*

recover *vt* wiedererlangen *vt*, eintreiben *vt*

recoverable eintreibbar *adj (z. B. Kosten)*, zurückzuverlangen *adj (z. B. Kosten)*

recovery Eintreibung *f*, Beitreibung *f*, Erstattung *f*

recreation area Erholungsgebiet *n*

recruit *vt* anwerben *vt*, einstellen *vt*

recruitment Anwerbung *f*, Einstellung *f*

rectification Nachbesserung *f*, Richtigstellung *f*, Nachbearbeitung *f*, Mängelbeseitigung *f*

rectify loss or damage, to *vt* Verluste oder Schaden beseitigen *vt*

reduce *vt* herabsetzen *vt*, reduzieren *vt*, vermindern *vt*

reduction Verringerung *f*, Minderung *f*

re-execution erneute Ausführung *f*

re-export Wiederausfuhr *f*

refer to *vt*, *vi* hinweisen auf *vt*, verweisen auf *vt*, beziehen auf, sich *vefl*

reference Bezug *m*, Empfehlung *f*, Hinweis *m*

refrigerator Kühlschrank *m*

refuse collection Müllabfuhr *f*

regard Beachtung *f*, Rücksicht *f*

regulation Bestimmung *f*, Durchführungsverordnung *f*, Rechtsverordnung *f*

reimburse to *vt* zurückzahlen *vt*, erstatten *vt*, vergüten *vt (Geldbetrag)*

reimbursement Erstattung *f*, Rückerstattung *f*, Rückzahlung *f*

reinforcing Bewehrung *f*

reinstate *vt* wiederherstellen *vt*, instandsetzen *vt*, wiederherrichten *vt*

reinstate to its original condition *vt* wiederherrichten in ursprünglichem Zustand *vt*

reinstatement Wiederherstellung *f*

reject materials *vt* Material(ien) zurückweisen *vt*, Material(ien) nicht abnehmen *vt*

rejection Zurückweisung *f*, Abnahmeverweigerung *f*, Nichtabnahme *f*

relate to *vi* sich beziehen auf *vrefl*

relating to in bezug auf *prep*
relative to bezüglich *prep*
release from entlassen aus *vt*, befreien von *vt*
Release from Performance Verzicht auf Vertragserfüllung *m*
relevant to anwendbar auf *adj*, erheblich für *adj*, sachdienlich für *adj*, rechtserheblich
    für *adj*
relief Rechtsschutz *m*, Unterstützung *f*
relieve of *vt* entbinden von *vt*, entlasten von *vt*
remain *vi* verbleiben *vi (i. S. von noch übrig sein)*
remainder Rest *m*, Restbestand *m*
remainder of the works Rest der Bauleistungen *m*, übrige Bauleistungen *fpl*
remedial work Abhilfemaßnahme(n) *t (pl)*, Nachbesserungsarbeit(en) *f (pl)*
remedy Rechtsmittel *n*, Rechtsschutz *m*, Rechtsbehelf *m*, Abhilfe *f*
remedy *vt* abstellen *vt (Mißstand)*, heilen *vt (auch juristisch)*, abhelfen *vt (einer Sache)*,
    beheben *vt (Mangel)*, beseitigen *vt (Mangel)*
remove *vt* entfernen *vt*
remuneration Entlohnung *f*, Vergütung *f (z. B. durch Geldbeträge)*,
    Honorar *n*
rendered inappropriate unangemessen gemacht
renewal Erneuerung *f*
rent Miete *f*
repatriation Heimführung *f*, Repatriierung *f*, Rückführung in die Heimat *f*
repay *vt* zurückzahlen *vt*
repetition Wiederholung *f*
replace *vt* ersetzen *vt*
replacement Ersatz *m*, Wiederbeschaffung *f*
replacement cost(s) Wiederbeschaffungskosten *fpl*
reproducible reproduzierbar *adj*, kopierfähig *adj*, pausfähig *adj*
repudation Unverbindlichkeitserklärung *f (z. B. bezüglich eines Vertrages)*,
    Nichtanerkennung *f*
repudiate the contract, to *vt* Vertrag für unverbindlich erklären *vt*
request Ersuchen *n*, Verlangen *n*, Bitte *f*
request *vt* bitten um *vt*, ersuchen um *vt*
require *vt*, *vi* benötigen *vt*, erfordern *vt*
requirement Erfordernis *n*, Bedingung *f*, Forderung *f*, Auflage *f*
requisite erforderlich *adj*, notwendig *adj*
responsibility Verantwortung *f*, Verantwortlichkeit *f*
responsible verantwortlich *adj*
restrict *vt* beschränken *vt*, einschränken *vt*
restricted to beschränkt auf *adj*
restriction Beschränkung *f*, Einschränkung *f*
resume *vt* wiederaufnehmen *vt*
resumption Wiederaufnahme *f (z. B. der Arbeiten)*
retain *vt* zurückbehalten *vt*, einbehalten *vt*, zurückhalten *vt*

Retention Money Einbehaltungsgeld *n*, Einbehalt von Geld *m*, einbehaltener Betrag *m*

retentions Einbehalte *mpl (von den Zwischenrechnungen)*

return Aufstellung *f (z. B. in Form einer Liste)*, Bericht *m*

reverse *vt* rückgängig machen *vt*, aufheben *vt*

revest the property in the Contractor, to *vt* Eigentum zurückübertragen an den Auftragnehmer *vt*

review *vt* durchsehen *vt*, überprüfen *vt*, nachprüfen *vt*

revised überprüft *adj*, verbessert *adj*

revoke *vt* widerrufen *vt*, zurücknehmen *vt*

reward Entgelt *n*, Belohnung *f*

riot Zusammenrottung *f*, Aufruhr *m*

riotous aufrührerisch *adj*, ausschweifend *adj*

royalty Lizenz *f*, Lizenzgebühr *f*

rubbish Abfall *m*, (Bau)schutt *m*

Ruling Language maßgebliche Sprache *f*, Vertragssprache *f*

safety at work Unfallverhütung *f*, Arbeitssicherheit *f*

samples of materials Materialproben *fpl*

sanitation sanitäre Einrichtungen *fpl*, Gesundheitmaßnahmen *fpl*

satisfaction Befriedigung *f*, Zufriedenheit *f*

satisfy *vt* zufriedenstellen *vt*, überzeugen *vt*

save harmless from *vt* bewahren vor *vt*

save in so far as abgesehen von Fällen, in denen ..., außer in Fällen, in denen ...

save that abgesehen davon, daß *conj*, nur, daß *conj*

scheme of reconstruction Sanierungsplan *m*

scope Umfang *m*, Bereich *m*, Gebiet *n*

scope of authority Bereich der Befugnis *m*, Umfang der Befugnis *m*

sea wall Küstenschutzmauer *f*, Deich *m*, Hafendamm *m*, Kaimauer *f*

search *vt* suchen *vt*

Section Teil *m*, Abschnitt *m (im Vertrag als solcher ausdrücklich festgelegt)*

secure *vt* sichern *vt*, schützen *vt*, sicherstellen *vt*

security Sicherheit *f*

sediment schichtige Ablagerung *f*, Sediment *n*

seek *vt* erbitten *vt*, ersuchen *vt*

semi-skilled labour sg = pl angelernte Arbeitskräfte *fpl*

semi-skilled workman angelernter Arbeiter *m*

sequence Abfolge *f*, Folge *f*, Reihenfolge *f*

set forth *vt* erklären *vt*, darlegen *vt*

set-off Anrechnung einer Gegenforderung *f*, Aufrechnung *f*, Verrechnung *f* *(Forderungen)*

set-off *vt* gegenrechnen *vt*, aufrechnen *vt*

setting-out Abstecken *n*, Absteckung *f*

settlement Klärung *t*, Regelung *f*

settlement of disputes Beilegung von Streitigkeiten *f*

shell Granate *f*, Sprenggeschoß *n*

shop Werkstatt *f*, Werkhalle *f*

shrinkage Schrumpfung *f*, Schwinden *n*, Schrumpfen *n*

sick bay Lazarett *n*, Krankenrevier *n*

sight-rail Visiergerüst *n*, Visiertafel *f*

Site Baustelle *f (u. U. weitere Flächen, die im Vertrag als zur Baustelle gehörig festgelegt sind)*

site operations Baustellentätigkeiten *fpl*, Arbeitsvorgänge auf der Baustelle *mpl*

skilled erfahren *adj*, Fachkenntnisse besitzend *adj*

skilled worker Facharbeiter *m (in England teilweise ohne Lehre)*, gelernter Arbeiter *m*

skilled workman Facharbeiter *m (in England teilweise ohne Lehre)*, gelernter Arbeiter *m*

sole alleinig *adj*

solely einzig und allein *adv*, ausschließlich *adv*

soluble lösbar *adj*, löslich *adj*

sonic speed Schallgeschwindigkeit *f*

source Quelle *f*, Ursprung *m*

Special Risks besondere Risiken *npl (Definition nach Klausel 65 der FIDIC-Bedingungen, nicht ganz identisch mit »Employer's Risk«, vgl. Klausel 20.4)*

specifically ausdrücklich *adv*, spezifisch *adv*

Specification technische Beschreibung *f*, technische Vertragsbedingung *f (etwa VOB Teil C entsprechend)*

specify *vt* genau beschreiben *vt*, spezifizieren *vt*

spray *vt* sprühen *vt*, versprühen *vt*, besprühen *vt*

stability Beständigkeit *f*, Stabilität *f*, Standsicherheit *f*

staff Belegschaft *f*, Mitarbeiterstab *m*, Personal *n*

stagnant stehend *adj*, stillstehend *adj*

standard Norm *f*, Anforderung *f*

state *vt* festlegen *vt*, festsetzen *vt*, darlegen *vt*

statement Aufstellung *f*, Darlegung *f*

Statement at Completion Aufstellung bei Fertigstellung *f*, Fertigstellungsmeldung *f (mit vorläufiger Schlußrechnung)*

Statute Gesetz *n*, Statut *n*

stipulation Bedingung *f*, Vereinbarung *f*, Vertragsklausel *f*

store *vt* einlagern *vt*, lagern *vt*

strengthen *vt* stärken *vt*, verstärken *vt*

subcontract Nachunternehmervertrag *m*, Subunternehmervertrag *m*

subcontracting Weitervergabe *f*

Subcontractor Subunternehmer *m*, Nachunternehmer *m*

subject to *adj* vorbehaltlich *adj*

submission Einreichung *f*, Vorlage *f*, Unterbreitung *f*

submit *vt* unterbreiten *vt*, vorlegen *vt*

subsequent nachträglich *adj*

subsequently anschließend *adv*, nachfolgend *adv*

substantial completion wesentliche Fertigstellung *f*

substantial quantities wesentliche Mengen *fpl*

substantially im wesentlichen *adv*, weitgehend *adv*

substantiate *vt* begründen *vt*, glaubhaft machen *vt*

substantiation Begründung *f*, Glaubhaftmachung *f*

substitute *vt* ersetzen *vt*

substitution Ersetzung *f*, Ersatz *m*

sub-surface conditions Untergrundverhältnisse *npl*

successor Nachfolger *m*, Rechtsnachfolger *m*

suffer *vt, vi* dulden *vt*, erlauben *vt*, gestatten *vt*

sufficiency Angemessenheit *f*, Vollständigkeit *f*, Zulänglichkeit *f*

sufficient genügend *adj*, ausreichend *adj*

suggestion Vorschlag *m*

suit Antrag *m*, Rechtsstreit *m*

suitability Angemessenheit *f*, Eignung *f*, Übereinstimmung *f*

suitable brauchbar *adj*, geeignet *adj*, angemessen *adj*

superintend *vt* beaufsichtigen *vt*, überwachen *vt*

superintendence Aufsicht *f*, Oberaufsicht *f*, Leitung *f*

supervise *vt* beaufsichtigen *vt*, überwachen *vt*

supplement *vt* ergänzen *vt*

supplementary ergänzend *adj*, nachträglich *adj*

supply Versorgung *f*, Lieferung *f*

supply *vt* bereitstellen *vt*, liefern *vt*

surety Bürge *m*, Bürgschaft *f*

surety bond for performance Erfüllungsbürgschaftsurkunde *f*

surface Oberfläche *f*

surplus materials Überschußmaterial(ien) *n, (pl)*

surroundings Umgebung *f*, Umgegend *f*

suspend *vt* unterbrechen *vt*

suspension of work Aussetzen der Arbeiten *n*, Unterbrechung der Arbeiten *f*

sustain destruction, to *vt* Zerstörung erleiden *vt*

Table of Exchange Rates Wechselkurstabelle *f*

take account of *vt* berücksichtigen *vt*

take effect *vt* Gültigkeit erlangen *vt*

take into account *vt* berücksichtigen *vt*, in Betracht ziehen *vt*

take into consideration *vt* berücksichtigen *vt*, in Betracht ziehen *vt*

take out insurance *vt* Versicherung abschließen *vt*

take over *vt* abnehmen *vt*, übernehmen *vt*

taking over of Sections Abnahme von Abschnitten *f*, Übernahme von Abschnitten *f*

Taking-Over Certificate Abnahmebescheinigung *f*

task Aufgabe *f*

temporary measure zeitweilige Maßnahme *f*

Temporary Works zeitweilige Bauten *mpl*, Hilfsbauwerke *npl*

Tender Angebot *n*

tender stage Ausschreibungsstadium *n*

tendering procedure Ausschreibungsverfahren *n*

terminate vt beenden vt *(Vertrag)*, kündigen vt *(Vertrag)*
termination Beendigung f, Kündigung f
terms of appointment Bedingungen der Beauftragung f
terms of insurances Bedingungen der Versicherungen fpl *(wie sie in den Ausschreibungsunterlagen gefordert werden)*
test readings Testergebnisse npl
tests not provided for nicht vorgesehene Prüfungen fpl *(laut Vertrag)*
Tests on Completion Prüfungen bei Fertigstellung fpl *(vor der Abnahme der Arbeiten)*
the like derartig(es) adj
third-party insurance Haftpflichtversicherung f
thoroughly gänzlich adv, völlig adv, vollkommen adv
Time for Completion Ausführungsfrist f, Fertigstellungszeit f, Vertragsfrist f
time for payment Zahlungsfrist f
to the extent in dem Ausmaß n, in dem Umfang m
tonnage Lastgebühr f, Schiffszoll m
toxic giftig adj, toxisch adj
trade Handwerk n, Baugewerbe n, Handel m
trademark Schutzmarke f, Warenzeichen n
tradesman Handwerker m, Einzelhändler m, Händler m
translation Übersetzung f *(z. B. eines Textes)*
trustee Treuhänder m, Vermögensverwalter m
unaltered unverändert adj
unavoidable result unvermeidbares Ergebnis n
UNCITRAL Arbitration Rules UNCITRAL – Schiedsgerichtsordnung f *(UNCITRAL = United Nations Commission on International Trade Law)*
uncover vt freilegen vt, aufdecken vt
under seal gesiegelt adj *(etwa: notariell beglaubigt)*
undertake an obligation vt Verpflichtung übernehmen vt, sich verpflichten vrefl
undesirable unerwünscht adj
undue unangemessen adj, unnötig adj
unexpired nicht abgelaufen adj, noch in Kraft befindlich adj
unfulfilled obligations nicht erfüllte Verpflichtungen fpl
unlawful rechtswidrig adj, ungesetzlich adj
unless sofern nicht conj, wenn nicht conj, außer wenn conj
unperformed unerfüllt adj, ungetan adj
unskilled workman ungelernter Arbeiter m, Hilfsarbeiter m
urgent dringend adj, eilig adj
use of sums Verwendung der Beträge f
usurp vt aneignen, sich vrefl *(widerrechtlich)*, an sich reißen vt
utilise vt benutzen vt, verwenden vt, ausnutzen vt
valid gültig adj, rechtsgültig adj
validity Gültigkeit f
valuation Bewertung f, Wertbestimmung f
value Wert m

value *vt* bewerten *vt*, einschätzen *vt*, Preis bestimmen *vt*

variation Bauvertragsänderung *f*, Leistungsänderung *f (gegenüber der ursprünglichen vertraglichen Leistung)*, Änderung *f*, Abwandlung *f*, Bauausführungsänderung *f*

vary *vt, vi* abändern *vt*, verändern *vt*, variieren *vi, vt*

vehicle Fahrzeug *n*, Beförderungsmittel *n*

verify *vt* beweisen *vt*, bestätigen *vt*

vest in s.o. *vt* übertragen, jemandem *vt*, verleihen, jemandem *vt*

vesting of Contractor's Equipment Übereignung der Geräte des Auftragnehmers *f*

vice versa umgekehrt *adv*, wechselseitig *adv*

vitiate *vt* ungültig machen *vt*, aufheben *vt*

void nichtig *adj*, ungültig *adj*

voluntary freiwillig *adj*, vorsätzlich *adj*

voucher Beleg *m*, Bescheinigung *f*, Zahlungsbeleg *m*

wage Arbeitslohn *m*, Lohn *m*

warranty Mängelhaftung *f*, Gewährleistung *f*

wastage Verlust *m*, Verschwendung *f*

waterborne traffic Wasserverkehr *m*

wayleave Wegerecht *n (ersetzt durch "right of way")*

welfare Wohlergehen *n*, Wohlfahrt *f*

whether ... or sei es ... oder *conj*

withdraw *vt* zurücknehmen *vt*, zurückziehen *vt*

withhold *vt* zurück(be)halten *vt*, vorenthalten *vt*

withholding Vorenthalten *n*, Zurück(be)halten *n*

without prejudice to unbeschadet *prep*, ohne Schaden für *m*

wording Formulierung *f*, Wortlaut *m*

working knowledge of a language praktisch anwendbare Kenntnisse in einer Sprache *fpl*

workmanlike fachgemäß *adj adv*, fachgerecht *adj adv*

workmanship Ausführung in bezug auf Qualität der Arbeit *f*, handwerkliches Fachkönnen *n*, Handwerksarbeit *f*

Works of Civil Engineering Construction Ingenieurbauarbeiten *fpl*, Ingenieurbauleistungen *fpl*

workshop Werkstatt *f*, Werkhalle *f*

wreckage Trümmer *npl*, Trümmerhaufen *m*

written discharge schriftliche, rechtswirksame Bestätigung *f*

written undertaking schriftliche Verpflichtung *f*

zoning permission Baunutzungsgenehmigung *f*

9. Musterbriefe und Mitteilungen in Englisch für den Auftragnehmer (mit Kommentar)
9. Standard Letters and Notices in English für Use by the Contractor (with comments)

Summary of the Standard Letters and Notices for use by the Contractor under the Conditions of Contract for Works of Civil Engineering Construction Fourth Edition.

Ref.	Subject	Contract Clause(s)
1.	Agreement or objection to assignment by the Employer	1.1 (a)
2.	Request for written notification of the delegated powers of the Engineer	2.2
3.	Dissatisfaction with an instruction of the Engineer's Representative	2.3 (b)
4.	Request for consent to sublet	4
5.	Request for clarification of ambiguity or discrepancy in the documentation and possible additional cost	5.2
6.	Request for additional information, disruption of progress	6.3
7.	Notice of delay in the issue of any drawing or instruction	6.4
8.	Submission of design work for approval	7.2
9.	Performance Security	10.1
10.	Advice that Performance Security has been provided	10.1
11.	Notice of Not Foreseeable Physical Obstructions or conditions on site	12.2/44
12.	Notice of legally or physically impossible work	13.1/55.1
13.	Submission of Programme	14.1
14.	Cash Flow Estimate to be submitted	14.3
15.	Request for reimbursement of costs in correcting inaccurate setting out data	17.1
16.	Reimbursement for Exploratory Works	18.1
17.	Letter advising of Empoyers liability to insure the works after issue of Taking-Over Certificate	20.1
18.	Claims loss or damage in respect of Employer's Risks	20.43
19.	Evidence and Terms of Insurance	25.1
20.	Notice of fossils, geological or archaeological interest	27.1
21.	Claims for reimbursement of additional costs and extension of time	27.1
22.	Request for the reimbursement of costs associated with Patent Rights	28
23.	Notification of damage to a road or bridge on the route to site	30.3
24.	Letter to Engineer requesting payment for services provided	31.2
25.	Return of Labour and Contractor's equipment	35.1
26.	Application for cost of samples	36.2
27.	Request for extensions of time and cost reimbursement where tests not provided for	36.5
28.	Examination of work before covering up	38.2
29.	Reimbursement of costs for opening up the works for inspection	38.2
30.	Disagreement with Engineers instruction to remove improper work	39.1
31.	Notice of Delay and Additional Cost arising from suspension of work	40.1

Clause 1

1.1   Definitions

1.2   Headings and Marginal Notes

1.3   Interpretation

1.4   Singular and Plural

1.5   Notices, Consents, Approvals, Certificates and Determinations

Clause 1 sets out the meanings of almost all the forms in the contract.

In reading the Contract Text it should be noticed that in general any word which begins with a capital letter represents a defined term which has the meaning given in Clause 1 and no other meaning. The only exceptions are the definitions under (g) "cost", "day", "foreign currency" and "writing" which begin with letters in the lower case.

The definitions of "Defects Liability Period" and "nominated Subcontractor" are to be found in Clause 49.1 and Clause 59.1 respectively.

Notices, consents, approvals, certificates and determinations must be given in writing and, with the exception of notices, must not be unreasonably withheld or delayed.

Clause 2

2.1   Engineer's Duties and Authority

2.2   Engineer's Representative

2.3   Engineer's Authority To Delegate

2.4   Appointment of Assistants

2.5   Instructions in Writing

2.6   Engineer to Act Impartially

This clause sets out the function duties and responsibilities of the Engineer.

In a number of the Clauses the Engineer is required to undertake due consultation with the Employer and the Contractor before making his determination and the extent of such consultations will be at the discretion of the Engineer.

Reference 1

To   Date ....
The Employer

Dear Sir

**Contractors Agreement/Objection to the Assignment
of the Contract by the Employer**

We refer to the request in your letter dated .... (/recent intimation) to
us whereby you confirmed your wish to assign your contractual rights to
.... pursuant to Clause 1.1(a) of the Conditions.

We are pleased to confirm our agreement to this request subject to satisfactory
assurances that .... are fully aware of their current and
future liabilities to us under the Contract Agreement.

(Alternatively – We regret that we are unable to agree to your request and
would suggest that we meet urgently to discuss this matter further.)

Yours faithfully

....
Contractor Ltd

Reference 2

To   Date …………
The Engineer

Dear Sir

**Request for notification of the
Delegated Powers of the Engineer**

With reference to Clause 2.2 of the Conditions we note that we have yet to receive written notice of the powers delegated to your Representative.

You will be aware that to permit the efficient administration of the Contract both the Employer and ourselves require written notice of such delegated powers as soon as possible as required by Clause 2.3 of the Conditions.

In the meantime we are contractually unable to accept instructions from your Representative other than those in respect of supervision, testing and examination of materials and workmanship incorporated into the works and the present situation may/will disrupt the progress of the works.

Yours faithfully

....
Contractor Ltd

Reference 3

To   Date...........
The Engineer

Dear Sir

**Dissatisfaction with an Instruction
of the Engineer's Representative**

We write to acknowledge receipt of Instruction No .... relating to
.... issued by your Representative.

We have considered this instruction carefully and believe this to be contrary to
the spirit and intention of the Contract and therefore question this pursuant to
Clause 2.3(b) of the Conditions and request that this be
confirmed/reversed/varied accordingly.

Yours faithfully

....
Contractor Ltd

Reference 4

To   Date ....
The Engineer

Dear Sir

Request for Consent to Sublet

In accordance with the requirements of Clause 4.1 of the Conditions we are
writing to seek your consent to subcontract the following work items to the
companies named -

              Item of Work   Company

We are satisfied that the Companies named have the resources and
competence to carry out the works in a satisfactory and timely manner.

Yours faithfully

....
Contractor Ltd

Reference 5

To   Date ....

The Engineer

Dear Sir

Request for clarification of Ambiguity
(and for reimbursement of extra cost)

May we draw your attention to an apparent ambiguity between the description given in Bill of Quantity Item .... and the contradictory specification item page number .... (or say between figured and scaled dimensions for.............).

We therefore request clarification of this discrepancy pursuant to Clause 5.2 of the Conditions and if you deem necessary the issue of an instruction.

Should any such instruction cause extra cost which could not have been reasonably foreseen we assume that you will be certifying an additional sum to cover the amount involved.

Yours faithfully

....

Contractor Ltd

Reference 6

To   Date ....
The Engineer
(Copy to Employer)

Dear Sir

Request for Additional Information
Disruption of Progress

Further to our discussion with your Representative and pursuant to Clause 6.3
of the Conditions we now write to confirm that the execution of the works is
likely to be delayed or disrupted unless details .... are issued by you
within a reasonable time. Such delay or disruption will incur additional
consequential costs.

Our requirements were indicated on the Programme issued to you on ....
and to avoid delay the details requested should be made available to us not
later than ....

Yours faithfully

....
Contractor Ltd

Reference 7

To   Date ....

The Enginee

Dear Sir

Notice of Delay in the issue of Information

Further to our letter reference .... dated .... and to our programme issued on the .... it has become apparent that the non receipt of the information requested is now delaying our work and we therefore give notice of delay and additional cost pursuant to Clause 6.3 of the Conditions.

It is considered that an extension of time may also be required and we therefore give notice of our request for this pursuant to Clause 44 of the Conditions.

We shall in support of the above keep contemporary records as may reasonably be necessary to support our claims pursuant to Clause 53.1 of the Conditions.

Yours faithfully

....
Contractor Ltd

Reference 8

To   Date ....
The Engineer

Dear Sir

Permanent Works Designed by the Contractor

In accordance with Clause 7.2 of the Conditions we have pleasure in enclosing our detailed drawings and design calculations for the .... and look forward to receiving your approval to these within the next seven days.

Yours faithfully

....
Contractor Ltd

Reference 9

To   Date ....
The Employer
(Copy to Engineer)

Dear Sir

Performance Security

We have pleasure in enclosing the Performance Security as required and in
accordance with Clause 10.1 of the Conditions.

This has been executed by the Institution approved by you and is in the Form
annexed to the Appendix to the Tender Documents.

We trust that this will be entirely satisfactory to you and would appreciate
your acknowledgement for our records.

Yours faithfully

....
Contractor Ltd

Reference 10

To   Date ....
The Engineer

Dear Sir

Performance Security

We are pleased to advise you that pursuant to Clause 10.1 of the Conditions
we have today provided to the Employer the Performance Security in the form
annexed to the Tender Documents and as agreed between the Employer and
ourselves as per the attached copy letter.

Yours faithfully

....
Contractor Ltd

Reference 11

To   Date ....
The Engineer

Dear Sir

Notice of Not Foreseeable Physical Obstruction or Conditions

In accordance with the requirements of Clause 12.2 of the Conditions we write to give notice that we have encountered physical obstructions on site which in our opinion were not foreseeable by an experienced contractor.

The physical obstruction is .... and located ....

Yours faithfully

....
Contractor Ltd

Reference 12

To   Date ....
The Engineer

Dear Sir

Legally/Physically Impossible Work

Pursuant to Clause 13.1 of the Conditions we write to give notice that having
examined your Drawings .... it is apparent that the work as designed
cannot be constructed because it fails to ..../or is physically
impossible to construct because ....

Since this is a matter for which we are not liable under Clause 13.1 may we
request an instruction to vary the works pursuant to Clause 51.1

Yours faithfully

....
Contractor Ltd

Reference 13

To   Date ....

The Engineer

Dear Sir

Submission of Programme

As required under Clause 14.1 of the Conditions we have pleasure in enclosing our Programme for the Works which is in the form and detail discussed with you.

As recently requested by you we also enclose a method study giving a general description of the arrangements and methods which we propose to adopt for the execution of the works.

This also gives dates for our specific requirements for information related to our programme and we shall be happy to discuss these further should this be necessary.

Yours faithfully

....

Contractor Ltd

Enc: Programme Ref ....
                Method Statement

Reference 14

To   Date ....
The Engineer

Dear Sir

Cash Flow Estimate

Pursuant to Clause 14.3 of the Conditions we have pleasure in enclosing our
Cash Flow Estimate for the Contract and trust that you will find this adequate
for your purposes.

We anticipate that there will be adjustments required from time to time and we
shall arrange to issue revised Cash Flow Estimates on a quarterly basis and
trust that this will be acceptable.

Yours faithfully

....
Contractor Ltd

Enc: Cash Flow Estimate

Reference 15

To   Date ....
The Engineer

Dear Sir

**Request for reimbursement of costs in correcting
inaccurate setting out data**

We refer to your drawing No .... which gives details of setting out points,
lines and levels of reference for all parts of the Works.

It has now become apparent that the drawing is inaccurate in so much that
.... and that we have as a direct result of working to the
information given incurred expense in correcting the setting out and correcting
faulty construction work.

May we therefore request that the additional costs that we have incurred be
reimbursed to us pursuant to Clause 17.1 of the Conditions.

To enable you to determine an addition to the Contract Price in accordance
with Clause 52 we are maintaining contemporary records and these are
available to you to assist your determination.

Yours faithfully

....
Contractor Ltd

Reference 16

To
The Engineer

Date ....

Dear Sir

Boreholes and Exploratory Excavation

Further to your Representative's recent request we are writing to confirm that we have completed the exploratory excavation work.

This work is not covered by either a Bill of Quantities item or included therein as a provisional sum.

May we therefore request an instruction under the provisions of Clause 51, pursuant to Clause 18.1 of the Conditions.

Yours faithfully

....

Contractor Ltd

Reference 17

To   Date ....

The Engineer

Dear Sir

**Employer's Liability to insure the Works after
the issue of the Taking-Over Certificate**

Now that you have confirmed that you will be issuing the Taking-Over
Certificate for Section .... of the Works/Taking-Over
Certificate for the whole of the works may we draw your attention to the fact
that the care and insurance of that Section/whole of the works will pass to the
Employer and that the Employer should be made aware of this to avoid the
possibility of the works being uninsured as a result of the operation of Clause
20.1 of the Conditions.

Yours faithfully

....

Contractor Ltd

Reference 18

To   Date ....
The Engineer

Dear Sir

**Claim for reimbursement of the cost of repairs
in respect of an Employer's Risk**

We refer to your instruction to carry out rectification works arising
from ....

Since this requirement has arisen as a direct result of one of the Employer's
Risks as listed under Clause 20.4 of the Conditions we shall require you to
determine the cost of the work involved and for this to be added to the contract
sum as provided for pursuant to Clause 20.3 of the Conditions.

Yours faithfully

....
Contractor Ltd

Reference 19

To   Date ....
The Engineer

Dear Sir

Evidence and Terms of Insurance

We are writing to confirm that pursuant to Clause 25.1 of the Conditions that we are providing the policies of Insurance to the Employer.

The Insurances effected are consistent with the general terms agreed prior to the issue of the Letter of Acceptance.

Yours faithfully

....
Contractor Ltd

Clause 27

27.1   Fossils

Items of value or interest discovered on the site are deemed to be the absolute property of the Employer.

The Contractor is required to take all reasonable precautions to preserve such articles and is required to tell the Engineer immediately and to follow his instructions.

The Contractor will be entitled to an extension of time under Clause 44 of the Conditions and reimbursement of his costs in complying with the Engineer's instructions.

Reference 20

To   Date ....
The Engineer

Dear Sir

**Notice of the Discovery of an Item of Geological
and/or Archaeological Interest**

In accordance with Clause 27.1 of the Conditions we write to give you notice
of the discovery on site of ....

We are complying with the general obligations of Clause 27.1 to take
reasonable precautions to protect the find and would ask for your immediate
instruction for dealing with this discovery.

As a result of this obligation we have to advise you that the works are now
being delayed and we shall be seeking an extension of time and
reimbursement of our additional costs.

Yours faithfully

....
Contractor Ltd

Reference 21

To
The Engineer

Date ....

Dear Sir

**Reimbursement of Additional Costs and Extension of Time arising
from the Discovery of an Item of Geological/Archaeological Interest**

We refer to the recent discovery on site of .... and your
subsequent instructions which we are able to confirm have now been complied
with.

As a result of complying with your instructions the works have been delayed
and additional costs have been incurred.

We have maintained such contemporary records as we feel necessary or as
may be required by you and these are attached to support our claim for
additional costs and for an extension of time pursuant to Clause 44.

We look forward to your early determination of this application pursuant to
Clause 27.1.

Yours faithfully

....
Contractor Ltd

Enc:

Clause 28

28.1   Patent Rights

The Contractor is required to indemnify the Employer from all claims for infringement of any patent rights design trademark or other protected rights in relation to the Contractor's equipment, materials or plant except where the infringement results from compliance with the Engineer's design or specification

28.2   Royalties

The Contractor is required to pay all costs for obtaining materials for the Works.

Reference 22

To   Date ....
The Engineer

Dear Sir

**Request for the Reimbursement of the Costs Associated with
Patent Rights/Royalties in respect of Varied Works**

As a result of your Instruction No .... which varies the works we have
incurred Patent Rights/Royalty charges and associated costs.

The total cost incurred amounts to .... and we are requesting
that such amount be added to the Contract price pursuant to Clause 28 of the
Conditions.

Yours faithfully

....
Contractor Ltd

Clause 30

The Contractor is required to take all reasonable precautions to avoid damage to roads or bridges and to select routes and distribute loads so as to limit the amount of extraordinary traffic which will arise.

Unless the Contract specifies otherwise the Contractor is responsible for and shall pay the cost of alterations and strengthening bridges and roads necessary for the transport to site of the Contractor's Equipment or Temporary Works and shall indemnify the Employer against any claim arising from damage.

Should damage arise due to the transport of plant or materials the Contractor is required to inform the Engineer and Employer. Clause 30.3 sets out the procedure.

The procedure is similar for Waterborne Traffic.

Reference 23

To   Date ....
The Engineer
(Copy to Employer)

Dear Sir

**Notification of Damage to a Road or Bridge
on the Route to Site**

We are writing to advise you that pursuant to Clause 30.3 of the Conditions we
have been made aware of damage caused to the road communicating with the
site (or bridge on the route to the site) located at .... and arising
from the transport of construction plant (or materials).

We have received a claim from the Ministry of Roads (name of Authority)
being the authority responsible and entitled to present such a claim and append
details of this for your information.

Yours faithfully

....
Contractor Ltd

Enc:

Clause 31

31.1   **Opportunities for Other Contractors**

31.2   **Facilities for Other Contractors**

Under these clauses the Contractor is required to allow other contractors employed by the Employer, the Employer's own workmen and also local Authority workmen working on or near the Site on any work not forming part of the contract all reasonable opportunities for carrying out their work.

The Contractor shall if requested by the Engineer make available any roads for which he is liable to maintain or if he permits the use of any Temporary Works or Contractor's Equipment, or provides any other services then the Contractor is to be paid.

Reference 24

To   Date ....
The Engineer

Dear Sir

Facilities provided for a duly Constituted Authority

In accordance with your Instructions dated .... we are writing to confirm
that we have now made available to ...., a duly constituted authority,
facilities for which we are responsible for the maintenance and (or special
facilities for which we are responsible) consisting of ....

We confirm that the charges involved for the use (or service provided) are as
the attached details pursuant to Clause 31.2 of the Conditions and we trust that
these will be added to the Contract price in accordance with the provisions of
Clause 52.

Yours faithfully

....
Contractor Ltd

Enc:

Clause 35

35.1   Returns of Labour and Contractor's Equipment

This clause requires the Contractor to maintain a record in a prescribed form of his labour and equipment and to submit this as required to the Engineer.

Reference 25

To   Date ....
The Engineer

Dear Sir

Return of Labour and Equipment

As discussed with you we attach herewith our return of staff, labour and
equipment on site for week ended .... pursuant to Clause 35.1
of the Conditions.

The form which is in the detail requested will now be submitted weekly in
arrears.

Yours faithfully

....
Contractor Ltd

Enc

Clause 36

All materials, plant and workmanship must be in accordance with the Contract and the Engineer's instructions and tested as required by the Engineer in accordance with the Contract.

The Contractor shall provide all the necessary facilities for testing and shall provide the samples for testing at his own expense if this is clearly intended by the Contract.

The Contractor is required to bear the cost of making any test if this is clearly intended by the Contract and in the case of load tests and tests on executed work, where such tests are described in sufficient detail to enable a price to be provided in the Tender.

The Contractor is required to bear the cost of all other tests if the work or materials fail to satisfy the Engineer.

Otherwise the Engineer after due consultation will determine an extension of time and reimbursement of cost to the Contractor.

Reference 26

To   Date ....
The Engineer

Dear Sir

Application for the Cost of Samples

We refer to your instruction for the supply of samples of ....

These have now been supplied and since the supply was clearly not provided for in the Contract application is made for the reimbursement of the cost of these pursuant to Clause 36.2 of the Conditions.

Yours faithfully

....
Contractor Ltd

Reference 27

To   Date ....
The Engineer

Dear Sir

**Request for determination pursuant to Clause 36.5
of the Conditions**

Further to your Instruction dated ....testing has been carried
out on .... and you have confirmed that these tests have been
completed to your satisfaction and that the materials/plant/workmanship were
found to be in accordance with the Contract requirements.

As these tests were not provided for in the Contract and as a result delay to our
programme and additional costs have been incurred, we are writing to request
that pursuant to Clause 36.5 of the Conditions you determine the extension of
time to which we are entitled and also the amount of the costs to be added to
the Contract Price.

We attach our record of the delay incurred and the total costs which were
involved.

Yours faithfully

....
Contractor Ltd

Enc

Clause 37

37.1   **Inspection of Operations**

37.2   **Inspection and Testing**

37.3   **Dates for Inspection and Testing**

37.4   **Rejection**

37.5   **Independent Inspection**

The Engineer and any person authorised by him shall have access to the site and off site workshops and places and the Contractor is to offer every facility for this.

The Engineer may inspect and test the materials and plant to be supplied and the Contractor shall obtain permission for this. Such inspection or test will not relieve the Contractor of his obligations.

The Engineer and Contractor are to agree times and places for inspection and testing and the Engineer should give notice. If the Engineer does not attend the Contractor may proceed with the test and forward the results to the Engineer who must accept them. If the test does not take place or is a failure the Engineer may issue rejection giving his reasons and the Contractor must remedy the failure. Any costs due to a repetition of the test must be borne by the Contractor.

The Engineer may delegate inspection and testing to an independent inspector in accordance with Clause 2.4, 14 days notice has to be given to the Contractor.

Clause 38

38.1   Examination of Work before Covering up

38.2   Uncovering and making openings

The Contractor shall afford full opportunity for the Engineer to check and measure any such part of the Works which is about to be covered up.

The Contractor should give notice to the Engineer who should either attend without reasonable delay.

The Contractor is to uncover any part of the Works and make good any part of the Works as the Engineer should instruct.

If Clause 38.1 has been complied with and the work inspected has been found to be in accordance with the Contract then the Contractor will be paid for the opening up and reinstatement.

Reference 28

To   Date ....
The Engineer

Dear Sir

Examination (and measurement) of Work before Covering Up

We are writing to give you notice pursuant to Clause 38.1 that the following
works .... located at .... are about to be
covered up and that these works are available or will be available on
.... for examination by you.

Will you please arrange to attend for examination and/or measurement without
delay or advise us should you feel your attendance is not necessary.

Yours faithfully

....
Contractor Ltd

Clause 39

Clause 39.1	**Removal of Improper Works Materials and Plant**
Clause 39.2	**Default of the Contractor in Compliance**

The Engineer may issue instructions for the removal and proper re-execution of any materials, plant or workmanship or design by the Contractor which are not in accordance with the Contract.

In the case of Default by the Contractor in failing to comply with the Engineer's Instructions within the time specified or a reasonable time the Employer may engage others to execute the work at the Contractor's expense.

Reference 29

To   Date ....
The Engineer

Dear Sir

**Reimbursement of Costs for Opening Up the
Works for Inspection**

We refer to your Instruction .... being the opening up of works for
Inspection.

Further to your inspection you have expressed satisfaction with the work
opened up and having complied with Clause 38.1 of the Conditions we now
request that the costs together with the cost of making good be added to the
Contract Sum pursuant to Clause 38.2 of the Conditions.

Our records to substantiate the costs incurred are attached and we trust will be
of assistance in the determination of the cost.

Yours faithfully

....
Contractor Ltd

Reference 30

To   Date ....

The Engineer

Dear Sir

Removal of Improper Work

We refer to your Instruction No .... requiring us to remove .... on the basis that we have improperly constructed this by using materials which do not comply with the Specification.

We have now looked at this matter carefully and it is our opinion that the materials used comply fully with the Contract Conditions and that as such their removal should not be required pursuant to Clause 39.1 of the Conditions but should be the subject of a Variation order issued under Clause 51.1 of the Conditions.

Yours faithfully

....
Contractor Ltd

Clause 40

40.1   Suspension of Work

40.2   Engineer's Determination following suspension

40.3   Suspension lasting more than 84 days

If the Engineer instructs, the Contractor is to suspend the progress of the works or any part of it and to properly protect and secure the works as the Engineer feels necessary for the period of the suspension.

Unless the suspension is either provided for in the contract or is the Contractor's responsibility, or is necessary due to the weather, the proper execution or safety of the works (for a reason not being the Employer's responsibility) the Contractor will be reimbursed.

The Engineer will determine the extension of time and costs to be granted to the Contractor.

If a suspension of all or any part of the works for which the Contractor is to be compensated lasts for 12 weeks, the Contractor can give notice requiring permission to proceed within four weeks. If permission is not given, the Contractor may give notice and treat the part of the works as omitted or, where all the works were suspended, terminate the works under Clause 69.1

Reference 31

To   Date ....
The Engineer

Dear Sir

Notice of Delay and Additional Costs
arising from Suspension of Work

We refer to your instruction .... to suspend the progress of the
contract works/that part of the works and write to give notice of delay and
extra cost arising from your instruction pursuant to Clause 40.1 of the
Conditions.

This suspension is not to the best of our knowledge attributable to items (a) –
(d) of Clause 40.1.

We shall maintain such contemporary records as may be required by you to
substantiate our additional costs and to support our request for an extension of
time pursuant to Clause 44.

Yours faithfully

....
Contractor Ltd

Reference 32

To   Date ....
The Engineer

Dear Sir

Request for Permission to Proceed with Suspended Works

We refer to your instruction .... to suspend the progress of the contract works/that part of the works and note that 84 days have now elapsed from the date of your instruction.

We write therefore to give notice pursuant to Clause 40.3 of the Conditions requiring permission within 28 days to proceed with the suspended work.

Yours faithfully

....
Contractor Ltd

Reference 33

To   Date ....
The Engineer

Dear Sir

Notice to Treat Suspended Work as Omitted from Contract

We refer to our letter dated .... seeking your agreement to
proceed with the contract works/part of the works and note that the period of
28 days have now elapsed since our request to proceed.

We write therefore to give notice pursuant to Clause 40.3 that we elect to treat
the suspension as an event of default by the Employer and terminate our
employment under the Contract in accordance with the provisions of Clause
69.1 of the Conditions/an omission of the suspended part of the Contract under
Clause 51.

Yours faithfully

....
Contractor Ltd

Clause 41

41.1   Commencement of Works

This clause defines the commencement date for the start of the Project.

Once the tender has been accepted the Employer has a period of time as defined in the Appendix to Tender to instruct the Engineer to issue a notice to commence.

When the Contractor has received the Engineer's Notice, time commences to run and the Contractor is obliged to proceed with the Works with due expedition and without delay.

Reference 34

To   Date ....
The Engineer

Dear Sir

Acknowledgement of Commencement of Works

We acknowledge with thanks your notice to commence the Works issued
pursuant to Clause 41.1 of the Conditions requesting us to commence as soon
as this is reasonably possible.

Your notice was received today and we confirm that the date of receipt will be
the Commencement Date for the purposes of the Contract.

Yours faithfully

....
Contractor Ltd

Clause 42

42.1	**Possession of Site and Access Thereto**
42.2	**Failure to Give Possession**
42.3	**Rights of Way and Facilities**

Unless specifically provided otherwise the Employer is required to hand over possession of so much of the site and such access as necessary to enable the Contractor to commence and proceed with the execution of the Works in accordance with his programme or reasonable proposals for the Contract.

If the Contractor suffers delay and/or incurs costs from the failure of the Employer to give possession as required by Clause 42.2 the Engineer is required to grant an extension of time and costs.

The Contractor shall bear all costs and charges for any special or temporary rights of way and/or additional facilities outside of the site for the purposes of the Works.

Reference 35

To   Date ....
The Engineer
(Copy to Employer)

Dear Sir

Proposals for Commencement

In accordance with Clause 42.1 we are writing to give you notice of our
reasonable proposals for commencing and proceeding with the execution of
the Works.

These are set out in the attached sheets which we trust will be found
satisfactory.

Yours faithfully

....
Contractor Ltd

Clause 43

43.1 Time for Completion

This clause sets out the obligation upon the Contractor to complete the works within a particular time as stated in the Appendix to Tender.

The Contractor is required to substantially complete the works within the time stated subject to any extensions of time granted.

If the Works have been divided into Sections then each Section is required to be completed within the period stated subject to any extensions of time granted for that Section.

Clause 44

44.1   Extension of Time for Completion

44.2   Contractor to Provide Notification and Detailed Particulars

44.3   Interim Determination of Extension

Clause 44 provides the system for extension of time to be granted. If one of the events occurs such as to fairly entitle the Contractor to an extension of time for completion then the Engineer having first consulted with the parties must grant one.

The events giving grounds for an extension are:-

Additional or Extra Work

Other causes »referred to in these Conditions«

Exceptionally adverse climatic conditions

Delays caused by the Employer

Special Circumstances.

The Contractor is to give notice of the delay within 28 days and is to give detailed particulars within 28 days later.

If the event has a continuing effect provision is made for interim particulars and then final particulars and for the Engineer to make interim determinations and after due consultation final determinations. No final review of extension may reduce extensions already determined.

Reference 36

To   Date ....
The Engineer
(Copy to Employer)

Dear Sir

Application for Extension of Time

In accordance with the provisions of Clause 44.2(a) we write to give notice that an event has occurred within the last 28 days which is such as fairly to entitle us to an extension of the time for completion of the works or a section thereof.

The event was .... and item (a) – (e) of Clause 44.1 applies.

Yours faithfully

....
Contractor Ltd

Reference 37

To   Date ....
The Engineer

Dear Sir

Detailed Particulars of Claim

Further to our letter dated .... giving notice of an event which
fairly entitles us to an extension of time we now write in accordance with
Clause 44.2(b) to enclose detailed particulars of the extension of time to which
we consider ourselves entitled in relation to (give details of the nature of the
event referred to in the notice given under Clause 44.2(a)).

Yours faithfully

....
Contractor Ltd

Enc

Reference 38

To   Date ....
The Engineer

Dear Sir

Interim/Final Particulars of Claim

In accordance with the requirements of Clause 44.3 we enclose interim/final particulars in respect of the event referred to in our letter dated ....

The event referred to has had a continuing effect such that it has not been practicable for us to submit detailed particulars within the period of 28 days referred to in Clause 44.2(b).

Yours faithfully

....
Contractor Ltd

Enc

131

Clause 45

45.1   Restriction on Working Hours

Subject to any provision to the contrary in the Contract the Contractor is not entitled to work at night or on locally recognised days of rest such as weekends without the agreement of the Engineer, except in a case of emergency in which case the Contractor has to immediately advise the Engineer.

Where it is customary to work multiple shifts the restriction is not applicable.

Reference 39

To

The Engineer

Date ....

Dear Sir

Request for Permission to Work Night/Weekend Shifts

We are writing to request that in order to complete the works to comply with the Time for Completion/in response to your letter to expedite progress of the Works in accordance with Clause 46.1, permission be given for work to continue on night/weekend shifts pursuant to Clause 45.1 of the Conditions.

Yours faithfully

....

Contractor Ltd

Clause 46

46.1   Rate of Progress

If for any reason, which does not entitle the Contractor to an Extension of Time, the rate of progress of the Works is at any time in the opinion of the Engineer too slow to comply with the Time for Completion, Clause 46 enables the Engineer to require the Contractor to accelerate the pace of the Works to complete on time.

The Contractor may be given permission to work twenty four hours per day.

The Employer is entitled to recover any extra supervision costs which may arise.

Clause 47

47.1   **Liquidated Damages for Delay**

47.2   **Reduction of Liquidated Damages**

Should the Contractor fail to complete the Works or any specified section of the Works by the Time for Completion the Employer may deduct or recover from the Contractor the daily amount specified in the Contract as Liquidated Damages up to the limit specified.

If parts of the works are handed over the amount of liquidated damages is reduced proportionately.

Clause 48

48.1   **Taking-Over Certificates**

48.2   **Taking Over of Sections or Parts**

48.3   **Substantial Completion of Parts**

48.4   **Surfaces requiring Reinstatement**

Clause 48 provides for the Engineer to issue a Certificate referred to as a Taking-Over Certificate which states the date on which in his opinion the Works were substantially complete.

The procedure is for the Contractor to give notice when he feels the work to be complete and the Engineer agrees and issues his Certificate or gives notice specifying the works which are necessary to be done before he is able to issue his Certificate.

The Contractor is entitled to receive a Taking-Over Certificate within 21 days of completing the specified work.

Taking-Over Certificates may be issued for any Section of the Works, or any substantial part of the Works which have been completed to the satisfaction of the Engineer or uncompleted parts of the Works which have been occupied by the Employer.

Under Clause 48.3 discretion is given to the Engineer to issue an early Taking-Over Certificate in respect of complete but unoccupied parts of the Works. The Certificate would not cover ground or surfaces requiring reinstatement unless the Certificate expressly says so.

Reference 40

To   Date ....
The Engineer
(Copy to Employer)

Dear Sir

Taking-Over Certificate

We are writing to give you notice pursuant to Clause 48.1 of the Conditions that the whole of the Works have now been substantially completed, and have satisfactorily passed the Tests on Completion specified in the Contract.

Should this be necessary we undertake to finish any outstanding work during the Defects Liability Period.

Yours faithfully

....
Contractor Ltd

Reference 41

To   Date ....
The Engineer
(Copy to Employer)

Dear Sir

Taking Over of Sections or Parts

We are writing to give you notice pursuant to Clause 48.2 of the Conditions that .... (Section or Part) has been substantially completed and has satisfactorily passed the Tests on Completion specified in the Contract and/has been occupied or used by the Employer.

Should this be necessary we undertake to finish any outstanding work during the Defects Liability Period.

Yours faithfully

....
Contractor Ltd

Clause 49

This Clause gives a definition of the Defects Liability Period as an agreed period which will extend from the date/dates given on the Taking-Over Certificates.

The Contractor has to complete any items of outstanding work and to remedy any defects during this period or within 14 days of its expiration.

This work of remedying defects is carried out at the Contractor's cost unless it was not his responsibility in which case it would be treated as a variation.

Should the Contractor fail to carry out the remedial works within a reasonable time the Employer may engage others and charge the Contractor accordingly.

Reference 42

To   Date ....
The Engineer

Dear Sir

Clarification of Works of Repair

We refer to the Schedule of Defects issued pursuant to Clause 49.2 and write
to advise you that in our opinion the following items ....

        (a)   ....
        (b)   ....
        (c)   ....

are defects which are not attributable to any neglect or failure on our part to
comply with any obligation expressed or implied under the Contract.

As we regard these items of defects to have arisen from other causes we
request that the value in making good be therefore assessed and paid for as
additional work in accordance with Clause 52 pursuant to Clause 49.3 of the
Conditions.

Yours faithfully

....
Contractor Ltd

Clause 50

50.1   Contractor to Search

This clause requires the Contractor if instructed by the Engineer in writing to search for the cause of any defect, shrinkage or other fault in the Works which appear at any time prior to the end of the Defects Liability Period.

Subject to whose responsibility the fault turns out to be the Contractor will either be required to bear the cost of repair or rectification himself or will receive additional payment.

Reference 43

To

Date ....

The Engineer

Dear Sir

Request for Reimbursement of the Costs Associated with Instruction to Search for the Cause of a Defect

Further to your instruction dated .... requiring us to provide the appropriate facilities to determine the cause of the defect noted we are writing to confirm that this has now been done and we must advise you as follows:-

The search and investigation have shown that the defect reported to us cannot be attributed to any neglect or failure on our part under the Contract nor to the use of materials or workmanship not in accordance with the Contract and accordingly we request that the costs which we have incurred be added to the Contract Sum pursuant to Clause 50.1 of the Conditions.

Yours faithfully

....

Contractor Ltd

Clause 51

51.1   **Variations**

51.2   **Instructions for Variations**

This clause empowers the Engineer to order any variation of the form, quality or quantity of the Works or any part thereof that may, in his opinion, be necessary and for that purpose, or if for any other reason it shall, in his opinion, be appropriate, he shall have the authority to instruct the Contractor to do and the Contractor shall do any of the following:

(a)   increase or decrease the quantity of any work included in the Contract

(b)   omit any such work (but not if the omitted work is to be carried out by the Employer or by another Contractor)

(c)   change the character or quality or kind of any such work

(d)   change the levels, lines, position and dimensions of any part of the Works

(e)   execute additional work of any kind necessary for the completion of the Works

(f)   change any specified sequence or timing of construction of any part of the Works

Such variations are to be valued in accordance with Clause 52 unless the issue of an instruction to vary the Works is necessitated by some default of or breach of contract by the Contractor.

The Contractor should obtain the Engineer's written instruction for a variation unless this is purely for an increase or decrease in the quantities stated in the Bill of Quantities.

Clause 52

52.1	**Valuation of Variations**
52.2	**Power of Engineer to Fix Rates**
52.3	**Variations Exceeding 15 per cent**
52.4	**Day Work**

This clause lays down the basis for the Valuation of Variations. The rates and prices set out in the Contract are to be used where the varied work is of a similar nature failing which suitable rates and prices are to be agreed or fixed by the Engineer. Until such time as rates are agreed or fixed on account payments are to be made.

If the rates and prices contained in the Contract are inappropriate or inapplicable to the varied work suitable rates or prices shall be agreed – in the event of disagreement the Engineer shall have the power to fix an appropriate rate or price and to advise the Contractor accordingly, as before the Engineer is required to make on account payments for the varied work.

The Contractor is required to give notice within 14 days of the Engineer's instruction and before he starts work if he intends to claim extra payment or a varied rate or price. Similarly the Engineer is required to give notice of his intention to omit work or to vary a rate or price.

If on the issue of the Taking-Over Certificate for the whole of the Works it is found that the variations amount to more than 15 per cent of the adjusted contract price an addition or omission to the contract sum may be agreed or determined by the Engineer having regard to the Contractor's site and general overhead costs of the Contract.

The Engineer is empowered to issue an instruction that any varied work shall be executed on a day work basis at the rates and prices set out in the day work schedules attached to the Contract.

Reference 44

To   Date ....

The Engineer

Dear Sir

Confirmation of Instruction

We write to confirm your oral instructions issued by .... in respect of .... in accordance with the provisions of Clause 51.2 of the Conditions.

May we ask that as required by Sub-Clause 2.5 of the Conditions that you issue the instruction in writing and may we confirm that it will be our intention to claim extra payment under Clause 52.2 for these varied works.

Yours faithfully

....

Contractor Ltd

Reference 45

To   Date ....
The Engineer

Dear Sir

Notification of a Varied Rate

In accordance with the requirements of Clause 52 we write to give notice
pursuant to Clause 52.2(a) of the Conditions of our intention to claim a varied
rate for .... since the nature of the work arising from your Variation
Instruction is such as to render the Contract rate inapplicable for the following
reason............

Yours faithfully

....
Contractor Ltd

Reference 46

To   Date ....
The Engineer

Dear Sir

Notification of Variations Exceeding 15 per cent

It has become apparent that on the issue of the Taking-Over Certificate for the whole of the Works it will be found that there has been an increase (decrease) greater than 15 per cent of the Effective Contract Price, i.e. the Contract Price excluding Provisional Sums and day works allowances.

In the event of this occurring we will wish the amount of the Contract Price to be adjusted having regard to our site and general overheads.

We deem this to be the notice, if required, pursuant to Clause 52.3 of the Conditions.

Yours faithfully

....
Contractor Ltd

Reference 47

To   Date ....
The Engineer

Dear Sir

Daily Notification of Resources Expended on Day Work

As required pursuant to Clause 52.4 of the Conditions we attach our day work records noting

(a)	Items of day work being undertaken
(b)	Details of labour expended
(c)	Details of plant, materials being used for works carried out on ....

May we ask that the duplicate copy be signed and returned to our office on site.

Yours faithfully

....

Contractor Ltd

Enc

Reference 48

To   Date ....
The Engineer

Dear Sir

Monthly Day Work Statement

As required pursuant to Clause 52.4 we have pleasure in enclosing the priced
statement of the labour, material and Contractor's equipment which is covered
by our Daily Notifications of Resources Expended on Day Work for the period
dated ....

Yours faithfully

....
Contractor Ltd

Enc

Clause 53

The Intention of these clauses is to set out a disciplined procedure of dealing with claims which will be of advantage to both parties to the Contract.

A Contractor intending to make a claim for additional payment pursuant to any Clause of these Conditions or otherwise must give notice that he will do so within 28 days of the event.

Once the event has happened he must keep such contemporary records as may reasonably be necessary to support any claim he may subsequently wish to make and any such records that the Engineer may require. The Contractor is to allow the Engineer to inspect these records and to provide any copies required.

Within 28 days or such other time as may be agreed the Contractor is required to send a detailed claim to the Engineer. Where the event giving rise to the claim has a continuing effect the Contractor is required to send regular interim accounts followed by a final claim within 28 days of the end of the effects resulting from the event.

If the Contractor has failed to give notice and keep records or provide details of any claim that he wishes to make then his entitlement will be limited to that which can be proved by contemporary records that do exist.

The Contractor shall be entitled to have included in any interim payment such claim or parts of claims for which he has supplied sufficient particulars to enable the Engineer to determine the amount due.

Reference 49

To   Date ....
The Engineer
(Copy to Employer)

Dear Sir

Notice of Claim

In accordance with the requirement set down in Clause 53.1 of the Conditions
we are writing to give you notice of our intention to claim additional payments
pursuant to Clause ....
The event which is as follows .... occurred on the
.... and we are keeping such contemporary records as we feel
necessary to substantiate our claim.

Yours faithfully

....
Contractor Ltd

Reference 50

To   Date ....
The Engineer

Dear Sir

Substantiation of Claim
Ref No ....

Further to our letter dated .... giving notice of our intention to
submit a claim, we now enclose pursuant to Clause 53.3 of the Conditions our
account giving full and detailed particulars of the amount claimed together
with full details of the reasons and grounds upon which our claim is based.

Yours faithfully

....
Contractor Ltd

Enc

**The above or the following notice is to be given within 28 days or such
other time as may be agreed with the Engineer for the giving of such
notice under Clause 53.1 of the Conditions.**

Reference 51

To   Date ....
The Engineer

Dear Sir

Substantiation of Claim
Ref No ....

Further to our letter dated .... giving notice of our intention to submit a claim, we now enclose pursuant to Clause 53.3 of the Conditions our account giving full and detailed particulars of the amount claimed together with full details of the reasons and grounds upon which our claim is based.

As the event is of a continuing nature this account is submitted as an interim account and further accounts will be forwarded to you in due course. In accordance with Clause 53.3 we shall send to you a Final Account within 28 days of the end of the effects resulting from this event.

May we ask that you advise us as to the intervals at which you require further interim accounts and whether the attached and any further accounts are to be copied to the Employer.

Yours faithfully

....
Contractor Ltd

Clause 54

All Contractor's Equipment, Temporary Works and Materials that the Contractor brings onto the site are for the exclusive use and execution of the Works and may only be removed with the consent of the Engineer.

The Employer will not generally be liable for the loss of or damage to any of the said Contractor's Equipment, Temporary Works or materials.

The Employer will use his best endeavour to assist the Contractor obtain clearance of his equipment materials and other things required for the Works through Customs and where equipment has been imported will assist the Contractor to obtain Government consent for the re-export of such equipment pursuant to the term of the Contract.

All equipment hire contracts must be arranged so as to permit the Employer to continue the hire of the equipment in the event of a termination under Clause 63.

In the event of the Employer entering into any agreement to continue the hire of the equipment any costs incurred will be recoverable from sums otherwise due to the Contractor under Clause 63.

All subcontracts are to include a similar clause permitting the Employer to take over the equipment and materials of subcontractors.

Nothing in Clause 54 shall be deemed to imply any approval of the Engineer of the materials or other matters referred to therein.

Reference 52

To   Date ....

The Employer

Dear Sir

Assistance with Customs Clearance

We refer to our Contract with you for the construction of ....

As a requirement for the Works we have placed orders for various items of construction plant and materials and we would ask for your assistance in obtaining clearance through Customs for the items concerned pursuant to Clause 54.3 of the Conditions.

May we request an early meeting with you to discuss this matter more fully.

Yours faithfully

....

Contractor Ltd

Reference 53

To   Date ....

The Employer

Dear Sir

Assistance with Re-Export of Construction Equipment

We refer to our Contract with you for the construction of .... and write to confirm our wish to re-export the following items of constructional equipment imported for the purpose of the works

       (a)   ....
       (b)   ....
       (c)   ....

May we ask for your assistance in obtaining Government consent to such re-export pursuant to Clause 54.4 of the Conditions and to request an early meeting with you to discuss the matter more fully.

Yours faithfully

....
Contractor Ltd

Reference 54

To   Date ....
The Engineer

Dear Sir

**Consent for the removal of Temporary Works and
Equipment from Site**

We have now completed the sections of work for which the following items of
temporary works and equipment were brought onto site and now wish to
remove them for re-export

        (a)   ....
        (b)   ....

May we therefore have your consent for the removal from site of these items
pursuant to Clause 54.1 of the Conditions.

Yours faithfully

....
Contractor Ltd

Clause 55

55.1   Quantities

The quantities set out in the Bills of Quantities are the estimated quantities for the Works and are not to be taken as the actual and correct quantities of the Works to be executed.

Clause 56

56.1 Works to be Measured

The Works are to be measured by the Engineer in accordance with Clause 60 and when any measurement is to take place the Engineer is to give notice to the Contractor who is required to attend to assist the measurement and supply all particulars required.

Should the Contractor fail to attend the Engineer's measurement will be taken as correct.

Where measurements are to be based on records and drawings prepared by the Engineer, the Contractor when called upon to do so in writing shall within 14 days attend to, examine and agree such records and drawings. Should he not attend as required the records and drawings shall be taken as correct.

If after examination of such records and drawings the Contractor does not agree the same or does not sign the same as agreed they shall nevertheless be taken to be correct unless the Contractor within 14 days of such examination, lodges notice with the Engineer of the respects in which such records and drawings are claimed by him to be incorrect. The Engineer on receipt of such notice shall review the records and drawings and either confirm or vary them.

Reference 55

To   Date ....
The Engineer

Dear Sir

Notice of Disagreement with Measurement Records
Clause 56.1

We refer to the measurement records and drawings issued to us under your
reference No .... and dated .... and regret that we have been unable to
agree these considering them to be incorrect in the following respects:-

        (a)   ....
        (b)   ....
        (c)   ....
        (d)   ....

Yours faithfully

....
Contractor Ltd

**Alternatively should the Contractor agree the records and drawings he
should confirm his agreement to the records and drawings as issued and as
signed by him.**

Clause 57

57.1   **Method of Measurement**

57.2   **Breakdown of Lump Sum Items**

The Works shall be measured net notwithstanding any general or local custom, except where otherwise provided for in the Contract.

The Contractor is required to give a breakdown of the lump sum items in his Tender within four weeks of the letter of acceptance.

Clause 58

58.1	**Definition of "Provisional Sum"**
58.2	**Use of Provisional Sums**
58.3	**Production of Vouchers**

The term "Provisional sum" is defined, and the Contractor will be entitled to only such amounts determined by the Engineer in respect of work covered by the provisional sums. The Engineer may issue instructions in relation to provisional sums for the execution of work or for the supply of goods, materials, plant or services by

(a)   the Contractor who will then be entitled to an amount equal to the value thereof determined in accordance with Clause 52

(b)   a nominated Subcontractor, as hereinafter defined, in which case the sum to be paid to the Contractor shall be determined and paid in accordance with Sub-Clause 59.4.

Unless the work is valued in accordance with the contract rates and prices, the Contractor is required to produce to the Engineer all quotations, invoices, vouchers and accounts or receipts in connection with expenditure in respect of Provisional Sums.

Clause 59

The term "Nominated Subcontractors" is defined.

The Contractor is not required to employ any nominated Subcontractor against whom he may raise reasonable objection or who refuses to enter into a sub-contract which is in accordance with the conditions of the main contract and which indemnifies the Contractor from any negligence by the nominated Subcontractor, or his workmen and against any misuse by him or them of any Temporary Works provided by the Contractor.

Should any nominated sub-contract include a design or specification obligation the contract and the nominated sub-contract should expressly say so. The nominated Subcontractor must indemnify the Contractor in respect of such design and specification obligations.

For all work executed by any nominated Subcontractor the Contractor will be entitled to the price due to the Subcontractor, payment under Clause 52 for any attendance and the profit percentage specified in the Bill of Quantities or Appendix to Tender.

Before issuing any certificate to the Contractor under Clause 60, the Engineer is entitled to proof that previously certified sums for nominated Subcontractor's work have been properly discharged. Unless the Contractor can show that he has reasonable grounds for refusing to make such a payment and proves that he has so notified the nominated Subcontractor, the Employer may make direct payment and deduct the equivalent sum from any sums due to be paid by him to the Contractor.

The Engineer will show this deduction on his next certificate which should not be delayed.

Reference 56

To   Date ....
The Engineer

Dear Sir

Objection to the Nomination of a Nominated Subcontractor

We refer to your Instruction No ....and dated .... nominating ....
for .... and regret to advise you of our objection to the
nomination pursuant to Clause 59.2 of the Conditions on the ground that:-

Possible objections are:-
  (a) The nominated firm will not enter into a subcontract with the same
       liabilities, obligations towards the Contractor which are imposed on
       the Contractor towards the Employer by the main contract.
  (b) The nominated firm will not indemnify the Contractor from and
       against any negligence by the nominated Subcontractor or his
       workmen and from and against any misuse by him or them of any
       constructional plant or temporary works provided by the Contractor.
  (c) The nominated Subcontractor is believed to have financial problems.
  (d) The nominated Subcontractor has been unable to demonstrate that
       it has the skilled labour, management capabilities for the work
       involved.
  (e) The nominated Subcontractor is unable to meet the main contract
       programme dates.

Under the circumstances we would appreciate your further instruction.

Yours faithfully

....
Contractor Ltd

Reference 57

To   Date ....

The Engineer

Dear Sir

Design Liability under a Nominated Subcontract

We acknowledge receipt of your Instruction No .... dated ....
nominating Messrs .... for the ....

May we draw your attention to the fact that several matters in the proposed
subcontract documents relate to design and specification matters that were not
expressly stated in the Main Contract pursuant to Clause 59.3. Likewise in
respect of these matters the documents are not specific on the questions of
indemnity as to the adequacy of the design.

Under the circumstances therefore we must either receive from you a
statement from the Employer indemnifying us against any liability for the
adequacy of the subcontract design or object to the nomination of this
particular Company under Clause 59.2 of the Conditions.

Yours faithfully

....
Contractor Ltd

Reference 58

To   Date ....
The Engineer

Dear Sir

Proof of Payment to a Nominated Subcontractor

Further to your letter dated .... requesting proof of payment to nominated Subcontractors pursuant to Clause 59.5 of the Conditions we now enclose copies of receipted remittance advice forms in respect of the following companies:

        (a)   ....
        (b)   ....
        (c)   ....

We trust that the above is satisfactory.

Yours faithfully

....
Contractor Ltd

Enc

Reference 59

To   Date ....
The Engineer

Dear Sir

Notice of withholding payment to a Nominated Subcontractor

With reference to Clause 59.5(a) of the Conditions we are writing to advise
you that in our opinion we have reasonable cause for withholding payment to a
nominated Subcontractor and have withheld the sum of .... from ....
for the following reason .... against Certificate No ....

Attached for your further information is a copy of the letter dated ....
which we have written to the nominated Subcontractor advising of our action
as required pursuant to Clause 59.5(b).

Yours faithfully

....
Contractor Ltd

Enc

Clause 60

This clause is of particular interest to the Contractor since it sets down a mechanism for payment.

Each month the Contractor is required to submit to the Engineer, six copies of his monthly valuation including on site materials, fluctuations and claims.

The Engineer shall then within 28 days of receiving the Contractor's statement certify to the Employer the sum due less retention and any sums other than liquidated damages which the Contractor owes the Employer.

The Engineer will not certify if the net amount of the Certificate is less than the Minimum Amount of Interim Certificates stated in the Appendix and the Contractor has submitted his performance security.

Upon the issue of the Taking-Over Certificate one half of the retention money will be certified or if the Certificate relates to a Section or part only then the appropriate proportion of the retention money will be released.

The remaining retention monies will be certified at the end of the last Defects Liability Period although it should be noted that the Engineer may retain sufficient retention monies to cover the cost of any outstanding defect.

The Engineer may by any Interim Payment Certificate make any correction or modification in any previous certificate issued by him.

Within 84 days of the Taking-Over Certificate the Contractor shall submit to the Engineer a Statement at Completion which will be his valuation of all of the Works and Claims up to substantial completion. Additionally he shall provide an estimate of any future entitlements. The Engineer is then to provide a further Interim Payment Certificate.

Within 56 days of the issue of the Defects Liability Certificate the Contractor is required to submit to the Engineer his draft final statement together with supporting documents.

Once this is agreed the Contractor has then to prepare and submit to the Engineer the final statement as agreed referred to as the Final Statement.

The Contractor has then to provide a written discharge confirming that once the amount set out in the Final Statement has been paid and the performance security has been returned then he will have been paid in full and final settlement.

Within 28 days of receiving the Final Statement and written discharge the Engineer has to issue a Final Certificate setting out the total contract valuation and the balance of any monies outstanding between the Employer and the Contractor.

The Employer will not be liable to the Contractor for any claim which was not included in the Final Statement, and unless this arose after the issue of the Taking-Over Certificate in the Statement at Completion.

Interim Payment Certificates shall be paid within 28 days of their delivery to the Employer or in the case of the Final Payment Certificate within 56 days. Interest at the rate entered in the Appendix will accumulate on all sums unpaid from the due date.

Reference 60

To   Date ....
The Engineer

Dear Sir

Monthly Statement

We enclose for your necessary action our Statement No .... for period
dated .... pursuant to Clause 60.1 of the Conditions.

Yours faithfully

....
Contractor Ltd

Reference 61

To   Date ....
The Engineer

Dear Sir

Notification of Non Payment

We refer to our monthly statement No .... delivered to you on
the .... and regret to notice that we have not received payment against this
within the stipulated period of twenty eight days pursuant to Clause 60.10 of
the Conditions.

Under the circumstances interest entitlement at the rate stated in the Appendix
to Tender will be included in our next statement.

Yours faithfully

....
Contractor Ltd

Reference 62

To   Date ....
The Engineer

Dear Sir

Release of Retention Money

We write to acknowledge receipt of the Taking-Over Certificate for the whole/part of the Works and would ask that you now certify the payment of one half/appropriate proportion of the Retention Money pursuant to Clause 60.3 of the Conditions.

Yours faithfully

....
Contractor Ltd

Reference 63

To   Date ....
The Engineer

Dear Sir

Statement at Completion

We enclose our Statement at Completion together with supporting documents pursuant to Clause 60.5 of the Conditions.

This shows the Final Value of all work done in accordance with the Contract up to the date stated in the Taking-Over Certificate.

In addition we have stated the further sums which we consider to be due together with an estimate of amounts which we consider will become due to us under the Contract.

Yours faithfully

....
Contractor Ltd

Enc

Reference 64

To

Date ....

The Engineer

Dear Sir

Draft Final Statement

Further to issue of the Defects Liability Certificate we now enclose for your consideration our draft final statement, in the form agreed with you, together with supporting documentation pursuant to Clause 60.6 of the conditions.

This shows the value of all work done in accordance with the Contract and further sums which we consider to be due to us.

Should your require any further information please do not hesitate to contact us.

In the meantime the issue of a further interim certificate would be very much appreciated.

Yours faithfully

....

Contractor Ltd

Enc

Reference 65

To   Date ....
The Employer
(Copy to Engineer)

Dear Sir

Discharge pursuant to Clause 60.7 of the Conditions

The Final Statement has now been submitted to the Engineer and pursuant to Clause 60.7 of the Conditions we write to confirm that the total of the Final Statement represents full and final settlement of all monies due to us arising out of or in respect of the Contract. This discharge will only become effective after the payment due under the Final Certificate issued pursuant to Sub-Clause 60.8 has been made and the Performance Security referred to in Sub-Clause 10.1 has been returned to us.

Yours faithfully

....
Contractor Ltd

Clause 61

61.1   Approval only by Defects Liability Certificate

This clause together with Clause 62 makes it clear that there is only one Defects Liability Certificate which is issued at the expiration of the last Defects Liability Period.

Clause 62

62.1   Defects Liability Certificate

62.2   Unfulfilled Obligations

Clause 62 provides for the issue of the Defects Liability Certificate and recognition that the Contract has been completed.

The Certificate shall be issued to the Contractor within 28 days of the end of the Defects Liability Period, or the last of the periods if the Works have previously been handed over in sections, or after all works instructed under Clauses 49 and 50 have been completed to the Engineer's satisfaction.

The second portion of the Retention Money is released in accordance with the conditions set out in Sub-Clause 60.3 regardless of whether or not the Defects Liability Certificate is issued.

The issue of the Defects Liability Certificate does not affect the obligations to each other of the Employer and the Contractor.

Reference 66

To   Date ....
The Engineer

Dear Sir

Release of Second Half of Retention Money

May we draw your attention to the fact that the Defects Liability Period
expired on the .... and that the other half of the Retention
Money should be certified for payment pursuant to Clause 60.3 of the
Conditions.

We look forward to receiving payment of these monies within 28 days of the
above date.

Yours faithfully

....
Contractor Ltd

Reference 67

To
The Engineer

Dear Sir

Defects Liability Certificate

We now consider that all works of amendment, reconstruction, remedying defects, shrinkages and other faults required to be carried out under Clauses 49 and 50 of the Conditions have now been completed.

May we therefore request the issue of the Defects Liability Certificate pursuant to Clause 62.1 of the Conditions.

Yours faithfully

....
Contractor Ltd

Clause 63

This clause defines the events which under the conditions constitute events of default by the Contractor.

Should the Contractor become insolvent in one of the forms listed or in the event of the Engineer being able to certify one of the other breaches of Contract, then the Employer can give 14 days notice to the Contractor and then enter the site and the Works and terminate the employment of the Contractor and be free to complete the Works by other means using the Contractor's plant materials temporary works etc.

Once termination has taken place the Engineer has to certify the value of the Works completed and the value of used and partially used materials, any Contractor's equipment and any temporary works.

The Employer is not obliged to pay any further monies to the Contractor until after the Defects Liability Period and then only when the costs of completion and remedying defects, damages for delay (if any) and all other expenses incurred have been ascertained and deducted from the sum which would have been payable to the Contractor.

The contractor shall if instructed by the Engineer within 14 days of the termination assign sub-contracts and supply agreements to the benefit of the Employer.

Clause 64

64.1   Urgent Remedial Work

If during the course of the Works or during the Defects Liability Period the Engineer considers that urgent work is necessary for the safety of the works and the Contractor does not comply with an instruction to carry out the work at once, the Employer may use other Contractors.

If the Contractor was responsible for the work, the Employer may deduct his costs from monies that were due to the Contractor.

The Engineer is to notify the contractor of the occurrence of any such emergency as may be reasonably practicable.

Clause 65

The Contractor shall not be responsible for the consequences of special risks (other than to work condemned under the provisions of Clause 39) in respect of certain designated events.

The special risks are defined and the manner in which the Contractor will be compensated for any loss or damage sustained as a result of special risks is set out.

Damage caused by the impact or explosion of various explosives of war including missiles, mines, bombs etc. are special risks.

The Contractor is to be paid only costs of the execution of the Works which arise from the Special Risks and is to notify the Engineer of such costs forthwith.

If war should break out whether declared or not and materially affects the Works, the Contractor is to continue to use his best endeavours to complete the execution of the Works but the Employer shall be entitled to terminate the Contract by giving notice.

If war causes the termination of the Contract the Contractor is to remove his equipment and to give similar facilities to his Subcontractors. After termination the Contractor will be paid for all work executed, for all costs incurred and including all costs of demobilisation, less any outstanding balances due from the Contractor in respect of advance payments.

Reference 68

To   Date ....

The Engineer

Dear Sir

Damage to Works by Special Risks

We write to give notice that as a result of damage to the Works by a special risk in the form of .... , reimbursement is sought pursuant to Clause 65.3 of the Conditions.

May we ask that you determine the amount to be added to the Contract Price in accordance with Clause 52 of the Conditions together with a sum at fair market value for the cost of replacement of our items of Contractor's Equipment damaged at the same time.

Yours faithfully

....
Contractor Ltd

183

Reference 69

To   Date ....
The Engineer

Dear Sir

**Increased Costs arising from the Consequence of a
Special Risk**

We write to give notice pursuant to Clause 65.5 of the Conditions that we have
and are continuing to incur increased costs as a consequence of the occurrence
of a special risk namely ....

We are maintaining contemporary records to substantiate the costs involved
and to assist you to determine the amount which should be added to the
Contract Price.

Yours faithfully

....
Contractor Ltd

Clause 66

66.1 Payment in Event of Release from Performance

If a situation arises which makes it impossible or unlawful for one or both parties to meet their obligations under the Contract the parties are released from further performance and Clause 65.8 of the Conditions applies.

Clause 67

These clauses introduce a procedure for dealing with disputes.

Any dispute shall first be referred to the Engineer in writing with a copy given to the other party. The Engineer is requested to give notice of his decision within twelve weeks to both the Contractor and to the Employer.

Unless the Contract has already been ended the Contractor continues to proceed with the works and both the Contractor and the Employer are required to give effect to the Engineer's decision.

Should either the Employer or the Contractor be disatisfied with any decision of the Engineer or if the Engineer fails to give a decision within the time allowed then either party has ten weeks to give notice of their intention to commence arbitration. If the parties fail to give such notice then the Engineer's decision will become final and binding on the parties.

Once the notice of arbitration has been given the parties are required to try and settle the dispute amicably.

If neither the Engineer's decision or the attempt to settle the dispute by amicable settlement have resulted in a solution then the matter is referred to arbitration under the Rules of Conciliation and Arbitration of The International Chamber of Commerce.

Clause 67.3 sets down the powers that the Arbitrator will have and the arbitration may be commenced before or after the completion of the Works.

Where the Engineer's decision has become final and binding either party may, if the other party fails to comply with that decision, refer the matter to arbitration without the need for a further Engineer's decision or any attempt at amicable settlement.

Reference 70

To   Date ....
The Engineer
(Copy to Employer)

Dear Sir

Request for an Engineer's Decision

We are writing to advise you that a dispute has arisen between the parties to the Contract and pursuant to Clause 67.1 of the Conditions we are referring this to you for a decision.

The nature of the dispute is as follows:-

Yours faithfully

....
Contractor Ltd

Clause 68

68.1	**Notice to Contractor**
68.2	**Notice to Employer and Engineer**
68.3	**Change of Address**

Clause 68 might appear to be self evident but is most important particularly where overseas works are being carried out and specifies the addresses of the parties to which all certificates, notices or instructions are to be sent.

The addresses to which notices are to be sent for the Employer or to the Engineer must be set out in Part II of the Conditions.

Reference 71

(1) To   Date ....
    The Engineer

(2) To
    The Employer

Dear Sirs

Notices to Contractor

Pursuant to Clause 68.1 of the Conditions we nominate the following address -

to which all certificates, notices or instructions which are to be given to us
under the terms of the Contract by the Employer or the Engineer shall be sent.

Yours faithfully

....
Contractor Ltd

**The address will include telephone, facsimile and telex numbers as
applicable and as alternatives to post or hand delivery.**

Reference 72

To   Date ....
The Employer
(Copy to Engineer)

Dear Sirs

Change of Address

We write to give notice of change of our nominated address pursuant to Clause
68.3 of the Conditions from.............................. to..............................

Yours faithfully

....
Contractor Ltd

Clause 69

69.1 **Default of Employer**

69.2 **Removal of Contractor's Equipment**

69.3 **Payment on Termination**

69.4 **Contractor's Entitlement to Suspend Work**

69.5 **Resumption of Work**

Clause 69 gives the Contractor a right to terminate his employment under the Contract or to suspend work or reduce the rate of work. In the event of the Employer failing to pay a Certificate of the Engineer within 28 days of the due date, or if he interferes with a Certificate or becomes insolvent or gives notice to the Contractor that unforseen economic reasons have made it impossible for him to continue to meet his contractual obligations then the Contractor shall be entitled to terminate his employment after giving 14 days notice.

Upon the expiry of the 14 days notice the Contractor shall remove his Contractor's Equipment from the site.

In the event of such termination the Employer is required to pay the Contractor for all work done and for all losses and damages arising out of or in connection with the termination of the Works.

As an alternative under Clause 69.4 if the Employer fails to pay the Contractor the amounts due under any certificate within 28 days of the due date, the Contractor may give 28 days notice and then suspend work or reduce the rate of work. Should this happen he will be entitled to an extension of time and the amount of such costs arising from the suspension or reduced rate of the Works.

Should the Contractor adopt the alternative and the Employer subsequently pays the Certificate and interest due then the Contractor will no longer be able to terminate the Contract and shall resume normal working as soon as is reasonably possible.

Reference 73

To

Date ....

The Employer

Dear Sir

Notice of Termination of Contract

Pursuant to Clause 69.1 of the Conditions we write to give you notice that with effect from 14 days after the giving of this notice we shall terminate our employment under the Contract.

Such notice is given on the ground that you have failed to pay the amount due against the Engineer's Certificate .... dated .... within 28 days after the time stated in Sub-clause 60.10.

Yours faithfully

....

Contractor Ltd

Alternative grounds for termination will be:-

"You have interfered with and obstructed the issue of a certificate due under the contract."

"You have given us formal notice that for unforeseen economic reasons it has become impossible for you to continue to meet your contractual obligations."

"You have become bankrupt or being a company have gone into liquidation."

All of the above notices are required to be copied to the Engineer.

Reference 74

To
The Employer
(Copy to Engineer)

Date ....

Dear Sir

Entitlement to Suspend Work

Pursuant to Clause 69.4 we write to give you notice that as a result of your failure to pay us the amount due under Engineer's Certificate .... dated .... within 28 days after the expiry of the time stated in Sub-clause 60.10 within which payment is to be made and subject to any deduction that you are entitled to make under the Contract we shall suspend work or reduce the rate of work after 28 days of the giving of this notice.

We shall keep such records as may be required for the Engineer to determine any extension of time to which we may be entitled under Clause 44 and for the amount of such costs which shall be added to the Contract Price.

Yours faithfully

....
Contractor Ltd

Clause 70

70.1   **Increase or Decrease of Cost**

70.2   **Subsequent Legislation**

Should there be a rise or fall in the cost of labour and/or materials or any other matters affecting the cost of the execution of the Works then this is to be taken into account as an addition or deduction from the Contract Price in accordance with a clause set out in Part II of the Conditions.

If after 28 days prior to the date set for the return of tenders for the Contract changes in local laws or regulations in the country in which the Works are to be executed result in additional or reduced costs these shall be determined and added to or deducted from the Contract Price.

Clause 71

71.1   Currency Restrictions

This Clause is similar to Clause 70.2 and entitles the Contractor to be reimbursed by the Employer for any loss or damage arising from currency restrictions imposed by the Government of the country in which the Works are being executed and which have taken place after the date 28 days prior to the latest date for the submission of the tender for the Works.

Reference 75

To   Date ....
The Engineer

Dear Sir

Currency Restrictions

We are writing to give notice that as a result of an imposed currency restriction which has arisen after the date 28 days prior to the date for submission of our tender for the Works a loss is being incurred and we seek reimbursement pursuant to Clause 71.1 of the Conditions.

We shall keep such records as we feel necessary to substantiate our claim and shall submit these monthly to you for inclusion with our applications for payment.

Yours faithfully

....
Contractor Ltd

Clause 72

72.1   **Rates of Exchange**

72.2   **Currency Proportions**

72.3   **Currencies of Payment for Provisional Sums**

Where the Contract provides for payment to the Contractor in whole or in part to be made in foreign currency then the exchange rate will be fixed.

Where the Employer has required the Tender to be expressed in a single currency but with payment to be made in more than one currency then Part II of the Conditions allows an alternative of a fixed currency rate otherwise the rate will be that of the Central Bank of the country in which the Works are to be executed on a date 28 days prior to the latest date for submission of tenders.

Where payment is made for Works carried out against provisional sums and the Contract provides for the payment to be made in more than one currency then the principles set out in Clauses 72.1 and 72.2 will apply.

10. Musterbriefe und Mitteilungen in Englisch für den Beratenden Ingenieur (mit Kommentar)
10. Standard Letters and Notices in English or Use by the Engineer (with comments)

Summary of the Standard Letters and Notices for use by the Engineer under the Conditions of Contract for Works of Civil Engineering Construction Fourth Edition.

Ref.	Subject	Contract Clause(s)
1.	Engineer's Authority to Delegate	2.3
2.	Revocation of Delegation	2.3
3.	Engineer's response to Notice of Dissatisfaction with Instruction	2.3(b)
4.	Consent to Sub-let	4.1
5.	Clarification of Ambiguity	5.2
6.	Response to Notice of Delay in the Issue of Information	6.3
7.	Not forseeable Physical Obstructions	12.2
8.	Not forseeable Physical Obstructions, Determination of Entitlement	12.2
9.	Programme to be Submitted	14.1
10.	Setting Out	17.1
11.	Fossils	27.1
12.	Notification of damage arising from the transport of materials or plant	30.1
13.	Facilities for Other Contractors	31.2
14.	Returns of Labour and Contractors Equipment	35.1
15.	Cost of Tests not provided for	36.5
16.	Dates for Inspection and Testing	37.3
17.	Independent Inspection	37.5
18.	Uncovering and Making Openings	38.2
19.	Default of Contractor in Compliance	39.2
20.	Determination following Suspension	40.2
21.	Commencement of Works	41.1
22.	Failure to give Possession	42.2
23.	Extension of Time for Completion	44.1
24.	Rate of Progress	46.1
25.	Rate of Progress – additional supervision costs	46.1
26.	Taking-over Certificate	48.1
27.	Taking-over Certificate – additional defects	48.1
28.	Substantial Completion of Parts	48.3
29.	Cost of Remedying Defects	49.3
30.	Contractor's Failure to Carry Out Instructions	49.4

Reference 1

To   Date ....
The Engineer's Representative
(Copy to Employer and Contractor)

Dear Sir

Engineer's Authority to Delegate

Further to your appointment as my representative for the Works, I hereby
delegate to you pursuant to Clause 2.3 of the Conditions the duties and
authorities vested in me under the following clauses:- ....

This delegation shall take effect once a copy has been delivered to the
Employer and to the Contractor.

Yours faithfully

....
Engineer

**The clauses to be delegated might be some or all of the fifty clauses where
the Engineer is referred to. Delegation should not normally be considered
in respect of Clauses 41, 44, 48, 62, 63, 65, 67 and 69.**

Reference 2

To   Date ....
The Engineer's Representative
(Copy to Employer and Contractor)

Dear Sir

Engineer's Authority to Delegate

With reference to my letter dated .... I hereby revoke the
delegation to you of the duties and authorities made pursuant to Clause 2.3 of
the Conditions in respect of the following clauses ....

This revocation shall become effective when copies of this letter have been
delivered to the Employer and to the Contractor.

Yours faithfully

....
Engineer

**The clauses to be revoked may be some or all of the clauses previously
delegated.**

Reference 3

To   Date ....
The Contractor

Dear Sir

**Notice of Dissatisfaction with an Instruction issued by the
Engineer's Representative**

We write to acknowledge receipt of your letter dated ....
concerning an Instruction No .... given by my Representative
and concerning ....

Whilst your expression of dissatisfaction has been noted I confirm the
Instruction as issued and give this response pursuant to Clause 2.3 (b) of the
Conditions.

Yours faithfully

....
Engineer

**The Engineer's response may also be to withdraw the Instruction or to
vary it by issuing further instructions.**

Reference 4

To   Date ....
The Contractor

Dear Sir

Consent to Sub-let

Further to your letter dated .... seeking permission to
subcontract certain elements of the work we are writing to give our consent
pursuant to Clause 4.1 of the Conditions for the following items of Works to
be subcontracted.

Item of Work	**Company**

Yours faithfully

....
Engineer

**Regardless of the above consents the Contractor will be fully responsible
for any defaults of the Subcontractor as if they were caused by the
Contractor himself and it would be prudent for the Engineer to draw
attention to this fact.**

Reference 5

To   Date ....
The Contractor

Dear Sir

Clarification of Ambiguity

We thank you for your letter dated .... drawing our attention
to the difference between the description in the Bill of Quantities Item
.... and Specification Item .... page number ....

This is agreed and pursuant to Clause 5.2 of the Conditions we hereby instruct
you to ....

Yours faithfully

....
Engineer

**The Engineer may of course not accept that there is any ambiguity and
will then write to give a clarification if necessary and to instruct the
Contractor to proceed with the works as specified.**

Reference 6

To   Date ....

The Contractor

Dear Sir

Notice of delay in the Issue of Information

We thank you for your letter dated .... and issued pursuant to Clause 6.3 of the Conditions in which you have claimed that non receipt of information is causing you delay and additional cost to the Works.

We have examined your programme for the Works which illustrates that the information referred to is not yet required and your actual progress on site is not such as to reasonably require such information to be available.

Under these circumstances we are unable to accept that your notice is a valid one.

Yours faithfully

....
Engineer

Should the Contractor's notice be regarded as valid the Engineer is required to confirm this and determine the extension of time which should be granted and the amount of extra cost if any which should be added to the Contract Price.

Reference 7

To   Date ....
The Contractor

Dear Sir

Notice of Not Foreseeable Physical Obstructions or Conditions

We acknowledge receipt of your letter dated .... giving notice
pursuant to Clause 12.2 of the Conditions of the encountering of physical
obstructions in the form of .... which in your opinion were
not foreseeable by an experienced Contractor.

We have carefully examined the information which was made available to you
at the tender stage namely .... and have to advise you that we
consider the matter to be one which was wholly foreseeable pursuant to Clause
12 of the Conditions and have therefore to reject your notice and claim for an
extension of time and additional cost.

Yours faithfully

....
Engineer

Reference 8

To   Date ....
The Contractor
(Copy to Employer)

Dear Sir

Notice of Not Foreseeable Physical Obstructions or Conditions

I acknowledge receipt of your letter dated .... giving
notice pursuant to Clause 12.2 of the Conditions of the encountering of
physical obstructions in the form of .... which in your
opinion were not foreseeable by an experienced contractor.

I have examined the facts put forward by you and after my consultations with
you and the Employer I have determined pursuant to Clause 12.2 that the
extension of time to which you are entitled under Clause 44 shall be
.... and the amount of the costs to be added to the
Contract Price shall be ....

Yours faithfully

....
Engineer

Reference 9

To   Date ....
The Contractor

Dear Sir

Programme to be Submitted

We are writing to draw your attention to the requirement pursuant to Clause 14.1 of the Conditions to submit within the time stated in Part II of the Conditions a programme for the Works together with a method statement setting out a general description of the arrangements and methods which you are proposing for the execution of the Works.

The form and method of programme presentation required is that set out in the tender documentation but should you require any further clarification please do not hesitate to contact me.

Yours faithfully

....
Engineer

Reference 10

To   Date ....
The Contractor
(Copy to Employer)

Dear Sir

Setting Out

We refer to your letter dated .... in which you advise us
of an error in setting out and construction as a result of incorrect data on our
drawing No ....

We therefore require you to rectify this error and pursuant to Clause 17.1 I
have determined that the amount of .... shall be added to
the Contract Price in accordance with Clause 52 of the Conditions.

Yours faithfully

....
Engineer

**The Contractor is required to rectify any error, if required to do so by the
Engineer, at his own cost unless the error is based on incorrect information
or data supplied in writing by the Engineer.**

Reference 11

To   Date …………

The Contractor

(Copy to Employer)

Dear Sir

Fossils

Thank you for your letter dated ………………………… advising of the discovery on site of ………………………….

Following my consultation with you and the Employer, I have determined pursuant to Clause 27.1 that the extension of time to which you shall be entitled under Clause 44 of the Conditions will be ………………………… and the amount of the costs to be added to the Contract Price will be …………………………

Yours faithfully

…………………………………………………………

Engineer

Reference 12

To   Date ....
The Contractor
(Copy to Employer)

Dear Sir

Notification of damage arising from the transport of materials or plant

Thank you for your letter dated .... enclosing details of a claim received from the Roads (or Bridges) Authority.

As provided for in Clause 30.3 it is my opinion that the claim received from the Authority is due to your failure to comply with the obligations under Clause 30.1.

Following my discussions with you and the Employer I have determined that the sum recoverable from you as a result of your failure will be .... and the amount will be deducted by the Employer from sums which may become due to you.

Yours faithfully

....
Engineer

Reference 13

To   Date ....

The Contractor

(Copy to Employer)

Dear Sir

Facilities for Other Contractors

We acknowledge receipt of your letter dated ....
confirming that the following facilities .... have been
made available to ....

Following an examination of the detailed records that you have provided I
have determined that pursuant to Clause 31.2 the amount of
.... should be added to the Contract Price in accordance
with Clause 52.

Yours faithfully

....

Engineer

Reference 14

To   Date ....
The Contractor

Dear Sir

Returns of Labour and Contractor's Equipment

As previously advised, I require you to provide weekly returns of staff, labour and plant employed on the Works and in the format discussed with you.

These returns are to cover the whole of your own resources and also those of approved subcontractors and are requested pursuant to Clause 35.1 of the Conditions.

Yours faithfully

....
Engineer

Reference 15

To   Date ....

The Contractor

(Copy to Employer)

Dear Sir

Cost of Tests not Provided for

I refer to your letter dated .... confirming that testing has been carried out in accordance with my Instruction No ....

As these tests were not provided for in the Contract I have, after examination of records and consultations with you and the Employer determined pursuant to Clause 36.5 that the extension of time to which you are entitled under Clause 44 will be .... and the amount of the costs which shall be added to the Contract Price will be ....

Yours faithfully

....

Engineer

Reference 16

To   Date ....
The Contractor

Dear Sir

Dates for Inspection and Testing

Following our agreement on the time and place for the inspection and/or testing of the .... I am now writing pursuant to Clause 37.3 to give you the required notice (not less than 24 hrs) of my intention to carry out the inspection/or attend the tests.

Yours faithfully

....
Engineer

Reference 17

To   Date ....
The Contractor

Dear Sir

Independent Inspection

I am unable to provide the specialised equipment for the inspection and testing
of ....

I am therefore in accordance with Clause 37.5 writing to give you notice that I
have delegated this responsibility to .... an independent
inspector whose duties and scope of authority will be
....

This appointment will become effective on the ....

Yours faithfully

....
Engineer

Not less than 14 days notice is to be given

Reference 18

To   Date ....

The Contractor

(Copy to Employer)

Dear Sir

Uncovering and Making Openings

I refer to my instruction to you to uncover .... (or make
an opening through) pursuant to Clause 38.2 of the Conditions.

As the work has been found to have been executed in accordance with the
Contract I have after due consultation with you and the Employer determined
that .... representing your costs in respect of such
uncovering (or making openings) reinstating and making good the same shall
be added to the Contract Price.

Yours faithfully

....

Engineer

Reference 19

To   Date ....
The Contractor
(Copy to Employer)

Dear Sir

Default of Contractor in Compliance

I refer to my Instruction .... and dated ....

We have agreed that the materials referred to were not in accordance with the Contract and that you are in default by not removing these within the time specified.

I have therefore after consultation with you and the Employer determined pursuant to Clause 39.2 that the costs which the Employer shall be entitled to recover from you and which may be deducted by the Employer from any monies due or to become due to you shall be ....

Yours faithfully

....
Engineer

218

Reference 20

To   Date ....
The Contractor
(Copy to Employer)

Dear Sir

Engineer's Determination following Suspension

Further to my Instruction .... to you and your subsequent
letter giving notice of delay and extra cost arising from my instruction I have
after due consultation with you and the Employer determined pursuant to
Clause 40.2 of the Conditions that the extension of time to which you shall be
entitled under Clause 44 will be .... and that the amount
of cost which shall be added to the Contract Price by reason of this suspension
shall be ....

Yours faithfully

....
Engineer

Reference 21

To   Date ....

The Contractor

Dear Sir

Commencement of Works

In accordance with Clause 41.1 of the Conditions I hereby give you notice to commence the Works as soon as is reasonably possible.

You are required to proceed with the Works with due expedition and without delay.

For the purposes of the Contract the Commencement Date will be the receipt by you of this notice.

Kindly acknowledge receipt.

Yours faithfully

....

Engineer

Reference 22

To   Date ....

The Contractor

(Copy to Employer)

Dear Sir

Failure to give Possession

Thank you for your letter dated .... advising that you have suffered delay and incurred costs from the failure on the part of the Employer to give possession of Site Area ....

This has arisen due to factors beyond the Employer's control and the matter has now been resolved.

Following my consultations with you and the Employer I have determined pursuant to Clause 42.2 that the extension of time to which you are entitled under Clause 44 shall be .... and that the amount of cost to be added to the Contract Price is ....

Yours faithfully

....
Engineer

Reference 23

To   Date ....
The Contractor
(Copy to Employer)

Dear Sir

Extension of Time for Completion

I refer to your letter dated .... and issued pursuant to
Clause 44.2 (a) of the Conditions advising of the following event
.... which was such as to fairly entitle you to an
Extension of Time for Completion of the Works.

After my consultation with you and the Employer, I have determined pursuant
to Clause 44.1 that the extension of time to which you shall be entitled will be
.... in respect of the following event
....

Yours faithfully

....
Engineer

**A similar letter pursuant to Clause 44.3 of the Conditions would be issued
in respect of an interim/final determination for an Extension of Time.**

Reference 24

To   Date ....
The Contractor

Dear Sir

Rate of Progress

Reference is made to Site Meeting Minutes No .... which sets out in detail current progress of the Works.

Having considered these I give you notice that for reasons which do not entitle you to an Extension of Time the rate of progress of the Works (or any Section) is in my opinion too slow to comply with the Time for Completion.

You are therefore required to take such steps as are necessary, subject to my consent to expedite progress so as to comply with the Time for Completion.

This notice is given as required by Clause 46.1 of the conditions and it should be noted that you shall not be entitled to any additional payment for taking such steps.

Yours faithfully

....
Engineer

Reference 25

To   Date ....
The Contractor
(Copy to Employer)

Dear Sir

Rate of Progress

Further to my letter to you dated .... requiring you to
take such steps as are necessary to expedite progress I must advise you that the
measures consented to will involve additional supervision costs.

Following my consultation with you and the Employer regarding these I have
determined pursuant to Clause 46.1 that the additional supervision costs which
shall be recoverable from you by the Employer and may be deducted by the
Employer from monies due or to become due to you amount to
....

Yours faithfully

....
Engineer

Reference 26

To   Date ....
The Contractor
(Copy to Employer)

Dear Sir

Taking-Over Certificate

We refer to your letter dated .... and issued pursuant to
Clause 48.1 of the Conditions advising that the whole of the Works have been
substantially completed and have satisfactorily passed the Tests on
Completion specified in the Contract.

We are in agreement with the above and hereby certify that in our opinion the
Works were substantially completed in accordance with the Contract on
....

Yours faithfully

....
Engineer

The Engineer may issue instructions in writing to the Contractor
specifying all the work which, in the Engineer's opinion, is required to be
done by the Contractor before the issue of such Certificate.

The Engineer shall also notify the Contractor of any defects in the Works
affecting substantial completion that may appear after such instructions
and before completion of the Works specified therein.

Reference 27

To   Date ....
The Contractor

Dear Sir

Taking-Over Certificate

We write pursuant to Clause 48.1 of the Conditions to give you notice that the following items of defect have appeared in the Works:-

Item 1 ....

Item 2 ....

These have appeared since instructions were issued to you specifying all the work which in our opinion was required to be done before the issue of a Taking-Over Certificate.

These defects will affect substantial completion.

Yours faithfully

....
Engineer

Reference 28

To   Date ....
The Contractor
(Copy to Employer)

Dear Sir

Substantial Completion of Parts

Further to your letter dated .... we are now able to
certify pursuant to Clause 48.3 of the Conditions that the following parts of the
Works:-

> 1. ....
>
> 2. ....
>
> 3. ....

have been substantially completed and have satisfactorily passed any Tests on
Completion prescribed by the Contract on ....

By the issue of this Certificate you are now deemed to have undertaken to
complete with due expedition any outstanding work in the parts of the
Permanent Works listed above during the Defects Liability Period.

Yours faithfully

....
Engineer

Reference 29

To
The Contractor
(Copy to Employer)

Date ....

Dear Sir

Cost of Remedying Defects

It has been agreed that the following items of work ....
carried out after the expiration of the Defects Liability Period are attributable
to fair wear and tear.

Accordingly we have pursuant to Clause 49.3 of the Conditions determined
that .... should be added to the Contract Price in
accordance with Clause 52.

Yours faithfully

....
Engineer

Reference 30

To   Date ....

The Contractor

(Copy to Employer)

Dear Sir

Contractor's Failure to Carry Out Instructions

Following your failure to carry out our Instructions to remedy defects, we have after consultation with you and the Employer, determined pursuant to Clause 49.4 of the Conditions that the costs which the Employer shall be entitled to recover from you and which may be deducted by the Employer from any monies that are or will become due to you are ....

Yours faithfully

....
Engineer

Reference 31

To   Date ....

The Contractor

(Copy to Employer)

Dear Sir

Contractor to Search

We refer to the issue of an Instruction No ....

It is now apparent that the defect in question is one for which you are not liable under the Contract.

We have therefore after consultation with you and the Employer determined pursuant to Clause 50.1 of the Conditions that the amount in respect of the costs of the search carried out by you to be added to the Contract Price is ....

Yours faithfully

....

Engineer

Reference 32

To   Date ....
The Contractor

Dear Sir

Variations

You are hereby instructed to carry out the works listed in the attached
Variation Order which is issued pursuant to Clause 51.1 of the Conditions.

The effect, if any, of these variations shall be valued in accordance with
Clause 52.

Yours faithfully

....
Engineer

**Clauses 52.1, 52.2 and 52.3 require that the Engineer gives notice to the
Contractor that after consultation with both the Contractor and the
Employer suitable rates or prices have been agreed and in the event of non
agreement the Engineer will determine the rates or prices or such sums are
to be added to the Contract Price.**

These notices will be copied to the Employer.

Reference 33

To   Date ....

The Contractor

(Copy to Employer)

Dear Sir

Payment of Claims

Having received from you detailed particulars of the amounts claimed and the grounds upon which your claim is based we have pursuant to Clause 53.5 of the Conditions determined that the amount in respect of your Claim No .... to which you are entitled to have included in Interim Payment Certificate No .... will be ....

Yours faithfully

....
Engineer

Reference 34

To   Date ....
The Contractor's Authorised Agent

Dear Sir

Works to be Measured

In accordance with Clause 56.1 of the Conditions we give notice of our requirement for the following parts of the Works to be measured:-

....

You are required to attend forthwith or send a qualified representative to assist in making such measurements and to supply the following particulars
....

Yours faithfully

....
Engineer

Should the Contractor or his representative fail to attend, then the measurements taken shall be regarded as the correct measurement of the Work.

Where for the purpose of measurement the Engineer has prepared records and drawings as the work proceeds he is required to give notice to the Contractor pursuant to Clause 56.1 to attend and agree these.

Reference 35

To   Date ....
The Contractor
(Copy to Employer)

Dear Sir

Definition of 'Provisional Sum'

In accordance with Clause 58.1 of the conditions we have determined that the amounts to which you are entitled in respect of the work, supply or contingencies to which the following provisional sums relate are as follows:

        Provision Sum Ref:- ....

        Work involved:-   ....

        Amount determined:- ....

Yours faithfully

....
Engineer

Reference 36

To   Date ....
* (Copy to Contractor and Employer)

Dear Sirs

Certification of Payments to Nominated Subcontractor

We certify that pursuant to Clause 59.5 of the Conditions the Contractor has failed to provide reasonable proof that payment, less retentions, included in previous certificates due to .... a nominated Subcontractor has been paid or discharged, and has failed to satisfy us in writing that he has reasonable cause for withholding or refusing to make such payments or to produce to us reasonable proof that he has so informed the above named nominated Subcontractor in writing.

Accordingly the Employer shall be entitled to pay to the above named Subcontractor directly the sum of .... which the Contractor has failed to pay, and to deduct the amount stated from any sums due or to become due from the Employer to the Contractor.

Yours faithfully

....
Engineer

 * **The Conditions do not indicate to whom this notice should be addressed.**

Reference 37

To   Date ....
The Employer
(Copy to Contractor)

Dear Sir

Final Payment Certificate

In accordance with Clause 60.8 of the Conditions we hereby certify that the
amount finally due under the Contract is as follows:-

    Final value of the Works   ....

    Less amounts previously paid by Employer   ....
                                     _____
                                       ....

    Less sums to which the Employer is entitled
    under the Contract (excluding Liquidated
    Damages under Clause 47)   ....
                                       _____

    Balance due from the Employer to the Contractor
    (or from the Contractor to the Employer)   ==================

Yours faithfully

....
Engineer

Reference 38

To   Date ....
The Employer
(Copy to Contractor)

Dear Sir

Defects Liability Certificate

We have pleasure in certifying pursuant to Clause 62.1 of the Conditions that
the date on which the Contractor has completed his obligations to execute and
complete the Works and remedy any defects therein to our satisfaction was
....

Yours faithfully

....
Engineer

Reference 39

To   Date ....
The Employer
(Copy to Contractor)

Dear Sir

Default of Contractor

We hereby certify in accordance with Clause 63.1 of the Conditions that in our opinion the Contractor has

(a)   repudiated his Contract
       or list other defaults under Clause 63.1 (b) – (e).

Yours faithfully

....
Engineer

The Employer shall then be required pursuant to Clause 63.1 to give notice to the Contractor that he will after fourteen days enter upon the Site and the Works and terminate the Contractor's employment.

Reference 40

To   Date ....
* (Copy to Employer and Contractor)

Dear

Valuation at Date of Termination

We hereby certify in accordance with Clause 63.3 of the Conditions that at the
time of the Employer's entry upon the Site and termination of your
employment the amount which had been reasonably earned by you or which
reasonably accrue to you in respect of work than actually done by you under
the Contract was .... and that the value of any unused or
partially used materials, any Contractor's Equipment and Temporary Works is
....

Yours faithfully

....
Engineer

* **The Conditions do not indicate to whom this Certificate should be
addressed.**

239

Reference 41

To   Date ....
* (Copy to Employer and Contractor)

Dear

Payment after Termination

We hereby certify in accordance with Clause 63.3 of the Conditions that the Employer's costs of execution, completion and remedying of any defects, damages for delay in completion and all other expenses have amounted to
....

We hereby certify that the sum due to the Contractor upon the due completion of the Contract amounts to .... after the deduction of the Employer's costs stated above.

Yours faithfully

....
Engineer

* The Conditions do not indicate to whom this Certificate should be issued.

Should there be a balance of monies due to the Employer then this is payable on demand.

The Employer shall not be liable to pay the Contractor any further monies until the expiration of the Defects Liability Period when this Certificate should be issued.

Reference 42

To   Date ....

The Contractor

Dear Sir

Urgent Remedial Work

We write to give you notice pursuant to Clause 64.1 of the Conditions that an event of emergency has occurred in connection with the Works and in the nature of ....

This will in our opinion necessitate urgent remedial action by you for the safety of the Works.

Yours faithfully

....

Engineer

Should the Contractor be unable or unwilling at once to do such work the Employer shall be entitled to employ others.

If such work was, in the opinion of the Engineer, work for which the Contractor was liable then the Engineer shall after due consultation with the Employer and the Contractor determine the amount which shall be recoverable from the Contractor.

Reference 43

To   Date ....
The Contractor
(Copy to Employer)

Dear Sir

Damage to Works by Special Risks

We refer to your letter dated .... giving notice of damage
caused by a special risk as defined in Clause 20.4 of the Conditions namely
....

Now that the damage to the Works has been rectified we have pursuant to
Clause 65.3 of the Conditions determined that .... should
be added to the Contract Price in accordance with Clause 52.

Yours faithfully

....
Engineer

Reference 44

To   Date ....

The Contractor

(Copy to Employer)

Dear Sir

Increased Costs arising from Special Risks

We refer to your letter dated .... giving notice pursuant to Clause 65.5 of the Conditions that you have and are continuing to incur increased costs as a consequence of the occurrence of a special risk namely ....

After our consultations with you and the Employer, we have determined pursuant to Clause 65.5 that the amount of your costs which shall be added to the Contract Price will be ....

Yours faithfully

....

Engineer

243

Reference 45

To   Date ....
The Contractor

Dear Sir

Outbreak of War

I am writing to give notice pursuant to Clause 65.6 that due to the outbreak of
war which has materially affected the execution of the Works I am with
immediate effect terminating your Contract.

Yours faithfully

....
Employer

Reference 46

To   Date ....
The Contractor
(Copy to Employer)

Dear Sir

Payment for Terminated Contract

Further to the notice of termination issued by the Employer we have pursuant
to Clause 65.8 of the Conditions determined that you shall be entitled to
payment by the Employer for all work executed prior to the date of
termination and in addition for all items as applicable set out in sub paragraphs
(a) – (f) of this Clause insofar as such amounts or items have not already been
covered by payments on account to you.

The provisions of the Clause shall apply and once we have all the appropriate
information we shall after due consultation with you and the Employer
determine any sums which are payable.

Yours faithfully

....
Engineer

Reference 47

To   Date ....
The Contractor
(Copy to Employer)

Dear Sir

Engineer's Decision

Further to your letter to me dated .... and advising of a
dispute between the contracting parties concerning ....
my decision given pursuant to Clause 67.1 of the Conditions on the matter in
dispute is as follows ....

Yours faithfully

....
Engineer

**It is not required for the Engineer to expressly state the reason for his
decision which he is required to give within twelve weeks of the receipt by
him of written notice of the dispute.**

Reference 48

To   Date ....
The Employer

To
The Contractor

Dear Sirs

Change of Address

We are writing to give prior notice pursuant to Clause 68.3 of the Conditions
of our Change of Address from that set down in Part II of the Conditions to
our new address as follows ....

Yours faithfully

....
Engineer

Reference 49

To   Date ....
The Contractor
(Copy to Employer)

Dear Sir

Entitlement to Suspend Work

I acknowledge receipt of your copy letter addressed to the Employer and giving notice of your entitlement to suspend the Works.

I have after due consideration and consultation with both you and the Employer determined pursuant to Clause 69.4 of the Conditions that the extension of time to which you shall be entitled under Clause 44 will be .... days and that the amount of the costs which will be added to the Contract Price will be ....

Yours faithfully

....
Engineer

Reference 50

To   Date ....

The Contractor

(Copy to Employer)

Dear Sir

Subsequent Legislation

Further to your claim that the recently introduced Byelaw No ....
referring to .... has resulted in additional cost to your
Contract I have after due consideration and consultation with both you and the
Employer determined that pursuant to Clause 70.2 of the Conditions the
amount to be added to the Contract Price will be ....

Yours faithfully

....
Engineer

249

11. Literaturverzeichnis zu den FIDIC-Bedingungen und anderen Bauvertragsbedingungen
11. Literature concerning the FIDIC-Conditions and similar Conditions for Construction Contracts

[1] VOB – Verdingungsordnung für Bauleistungen Teil A (DIN 1960), Teil B (1961), Teil C DIN 18299 – DIN 18451, 1992

[2] Standard Method of Measurement of Building Works, (SMM7), London 1988, Reprinted 1989 with amendment sheets

[3] A Code of Procedure of Measurement of Building Works, London 1988, with amendments 1992

[4] World Bank, Sample Bidding Documents, for (major) Civil Works, "SBD-Works", Washington D. C. December 1991

[5] Heiermann/Riedl/Rusam, Handkommentar zur VOB 7. Auflage, Wiesbaden/Berlin 1994

[6] Ingenstau/Korbion, VOB-Kommentar, Teile A und B, 12. Auflage, Düsseldorf 1993

[7] Winkler, W., VOB-Gesamtkommentar, Braunschweig

[8] Bunni, N., The FIDIC Form of Contract, Oxford 1991

[9] International Construction Law Review, London

[10] Arbitration – The Journal of the Chartered Institute of Arbitrators, London

[11] World Arbitration and Mediation Report BNA International, London

[12] Arbitration and Dispute Resolution Law Journal, London

[13] FIDIC: Guide to the Use of FIDIC Conditions of Contract for Works of Civil Engineering Construction, Fourth Edition, Lausanne 1989

[14] Sawyer, J. G., Gillot, A., The FIDIC Digest: Contractual Relationships, Responsibilities and Claims under the Fourth Edition of the FIDIC Conditions, London 1990

[15] Brendan, J. K., FIDIC C.L.A.I.M. S. Software, Dublin 1990

[16] Euro Conferences, Claims an Disputes unter the FIDIC Contract Conditions for Works of Civil Engineering Construction, London 1989

[17] Corbett, E., FIDIC 4th, A Practical Legal Guide, London 1991

[18] ICE: CESMM3: Civil Engineering Standard Method of Measurements, London 1991

[19] FIDIC: Insurance of Large Civil Engineering Projects, Lausanne

[20] FIDIC: Marked-up Copy, Showing Changes from the third edition (Conditions of Contract for Works of Civil Engineering Construction Fourth Edition 1987)

[21] FIDIC: Conditions of Contract for Electrical an Mechanical Works, Third Edition 1987, Lausanne

[22] FIDIC: Guide to the Use of FIDIC Conditions of Contract for Electrical an Mechanical Works, Lausanne

[23] FIDIC: Standard Prequalification Form for Contractors, Lausanne

[24] FIDIC: Client/Consultant Model Services Agreement (The White Book) 2nd Edition, Lausanne 1991

[25]   FIDIC: The White Book Guide with notes on documents for Consultancy Agreements, Lausanne

[26]   Lange, K., Neue Fassung der FIDIC-Vertragsbedingungen für Ingenieurbauarbeiten, Bauwirtschaft 89, Heft 3

[27]   FIDIC: Guide to the Use of FIDIC Conditions of Contract for Works of Civil Engineering Construction (The Red Book Guide), Lausanne 1989

[28]   Corbett, E., FIDIC 4th – A Practical Legal Guide – A Supplement, London 1993

[29]   Hellard, R. B., Managing Construction Conflict, London 1988

[30]   Turner, R. H., FIDIC-Conditions in the Arabian Golf Region, The International Construction Law Review, 1992 p.p. 141 – 165

12. Verzeichnis von Wörterbüchern und sonstigen Veröffentlichungen zur Erleichterung der Korrespondenz
12. List of Dictionaries and other Publications to facilitate Correspondence

[101]   Buksch, H., Wörterbuch für Baurecht, Grundstücksrecht und Raumordnung
        Deutsch/Englisch – Englisch/Deutsch, Wiesbaden/Berlin 1986
[102]   Bucksch, H., Wörterbuch für Bautechnik und Baumaschinen
        Englisch/Deutsch – Deutsch/Englisch, Wiesbaden/Berlin 1982
[103]   Dietl, C.-E., Wirtschaftswörterbuch
        Deutsch/Englisch – Englisch/Deutsch, München 1989
[104]   Glass, G., Englische Rechtssprache, Wiesbaden/Berlin 1982
[105]   Sachs, R., Commercial Correspondence, München 1987
[106]   Chappel, D., Standard Letters for Building Contractors, London 1987
[107]   Hartman, W., Hartman, T., WARNE'S Complete Letter Writer, London 1983
[108]   Benson/Benson/Ilson, The BBI Combinatory Dictionary of English – A Guide to Word
        Combinations, Amsterdam, Philadelphia 1986
[109]   Eichborn, R. v., Der große Eichborn, Wirtschaft und Wirtschaftsrecht, Deutsch/Englisch
        – Englisch/Deutsch, Düsseldorf, Wien 1982
[110]   Eichborn, R. v., Der Kleine Eichborn, Deutsch/Englisch – Englisch/Deutsch,
        Taschenwörterbuch der Wirtschaftssprache, Burscheid, 1981
[111]   Kucera, A., Compact Wörterbuch der exakten Naturwissenschaften und der Technik,
        Englisch/Deutsch – Deutsch/Englisch, Wiesbaden 1989
[112]   Stock, K. H., Wörterbuch für alle Sparten der Versicherung,
        Deutsch/Englisch – Englisch/Deutsch, 1988
[113]   Schäfer, W., Financial Dictionary, Englisch/Deutsch – Deutsch/Englisch, 1990
[114]   Schäfer, W., Management and Marketing Dictionary,
        Englisch/Deutsch – Deutsch/Englisch, München 1991

13. Anlagen
13.1 Vergleich VOB – FIDIC

13. Appendices
13.1 Comparison VOB – FIDIC

Der nachstehende Vergleich erhebt keinen Anspruch auf Vollständigkeit. Es wird insbesondere auf die Problematik der unterschiedlichen Rechtssysteme hingewiesen, die eine direkte Übertragung oft unmöglich macht.

VOB	FIDIC
Deutsches Rechtssystem (BGB)	Englisches Rechtssystem Typisch englische Vertragssprache Rechtssystem muß vereinbart werden: »law in force in...« Part II, Clause 5.
Deutsche Sprache	Ruling Language Falls keine Rechtsnorm vereinbart ist, hängt der Vertrag im »luftleeren Raum«.
Zweiseitiger Vertrag: AG-AN	Zwei Parteien: AG, AN und Engineer, letzterer hat »Schiedsrichterfunktion« und ist meist Planer und Bauüberwacher
VOB Teile A, B und C	Entsprechung zu Teil A und C fehlt in FIDIC. Spezifikationen und Aufmaßregeln müssen vereinbart werden.
§ 1 Nr. 2 VOB/B Widersprüche im Vertrag: a) Leistungsbeschreibung b) Besondere Vertragsbedingungen c) etwaige zus. Vertragsbedingungen d) etwaige zus. Technische Vertragsbedingungen e) Allgemeine Technische Vertragsbedingungen für Bauleistungen (ATV) (VOB, Teil C) f) Allgemeine Vertragsbedingungen für die Ausführung von Bauleistungen (Teil B, VOB, Teil B)	Priority of Contract Documents (5.2) a) Contract Agreement b) Letter of Acceptance c) The Tender d) Part II of these Conditions e) Part I of these Conditions f) Any other document forming part of the contract

VOB	FIDIC

§ 1 Nr. 4 VOB/B
Nicht vereinbarte Leistungen

Meist: Nominated Subcontractor

Einschränkung:
… außer wenn sein Betrieb darauf nicht
eingerichtet ist.

Einschränkung fehlt, aber aus Clause 51.1
abzuleiten

§ 2 Nr. 3 VOB/B
1) Mengenabweichungen +/– 10 %
   → vertraglicher Einheitspreis
2) Über 10 % Überschreitung
   → neuer Preis auf Verlangen
3) über 10 % Unterschreitung
   → auf Verlangen Erhöhung E. P. für
   tatsächlich ausgeführte Menge, soweit
   nicht Ausgleich bei anderen Pos.

52.1 Mengenabweichungen +/– 15 % –
→ »Effective Contract Price« –
(Provisional Sums, Daywork, etc.) =
neuer berichtigter Gesamtpreis
→ Risikozuschlag in der Kalkulation bei
Vermutung von 15 % Mindermengen!

Hinweis: § 8 VOB/B. Der Begriff der
Teilkündigung für Wegfall von Arbeiten ist in
FIDIC nicht enthalten, er wird durch
»Variations« Clause 51.1 abgedeckt, mit
Preisanpassungsmöglichkeiten durch
Engineer.

§ 2 Nr. 5 VOB/B
Änderungen, neuer Preis unter Berücksichtigung der Mehr- und Minderkosten.
Vereinbarung soll vor Ausführung getroffen
werden.

51.2 Ähnliche Klausel:
Valuation of Variations
Preis wird nach Rücksprache mit AG u. AN
festgelegt.

§ 2 Nr. 6 VOB/B
1) Im Vertrag nicht vorgesehene Leistung
   → Anspruch auf besondere Vergütung →
   vorher ankündigen

Detaillierte Vorschriften für »Claims« (vgl.
Abschnitt 13.3)

§ 3 Nr. 3 VOB/B
AN hat Geländeaufnahme etc. zu überprüfen
und auf Mängel hinzuweisen.

Keine ausdrückliche Überprüfungspflicht,
jedoch Clause 11.1 ähnliche Forderung.

§ 4 Nr. 3 VOB/B
Bedenken des AN gegen vorgesehene Art der
Ausführung.

Keine ausdrückliche Pflicht zur Anmeldung
von Bedenken.
Bemerkung:
Nach der alten FIDIC (Third Edition) ist der
AN nur dann von der Verantwortung bei
Entwurfsfehlern des Engineer befreit, sofern
der Mangel zu 100 % auf diesem
Entwurfsfehler beruht! Ein kleines
Mitverschulden macht ihn voll ersatzpflichtig.
Neue Fassung: Aufteilung je nach Anteil des
Verschuldens.

VOB	FIDIC

§ 6 Nr. 2 VOB/B
Behinderung und Unterbrechung.
Streik und Aussperrung ausdrücklich erwähnt.

Streik und Aussperrung nicht ausdrücklich
erwähnt → Klausel in Vertrag aufnehmen!

§ 8 VOB/B
Kündigung durch AG 8.1 jederzeit, aber
vereinbarte Vergütung – ersparte
Aufwendungen.
Bei Nichterfüllung → Frist

Kündigung bei Nichterfüllung sonst
→ Suspension of Work more than 84 days
→ default of Employer → Termination (69.1,
69.2, 69.3). Weltbank verlangt Kündigungs-
klausel für AG-Kündigung

§ 9 VOB/B
Kündigung durch AN allgem. AG unterläßt
ihm obliegende Handlungen oder zahlt nicht,
Frist setzen.

Ähnliche Bestimmungen, meist zuerst:
Suspension of Work, dann: 14 Tage nach
Mitteilung Vertrag beenden.

§ 11 VOB/B
Vertragsstrafe BGB §§ 339 – 345 muß bei
Abnahme vorbehalten werden. Weiterer
Schadensersatz nicht ausgeschlossen

Liquidated Damages bei Verzug (no penalty),
d. h. vorher festgelegte Schadensersatzsumme
(47.1). Weiterer Schadensersatz wegen
Verzugs normalerweise ausgeschlossen.

§ 12 VOB/B
Abnahme
AN verlangt Abnahme → 12 Werktage →
Abnahme, Gefahrenübergang, Gewährleistung
beginnt, Schlußrechnung

»Substantial Completion«, Engineer stellt 21
Tage nach Mitteilung »Taking-Over
Certificate« aus. »Care of Works« geht auf
AG über, »Defects Liability Period« beginnt.
50 % Retention Money wird fällig. 84 Tage
danach: »Statement at Completion« Final
Payment erst nach »Defects Liability
Certificate« (vergl. Abschnitt 13.5)

§ 13 Nr. 4 VOB/B
Fristen für Verjährung der Gewährleistung in
VOB enthalten

Frist für Verjährung muß vereinbart werden.
Nach englischem Brauch verhältnismäßig
kurze Verjährungen

§ 13 Nr. 6 VOB/B
Unverhältnismäßiger Aufwand bei
Mängelbeseitigung → Minderung

Nicht ausdrücklich erwähnt, aber aus 13.1
evtl. abzuleiten
…physically impossible

§ 13 Nr. 7 VOB/B
(1), (2) Schadensersatz (darüber
hinausgehender Schaden)
a) Vorsatz oder grobe Fahrlässigkeit
b) Verstoß gegen anerkannte Regeln der
   Technik

Keine Angaben, wenn aber engl. Recht → law
of tort = Schadenersatzrecht.
Wichtig, ob »tort« oder »breach of contract« –
Negligence.
Kein gleichwertiger Begriff für grobe
Fahrlässigkeit (gross negligence)
im engl. Recht

VOB	FIDIC

c) Fehler einer vertraglichen zugesicherten Eigenschaft

d) soweit Auftragnehmer Schaden durch Versicherung gedeckt hat oder hätte ... decken können

§ 14 Nr. 1 VOB/B Abrechnung
AN hat Leistungen prüfbar abzurechnen, Mengenberechnungen sind beizufügen

§ 14 Nr. 2 Gemeinsame Feststellungen

56.1 The Engineer shall, except as otherwise stated, ascertain and determine by measurement the value of the works ...

Contractor assists the Engineer in making measurements ...

Contractor examines and agrees records.

Statement at completion 84 days after »Taking-Over Certificate«. Danach: »Draft Final Statement« (vgl. Abschnitt: 13.5)
→ Final Statement ist letzte Möglichkeit für »claims«.

---

§ 14 Nr. 3 VOB/B
Schlußrechnung je nach Ausführungsfrist

60.1 Monthly Statements

28 Tage danach Bescheinigung durch Engineer. Weitere 28 Tage nach Zugang des »Interim Payment Certificate« beim »Employer« Zahlung.

§ 16 VOB/B Zahlung

69.4 Nichtzahlung: Zinsen, Einstellung der Arbeiten oder Verlangsamen.

§ 16. Nr. 1 Abschlagszahlungen
Zahlung 12 Tage nach Zugang der Aufstellung. Nichtzahlung: Nachfrist, vom Ende der Nachfrist Zinsen 1 v. H. über dem Lormbardsatz der Dt. Bundesbank und Einstellung der Arbeiten.

→ Wichtig: Hoher Zinssatz, sonst Finanzierung durch Contractor.

69.1 Arbeitseinstellung mit 14 Tagen Frist.

10.1 »Performance Security«: 28 Tage nach »Letter of Acceptance«, zwei Muster für »Performance Security« in Part II FIDIC. Erstes Muster: Zahlung nur bei beiderseitigem Einverständnis (Employer und Contractor) oder »Arbitration Award«.

§ 17 Nr. 1 – 8 VOB/B Sicherheitsleistung:
Hinweis auf §§232 bis 240. Verzicht auf Einrede der Vorausklage: §771 BGB, d. h. auch ohne Zwangsvollstreckungsversuch.

Zweites Muster verlangt vom Bürgen die Fertigstellung der Arbeiten oder Vorlage von Angeboten zur Fertigstellung; u. U. Vertragsabschluß zwischen neuem Bieter und AG und Bereitstellung von Geld bis zur Höhe der Bürgschaft oder Zahlung an den AG zur Fertigstellung der Arbeiten.

13.2   Checkliste für Vertragsabschlüsse nach FIDIC

Neben den bei allen Auslandsverträgen erforderlichen Überprüfungen und Überlegungen, wie z. B. zur politischen und wirtschaftlichen Lage, Bonität des Auftraggebers, zu den geographischen und klimatischen Verhältnissen, erscheinen die folgenden Punkte wichtig:

1. Welche Ausgabe der FIDIC liegt vor? Häufig wird noch die dritte Auflage verwendet.
2. Welche Änderungen und Ergänzungen gegenüber dem Original-FIDIC-Vertrag sind vorgenommen worden (paralleles Lesen)? Vorsicht bei Kopien gegenüber der zweifarbigen Originalausgabe! Alle Änderungen sollten getrennt aufgeführt werden.
3. Sind die Vorbehalte und Einschränkungen des Angebots im Vertragstext bzw. im »Letter of Acceptance« enthalten?
4. Sind Preisgleitklauseln im Vertrag berücksichtigt?
5. Sind die Wechselkursrisiken abgesichert?
6. Welche Form der Sicherheiten (Securities) wird verlangt?
7. Ist die Entscheidungsmöglichkeit des »Engineer« durch den Auftraggeber vertraglich eingeschränkt?
8. Wie ist die »Design Responsibility« des »Engineer« im Vertrag geregelt? (Alte FIDIC-Fassung ist sehr ungünstig für den Unternehmer)
9. Sind die »Employer's Risks«, ausreichend definiert?
10. Sind die Kündigungsklauseln für beide Vertragsparteien angemessen?
11. Sind die »Liquidated Damages« angemessen?
12. Ist die »Special Risk«-Klausel auf das Land der Baustelle beschränkt oder umfaßt sie auch andere Länder, z. B. Herstell- und Lieferländer?
13. Ist die evtl. im Vertrag vorgeschriebene Versicherungsgesellschaft zuverlässig oder muß noch eine zusätzliche Versicherung abgeschlossen werden?
14. Welche Steuern sind nach dem Vertrag zu zahlen?
15. Ist bei dem Auftrag eine Unterschreitung der Abrechnungssumme bis zu 15 % denkbar (nicht gedeckte Gemeinkosten)?
16. Ist der Transfer von Gewinnen sowohl in einheimischer als auch in fremder Währung möglich?
17. Sind Verzögerungen durch Im- und Exportbeschränkungen (Lizenzen) zu erwarten?
18. Bestehen Beschränkungen bezüglich der Arbeitserlaubnisse für Ausländer?
19. Ist der Zinssatz bei Nichtzahlung des AG ausreichend hoch bemessen?

13.2 Checklist für Concluding Contracts under FIDIC

In addition to the necessary checks and considerations with all overseas contracts- e. g. political and economic situation, solvency of the Employer, geographical and climatic conditions - the following points appear to be of importance:

1. Which edition of the FIDIC Contract is the basis of the contract? Frequently the previous (third) edition is still used.
2. Which alterations and amendments against the official FIDIC-Contract have been made? (Parallel reading). Beware of copies, check against the two-coloured official version! All changes should be stated sparately.
3. Insure that tender qualifications are included in the letter of acceptance and contract documents.
4. Have price revision clauses been included in the contract?
5. Is the risk of foreign exchange rate fluctuations covered?
6. Which form of security is required?
7. Has the authority of the Engineer been restricted by contractual clauses?
8. How is the Engineer's "Design Responsibility" defined in the contract? The previous (third) edition is very unfavourable for the contractor.
9. Are the "Employer's Risks" defined adequately?
10. Are contract termination clauses fair to both parties?
11. Are liquidated damages fair or penal?
12. Is the "Special Risks"-clause confined to the country of the site or does ist also comprise other countries e. g. countries of manufacture and supply?
13. Is the insurance company which may be prescribed in the contract reliable or will the need of an additional insurance arise?
14. Have tax liabilities under the contract correctly been ascertained?
15. Is a decrease of the contract sum up to 15 % likely? (Uncovered fixed costs)
16. Is the transfer of profit in local currency and foreign currency possible?
17. Are delays as a consequence of import and export restrictions (licences) to be expected?
18. Are there restrictions regarding working permits for foreigners?
19. Is the rate of interest upon unpaid sums sufficient?

13.3 FIDIC – Normal Procedure for Claimes

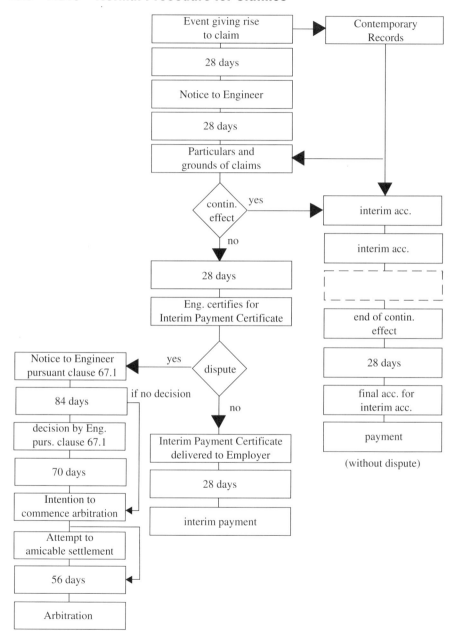

Event giving rise to claim

Contemporary Records

28 days

Notice to Engineer

28 days

Particulars and grounds of claims

contin. effect — yes → interim acc.

no

interim acc.

28 days

Eng. certifies for Interim Payment Certificate

end of contin. effect

28 days

dispute — yes → Notice to Engineer pursuant clause 67.1

final acc. for interim acc.

84 days

if no decision

payment

decision by Eng. purs. clause 67.1

(without dispute)

70 days

no

Intention to commence arbitration

Interim Payment Certificate delivered to Employer

Attempt to amicable settlement

28 days

56 days

interim payment

Arbitration

13.4 FIDIC – Types of Certificates

Interim Payment Certificate
Taking-Over Certificate
Defects Liability Certificate
Final Payment Certificate

Certificate of Valuation at Date of Termination

13.5   FIDIC – Normal Procedure for Final Payment

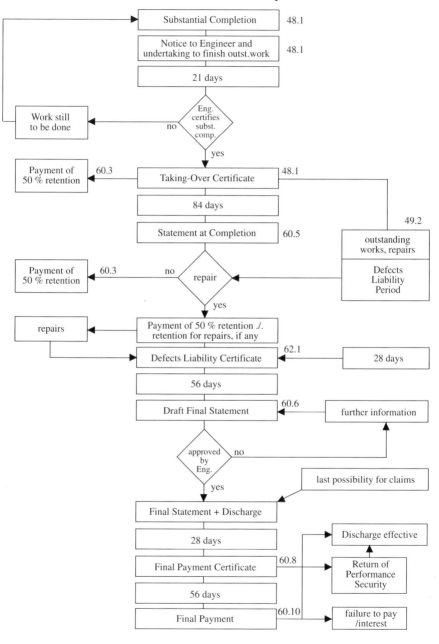